Zulu Frontiersman

Major C. G. Dennison, DSO, circa 1899, at the time he commanded Dennison's Scouts

Zulu Frontiersman

Major C. G. Dennison, DSO

Edited By

Ron Lock and Peter Quantrill

Frontline Books, London
Naval Institute Press, Annapolis, Maryland

Zulu Frontiersman

This edition published in 2008 by Frontline Books,
an imprint of Pen and Sword Books Ltd,
47 Church Street, Barnsley, S. Yorkshire, S70 2AS

Published and distributed in the United States of America and Canada
by the Naval Institute Press, Beach Hall, 291 Wood Road, Annapolis, Maryland
21402-5034
www.navalinstitute.org

Publishing History
An abridged version of Dennison's memoirs was published in 1904 by Longmans,
Green & Co., London, under the title *A Fight to a Finish: Reminiscences of the Great
Boer War of 1899–1902*. *Zulu Frontiersman*, published by Frontline Books, London,
is an unabridged edition of the Dennison's memoir which includes previously
unpublished material. This new edition also includes a new Introduction by Ron
Lock and Peter Quantrill and a new plate section.

Frontline edition
ISBN 978-1-84832-518-0

NIP edition
ISBN 978-1-59114-988-0
Library of Congress Control Number: 2008936927

CIP data records for this title is are available from the British Library and the Library
of Congress

For more information on our books, please visit www.frontline-books.com
or email info@frontline-books.com or write to us at the above address

Printed and bound in Great Britain by Biddles Ltd, King's Lynn

Contents

Illustrations

Acknowledgements

Our thanks are due to: first and foremost, Elizabeth Bodill who, despite all manner of aggravations, including moving house a hundred kilometres away and having her work continually interrupted by power cuts that threw her computer into confusion, completed the manuscript on schedule. Also to Elizabeth's daughter, Belinda, who frequently acted as courier, carrying the growing manuscript from her mother to the editors; to the staff of the National Archives Department of Arts and Culture, Pretoria, for their kind cooperation in making available a copy of Dennison's original manuscript; the ever smiling helpful staff of the Killie Campbell Library (now called The Campbell Collection) for producing some of the illustrations that we had despaired of finding; Audrey Portman for tracking down Dennison's papers describing the Stellaland Campaign, that had got separated from the main manuscript; Paul Naish, for his untiring interest in the project and for his assistance in procuring the picture of Dennison's grave; Lindsay Reyburn for his unflagging interest and visiting, on our behalf, the National Archives and, last, but not least, our patient and smiling wives who put up with quite a lot.

Introduction

It was said of George Dennison that he had seen more active service in southern Africa than any other living man. Not only was he an eminent soldier cast from a colonial mould of bitter experience, rather than of a formal military education, he was a frontiersman equal in standing to any legendary figure of the American West. For whereas the likes of Daniel Boone and David Crocket might have experienced a rare encounter with a puma or a rattler, in Dennison's early days brushes with man-eating lions, leopards, enraged buffaloes and a variety of snakes whose bite was an immediate passport to death were but daily affairs. He came from a military family, his forefathers having served in both the army and navy and with his grandfather, a colour-sergeant of the 55th Regiment, having being wounded at the Battle of Bunker Hill during the American War of Independence.

Dennison's military career saw him rise from an uncouth trooper to, fifty years later, a British officer with the rank of major and the added laurel of the Distinguished Service Order, an officer whose advice was sought by the likes of Lord Kitchener, Sir Garnet Wolseley and other British military names of fame.

Most likely Dennison, born in 1844 at Cradock, Cape Colony, was a first-generation descendant of 1820 settler immigrants, English rural folk who had been coaxed by a sly and unscrupulous British government to abandon their impoverished but safe existence in England and to travel halfway around the world to southern Africa, there to populate and occupy at the imminent risk of life and limb the vast spaces of newly acquired empire that were, in fact, already occupied by black rural folk who objected to the intrusion of the newcomers, so much so that it became perilous for whites to step outside their front doors. And, likewise, perilous for blacks should they show the slightest semblance of aggression.

Dennison encountered many foes during his half a century of soldiering, some he would have known as neighbours or men who had lately been comrades-in-arms. The more prolonged wars in which he was involved were mostly fought against white men, time and again of the same nationality but who were known by many names: Afrikaners; Dutchmen; Transvaalers; Voortrekkers and, most famous of all, Boers. His black foes were also diverse: the stealthy Xhosa of the eastern Cape; the battle-axe wielding Basutos from their lofty kingdom in the clouds; the Transvaal baPedi, masters of fortification and, most impressive of all, the military master race of southern Africa, the amaZulu warriors of King Cetshwayo.

Dennison's narrative of his battles against his heterogeneous adversaries shows little or no hint of hatred. One gets the impression that as soon as the conflict was over, all would be amicable. In fact, Dennison mostly concludes by expressing his admiration for the courage of his foes. Perhaps they were indeed the last of the 'Gentleman's Wars' if, as he himself remarks, there ever was such a thing.

Dennison wrote a book, taking in some of his exploits, titled *A Fight to the Finish*, published in 1904 and now a rare item of Afrikaner history. I was introduced to this volume by the Killie Campbell Library, Durban, in 1994, when I was researching the Battle of Hlobane in which Dennison fought and dramatically escaped but, to my astonishment and disappointment, there was no more than a passing reference to Hlobane. A mystery. There the matter rested for several years until what appeared to be the missing account of the Hlobane battle was discovered in the National Archives of South Africa, Pretoria (subsequently published by Huw Jones in *Natalia*, journal of the Natal Society) and which vividly described the incident. And the reason for its omission from *A Fight to the Finish* immediately became apparent – or so it seemed: Dennison had been highly critical of Colonel Evelyn Wood who, by the time Dennison published his book, was Field Marshal Sir Evelyn Wood, a father-figure of the British army. Once again, there the matter rested until a few years later, gathering material for *Zulu Vanquished*, co-authored with Peter Quantrill, I decided to obtain a copy of the 'missing chapter' and, to my surprise found it to be part of a bulky manuscript. In fact, it became obvious that the manuscript was intended to be the first half, or thereabouts, of a more lengthy *A Fight to the Finish*, so Peter Quantrill and I decided to unite the two and this book, *Zulu Frontiersman*, is the result. However, it soon became apparent that the manuscript – as with the book – was a minefield of grammatical gaffs and twisted English which would have to be put to rights. This we have attempted to do to a limited degree while trying to retain the raw stamp of a frontiersman who himself confessed to be of sparse education.

The reader will find the text littered with the word *kaffir* which is described in the current Concise Oxford English Dictionary as 'noun: offensive, chiefly in South Africa an insulting and contemptuous term for a black South African'. The dictionary goes on to say that the word was originally 'simply a descriptive term for a particular ethnic group'. We ask the reader's tolerance to see the word used thus as in the latter instance, having taken into account that the narrative begins 150 years ago. Nevertheless, we do apologise to those to whom the word unintentionally, gives offence. Yet, readers all, we crave your indulgence and ask you to contemplate the following: while the white man was calling his black brother a 'kaffir', what was the black man calling him in retaliation? We who live in Africa know that any black man worth his salt is capable of roaring a pithy response to any perceived insult. As Dennison, with pious indignation remarks: 'They danced around us, calling us all the bad names they could think of, mixed with the disgusting epitaphs for which they are noted!'

RON LOCK

Hillcrest, kwaZulu-Natal

Part I
A Fight for Survival:

The early wars in Southern Africa 1850–80
and
the Anglo-Zulu War 1879

Chapter 1

At the urgent wish of many of my friends and members of my family, I am again writing the history of my eventful life. I say again, for the manuscript of a lifetime was lost during the last war [the Anglo-Boer War 1899–1902] which I deeply regret for dates, as many of the details recorded in the lost manuscript, cannot be replaced. I must now trust solely to memory – which will be correct as far as it goes – but wanting in the fullness of my diary from which I formerly wrote and which was lost.

Well, to start, my earliest recollections begin from Cradock, in the Cape Colony, where I was born in the year 1844. My father was in business there. When I was four years old my family moved down to Grahamstown; my father, mother, and eldest sister, I being the youngest at the time. Some of the events of the journey are distinct in my memory such as the usual sticking in the rivers, and *sluits* [gullies]. Also getting stuck on the tracks called roads of that period and losing oxen, etc., etc. After being in Grahamstown for about six years, the war of 1850 broke out and the kaffirs overran the Colony. We had, I omitted to state, moved down a few months before to my uncle John Webber's farm below Grahamstown near the Kareiga River. It was from that farm we fled over to Salem where, with many other families, refugees like ourselves, we lived barricaded in the Salem Church until an opportunity offered to escape when my father and uncle, with their young families, trekked through in the dead of night to Grahamstown. As soon as the families were safely housed, they rode back to Salem to bring in the stock. Hardly had they arrived there when a report came in that the kaffirs had cleared off a farmer's stock near the town. Gravitt was the farmer's name. A party was hastily formed to go to the rescue. They found the *spoor* [tracks] and tracked the cattle and the kaffirs into one of the dry *kloofs* [gorges] on the Assegai River. As it was then very dark, they decided to go up a ridge between the kloof and another, and camp on top till next morning; but just as the party got near the top of the ridge and were in a narrow passage surrounded by bush, the kaffirs fired on them. One of the party, Frederick Short by name, fell with his back broken. My father had his right arm smashed and a bullet through the body. Before the kaffirs could rush in with their assegais, my uncle had lifted my father on to his horse and holding him, got back safely to Salem. Short was assegaied by the kaffirs, in fact cut to pieces, although vain attempts were made to get him out. A brother of the fallen man, and an old Hottentot servant, remained firing over him till forced back. The wounded man pleaded with his brother to put him out of his misery, but the kaffirs speedily did this for him.

It was about daybreak one morning when we heard a knock at our bedroom window. My mother arose, and asked who was there. 'Me, Missus, Jack,' was the reply.

'What is it?' my mother asked.

'Missus, Baas is shot,' was the reply. I distinctly remember this and saying to my mother: 'Never mind Mother, when I am big I will shoot kaffirs.' Thus at the early age of six years was the spirit of war instilled in me and exists in me up to the present. I never forgot that morning of grief and terror; grief for we dearly loved our father, and terror for we knew nothing but that he was fatally wounded. A few days later my father was brought in; he had been shot through the arm close above the elbow, and through the coating of his stomach by the same ball.

For many months he lay between life and death but owing to the ability and constant attention of Dr Campbell, the surgeon, and the careful nursing of my mother and friends, he recovered, but with a useless arm and shattered constitution. He died a few years later of an internal ulceration caused by the wound. Only the fact of his being a man of wonderful constitution, and inured to hardships, enabled him to recover at all and live the time he did. We were but one of many grief-stricken families of that war, for almost daily did we hear of murder and rapine, the murder of whole families, the ambushing of parties of regulars and others. The whole atmosphere reeked of war and rumour of war. Grahamstown was barricaded in all her principal streets.

The marching of troops, regulars, Fingoe levies and other irregulars composed of volunteers and burgers to the front was frequent. Boys drilled and played at war. School was a secondary matter; the fever of war was predominant in old and young. Servants left their masters and joined the enemy. A considerable section of the Hottentots of the old Frontier Armed and Mounted Police rebelled and joined the enemy under Uithalder and Hermanus, the Hottentot leaders of Kat River near Fort Beaufort, where a Hottentot settlement existed on the land grants made to them by the government. (The Hottentots rebelled in the first war of 1834 and joined the enemy's forces under the chief Hintza who, during a single-handed struggle with Colonel Sir Harry Smith, was shot by Southey who had rushed up in time to aid the Colonel who had lost his only weapon in the struggle.)

This kindly action of the government in allotting land grants to the Hottentots was repaid by the basest ingratitude of the Hottentots who joined the kaffirs in arms against the whites, and became a terror to helpless farmers.

My first recollection of 'The Dead March in Saul' was at the funeral of Colonel Fordyce in Grahamstown who was shot in the Waterkloof by one of the enemy, a Hottentot hidden in a tree, while leading his men up a path through the dense bush. So dense was the bush that a stalwart kaffir once leapt out, stabbed an officer at the head of his men, and escaped unscathed. Tales of single-handed heroism were frequent. Tales told in the hearing of the boys of the town – only too eager to hear them – many of whom became heroes and dauntless leaders in later years helping to swell the long list of brave deeds and to fill the local cemeteries. Many were from old Grahamstown which had provided not a few, and whose names were added to the scroll of fallen heroes. There was no racialism then among the whites [Boers and British]; all fought side by side for the one common cause.

My father, as I have already stated, recovered, but the recovery was but partial. He was, however, able to go with his wagons which, with all others, were pressed into military service. On one occasion when my father's wagon was in convoy going under strong escort to Fort Beaufort the rear guard, on nearing the town and thinking the danger past, had, with or without orders, joined the advance when the rear was attacked. The kaffirs rushed the last few wagons of the train, one of which was my father's. I was laying asleep between two cases in the front part of the vehicle. There were only tent wagons in those days; it was before buck wagons were in use. My mother could do nothing with me. I did not want to go to school and often played truant. Thus it was that my father took

5

me with him to try and cure me. The noise of attacking kaffirs woke me and I have still a vivid recollection of seeing one sawing with his assegai at the neck strap of one of the hind oxen when he was shot down by my father who, with a few others from the wagons, checked the onslaught of the enemy until the escort galloped back and drove the kaffirs off.

Boys often played truant in those days, as the excitement which prevailed was not conducive to learning. One little boy about seven years old disappeared; he had gone to school as usual but when the school came out he was missing. He did not turn up at his home and enquiries were made by the anxious parents. It was ascertained that the child had not been seen at school that day.

His father, who knew the boy's restless and reckless nature, said: 'Amos came in, wounded this morning, from the Woests Hill and the boy saw him.'

The father then left the house and cut across the road against the hillside leading out to Woests Hill on the Kareiga road, in search of his son's spoor. He found the child's tracks along the road leading away from the town. He hastily returned and with a few friends, mounted and armed, galloped away to the foot of Woests Hill where Amos and Bowles had been attacked while coming into town with the wagon; they had ventured out at great risk to bring in a load of firewood. If my memory serves me right, they had been travelling in the dark and had tied their oxen to the yokes and had laid down when the kaffirs attacked them. They both fortunately escaped. Amos was wounded through the flesh of the thigh but got away into thick bush and later gradually made his way to Grahamstown, seven miles off. He was found by an old native woman near the town and helped in by her.

It was early in the morning that the boy, ever an early riser during the war, had slipped away after breakfast and had got on to the tracks of the wounded man, guided along the road by blood spots. The boy was found at the foot of the hill with a pocket knife in his hand that he had picked up near the wagon, which was still where it had been left by Bowles and Amos. He was hastily lifted on to his father's horse and the party rode back towards town. Such was the spirit of the age that such boys, who became the men of Grahamstown and lower Albany, did service for the flag in after years, many of whom bled and died in the wars of later date.

Shortly after the close of '51 war, my father moved his family to Baviaans River in company with my uncle, Henry Dennison, who had hired the farm Clipton from the late Dots Pringle of Lyndock. For five years we lived at Clipton and then at Hindhope. The latter was situated between Baviaans River and the Mankazana to which we moved after living at Clipton for about three years. Baviaans River was the home of the Pringle family, relatives of the poet of that name who was also resident for a time with the others. A gravestone in the corner of the garden at Clipton marks the last resting place of one member of the Pringle family. This I remember well, for we thought it was the poet's grave but found out later that it was not. When I say 'we', I mean we children. I had read some of Pringle's poetry as a child and, hence, perhaps the reason why the grave is so fixed in my memory.

Many happy days were spent on the old Baviaans River farm whose steep hills we boys took great pleasure in climbing with our dogs in search of *dassies* [rock rabbits]. At night many were the hunts in the mealie lands for porcupine which, when brought to bay by the dogs, were quickly killed with an old bayonet fixed to the end of a long stick. Frequently, half a blade from of a pair of shears was used in the same way.

But it was by no means all play for us boys. My cousin, Henry Edward Dennison and myself had to do our share in the ploughing and harvesting of the land. Labour hands at the time were by no means plentiful. Besides, our fathers rightly taught us to work and said it kept us out of mischief which was, I cannot gainsay, but too true. On one occasion, a day or two before New Year, having been told that we could not have a holiday, we planned an escape from work. The oxen, which were grazing away up in the mountain kloofs, were wanted for some work or other and we, Henry and myself, were told to rise early on the New Year's morning to fetch them. This gave us the opportunity we sought for. So at the dawn of the day we set off with our dogs, spears and an old single-barrelled gun. We soon found the oxen and drove them away for some miles towards Quagga's Nek – a farm away towards the Winterberg on the mountain heights. We hunted all day and returned at night without the oxen. We did not tell the truth, for we said we could not find them. A Hottentot was sent in search of them next day and we were allowed to rest from work. The Hottentot returned that night without the oxen. We asked to be allowed to go out again and, accompanied by a native boy but not the Hottentot, continued the search. We found the oxen, of course, and got well praised for it! I have often thought since, how little we deserved it. Well, it was thus we were in those days; in my experience just like many boys at that time.

Our fathers did a great deal of transport riding and were often away from home between ploughing and harvesting. The times were grand for boys, of course, and many were the hunts we had in the old Baviaans River Mountains during the absence of our fathers. At times responsibilities fitting older shoulders were perforce, ours. At one time I remember during my father's absence from home, a piece of land had to be ploughed; we were then living at Hindhope and had a herd of cattle but only one herd boy. So alone I ploughed the land with a small no. 25 plough. My eldest sister helped me to inspan the oxen, and away I went to the land each morning. Often I sat down and cried out of pure vexation, when the old oxen leaders would not turn properly into the furrow and when, whip in hand, I had to run out and flog them round; then again out of pure cussedness, they would cross, and give me a rough time as they zigzagged about; but I ploughed that land, and got a crop from it. The results from the crop went towards my school fees. I was then a boy of about fourteen years and, though fond of reading knew little in the way of education. At that time many a child of six or eight years was further advanced than I was at the age of fourteen. The facilities for learning in those days were meagre in the extreme.

In the year 1859 we moved back to old Grahamstown and it was there my father, after a lingering illness resulting from the old wound, died. We were left in very poor circumstances, so with only the wagon and oxen left, I had, with the help of a native boy, to cut and ride firewood into the town market to help maintain my mother, one brother and three sisters. My eldest sister had married ere we had left Hindhope, and was with her husband, Joseph Miller, then living in the Kwelaga, in British Kaffraria.

Having secured a billet in Burghersdorp in 1861, I was able to give up the laborious work of firewood riding. For three years I remained a clerk in a general store and then the spirit of adventure took a keen hold on me. I gave up my billet and went with a man by the name of Neser and his brother-in-law, Hans Bender, on a trading trip into the Free State. Hans was the son of an old Hollander who lived in Burghersdorp. He had been one of Napoleon's secretaries and was with the Emperor on that memorable expedition to Moscow. Many were the stories told by old Mr Bender of his days of trial and suffering while with Napoleon. The old man was very deaf, in fact stone-deaf, and all questions had to be written on a slate, kept for the purpose, on a table at which he generally sat. In High Dutch the old man would, in a very loud tone of voice, give us some of his experiences. I still have in my possession a book of his entitled 'Tennant's Notary Manual' that he no doubt used in his work which consisted principally in the writing of wills for Boers.

On one trading expedition we arrived at Reddersburg where I was employed by the manager of Thos. Webster's store to open a trading station at Thaba Nchu, the chief town of Moroko, the Baralong chief. I was at Thaba Nchu for about a year when the war of 1865 broke out between the Free State and the Basutos, the good Sir John Brand being then President of the Orange Free State. I gave up the trading station, packed up the goods and left them with one of the missionaries, the Rev. Jas. Scott. I then went to Bloemfontein where I joined the Bloemfontein Rangers under Capt. Edward Hanger. Previous to my coming to Thaba Nchu I went with fourteen men on to the border line made by Sir P. Wodehouse between the Free State and Basutoland. I was elected leader of our little party.

We were for some time on the line near Governor's Kop and Wonderkop, and while there my spirit of adventure nearly cost me my life. A dispatch had come from Bloemfontein asking for volunteers to carry a dispatch to the Basuto chief Poulus Mopere, or 'Gentleman Paul' as he was called due to his fondness for European dress. Poulus was one of the under chiefs of Moshesh, who was Paramount Chief.

I went with one of my men, a Scotsman, Cumming by name. After sundry mishaps in the quicksands of the streams we crossed, we arrived at Mopere's the following evening and were well received and treated – food being sent by the resident missionary. The next morning we started back with the reply to the dispatch we had brought and when nearing a village that lay beyond a pass, we heard the noise of shouting and singing. It was a beer drink. We off-saddled in the pass, not thinking it safe to go on to the village, and there we waited hoping for some passing native who might give us the opportunity of letting Mahakabe, the head man, know that we were there. It was necessary for us to call at this kraal, as there we had left a lame horse. Barely had we off-saddled when a couple of Basuto boys came from the direction of the village and seeing us turned and ran, shouting '*Magona keau! Magona keau!*' ('Here are white men. Here are white men!') We shortly heard loud shouts approaching and in a few moments we were surrounded by a howling crowd of half-drunken Basutos armed with *kerries* [sticks], assegais and battleaxes. We sat down on the rocks and the kaffirs danced round us – one even went so far as to prick us with his assegai. My companion, Cumming, clenched his fist and would have risen but I stopped him for had we offered any resistance our chances would have been very small. It was a trying few minutes until we heard an imperative order shouted from behind the crowd. It was Marukabi, the head man, who had rushed into the crowd and, by striking right and left with a long kerrie, in all probability saved our lives for the kaffirs were becoming frenzied. As they danced around us they called us by all the bad names they could think of mixed with disgusting epithets for which the Basutos are noted. The crowd was quickly dispersed, our horses caught and accompanied by the head man we walked to the kraal. Marukabi was profuse in his expressions of regret at the occurrence and treated as well. We got our lame horse and resumed our journey feeling that we had had a very narrow escape. This happened but a few months before the war of 1865. White men's lives were held cheap by the Basutos at that time. Suffice to say we arrived safely in camp.

Now to return to my story. As already stated I had joined the Bloemfontein Rangers. We were, if I remember aright, about fifty strong, well-mounted and armed with Wesley Richards breechloading carbines with paper-covered cartridges as ammunition. If any of my old fellow Rangers ever read this story they will remember how often we cursed the cartridges when on cold frosty mornings the paper could not stand the pressure of being pushed into the cold breeches of our rifles and would burst, scattering the black powder to the ground. During this war our forces were everywhere successful for the Basutos, daring as they were, could not face the fire of our arms. On different occasions we shot down a number of them as, mounted on their hardy and active ponies, they made futile attempts to charge home with their battle axes. Their ponies were inured to hard work, and their ability to climb the steep mountains of Basutoland is well known. Sure-footed, and with powers of endurance beyond that of most African horses, which are generally known as strong and long goers but especially so were the old Hantam breed of Bosetje Koppen [Bushy Heads] so called owing to their heavy manes and forehead's tufts.

Frequent excursions were made into the mountain passes on cattle raiding expeditions. I remember on one occasion we started out about 2 o'clock on a bitterly cold June morning having received the usual order the night before to prepare three days' ration for the morrow's start. On such occasions rations of meal were issued with coffee and sugar if available, otherwise meal only. Our mode of preparing our bread was by making up the dough into balls and then, in a three-legged pot, frying them in fat. These were called 'storm jagers' by our Dutch friends. Anglicised, the name would mean 'stormers' as it would apply to a storming party, i.e., being quick, or quickly made, for it certainly was the quickest and easiest mode of making bread and the most convenient to carry about with us. Meat we could always get in any part of Basutoland by capturing enemy cattle.

Our course on this expedition was into the Double Mountains or the Quathlamba [now known as the Drakensberg Mountains], which divide Basutoland from Natal and, to the east, Pondoland from Basutoland. Away in the hidden kloofs of this mountain range of deep gorges and almost endless ridges, where the Basutos had hidden most of their many thousands of cattle, horses and small stock. As the sun rose with a cold biting wind, we heard shots ahead. All hands galloped on to the plateau we had earlier climbed and which was immediately above our camp. It was called the Berea or, otherwise Cathcart's Mountain, for it was here that the Lancers [12th Lancers], belonging to the Force under Sir George Cathcart, were cut up in 1848 [*sic* – actually 1852. During the Cape frontier wars between 1834 and 1853, an expedition led by Sir George Cathcart, in November 1852, moved against Chief Moshesh, the force included a contingent of the 12th Royal Lancers] – having gone up to drive down cattle which the wily Chief Moshesh had said were there. The cattle represented a fine that had been imposed on Moshesh, but as his men were afraid to drive the cattle down, so the General sent his lancers for them with the result that while the lancers were scattered about collecting and goading the cattle, the Basutos, who were hidden nearby, rushed on to the scattered soldiers killing a number of them. (During the campaign we found two old lances hidden in a mountain cave near Molopos, one of which had a broken shaft.) [Most likely captured during an earlier skirmish with another part of the column.]

History can give a fuller and more complete detail than I can. Suffice to say the mountain plateau retained the name of the officer in command. As I have said, away we galloped, the men casting off blankets and overcoats as they rode, while some of us rangers, with our numbed fingers, tried in vain to unbuckle our carbines which were carried in the old type of gun bucket. After frenzied attempts, we broke or tore away the straps and, as we reached the front we cast ourselves off our horses and, with numbed fingers, tried to load the cartridges made brittle by the piercing cold. We tried in vain to join in the firing which the others, armed with muzzle-loaders, had started pouring into the now flying Basutos mounted on their quick and nimble ponies. They had tried to intercept our advance along the mountain and now a wild chase ensued, but in vain, as the enemy had scattered and disappeared into the hills beyond.

We captured a large number of cattle on this expedition but the hardships endured by our men were severe for it rained heavily each day. In the mornings, as the sun rose over the cloud-topped mountains, it would shine down piercingly hot and towards noon the distant roar of thunder would be the forewarning of a wet afternoon and night. Not gentle showers, oh no! But heavy downpours each day. Then drenched to the skin and under wet blankets, often lying in water, we slept the sleep of the tired. Many of our men became ill and some deaths resulted from cold and exposure. Our horses too suffered severely and many of them were completely knocked up, the men being reduced to ride oxen.

As we were descending into a deep ravine on our return, our scouts reported a strong force of the enemy holding the summit pass. I was near Louis Wessels, the commandant of the Bloemfontein contingent, when a burger urged his horse past the herd of captured stock to where the commandant rode and hastily said: 'Commandant, the Basutos hold the Nek in a strong force.'

Without another word our plucky commandant, in a loud ringing voice, shouted his usual order of advance: '*Vorward kêrels, vorward allen buiten dachter hoeden.*' ('Forward chaps, forward all except the rear guard.') All hands pushed down the steep ravine as best they could, through and past the captured stock, eager and anxious to meet the foe. One young man, Isaac Vivier by name, ran down the hill until he reached the commandant's side. 'Commandant, give me a horse,' he pleaded.

'Where from can I get you a horse, Isaac? You know the horses are nearly all knocked up!'

'Then I will get there on foot,' Isaac replied, pointing to the hill above and away he ran. True to his word Isaac was there before many of the horsemen.

After a short stand, the Basutos fled leaving several of their numbers slain. Isaac was one of the true type of hardy warriors descended from the old Voortrekkers. I knew many such in days gone by. Our British forefathers too often misjudged the character of the Voortrekkers' descendants judging all, no doubt, by their experience of but a few. My experience does not guide me to condemn them. No! Far from it. However more of this anon.

Many an engagement we had in the war of 1865 including the two attempts on Thaba Bosigo (Mountain of Darkness). The first was made from the south-east, from one of the flat mountain points of the plateau which surrounds Moshesh's stronghold. Commandant Wessel's men, including the rangers, crossed the intervening *nek* [col] with their horses covered by a firing party from above. We reached the foot of Moshesh's famous stronghold, left our horses in charge of a guard, then quickly ascended the mountain ledges until we reached the last, immediately beneath the top of the mountain. Here the rocks overhung the ledge beneath and in places had immense cracks across which the Basuto lines of defence, consisting of stone walls, had been built. As our men passed beneath the enemy, they cast down stones upon them. Several of our party were hurt, including J. M. Howell, the correspondent of the Bloemfontein paper, *The Friend of the Free State*. A party of burgers under Captain Roos of the Fouresmith District should have occupied a sluit below the fences but had failed to do so. A party of the enemy got down from the mountain and opened fire on us from the sluit and we were obliged to retire. The attack was a failure. The mountain would have been ours that day had Roos done his duty. If my memory serves me right, the second attack was made about a month later.

It was then decided to call for volunteers and although about 800 responded, not so the rangers, for as our Captain said, we will be there if real business is meant. We left shortly after midnight crossing the Caledon River close to our camp and rode on in silence until we were opposite Job's Point on Moshesh's mountain. Here we halted, dismounted, holding our horses. We stood or lay down in the bitter cold of a Basutoland mid-winter morning, wondering what the delay was about. At last, as the grey of dawn showed in the east, we were told that the volunteers' idea had fallen through and that the whole commando was to attack. The delay, as we afterwards learned, was because the officers could not agree as to who should lead the attack. Some were for Wessels, our commandant, others were for Joubert or Cronstadt and some for Wippenaar who commanded the Smithfield division. But it was then decided that the whole force should attack under Wippenaar.

Orders were then given to move. We turned to the left and shortly

13

halted near the crossing of a mountain sluit, why we knew not. It was almost daylight and a few of us had gathered some dung and made a fire around which we sat to gain what warmth we could for our numbed fingers. Suddenly a shot with a resounding report came from the mountain. The bullet had struck our fire scattering hot particles all over us. Immediately an imperative order was shouted to put out the fire. The shot was a signal for a general fusillade from the enemy. Hastily all hands scattered about. 'Mount and charge!' was the shout and away we went, in any sort of order, for the sluit.

'Halt, dismount and follow me,' came the instruction from our gallant leader, Wippenaar, which was eagerly responded to by the Smithfield men who had led, closely followed by the rangers.

'Halt men!' shouted Captain Hanger, 'and cover Commandant Wippenaar.' This order was given as we gained the rocks below the point which appeared to me to be a much worse place to attack than had we attacked Job's. Two jutting *krantzes* [cliffs] with a natural pathway, full of loose stone, was the point towards which the commandant and his men, under heavy fire from the enemy above, were climbing. Our opponents' aim was by no means accurate owing to the fire from our cannons, a Whitworth and an Armstrong, which were worked with great accuracy by the gunners. The Whitworth, under the command of a young Boer by the name of van Rensburg, was fired with notable accuracy.

Shell after shell burst on the mountain and under this covering fire Wippenaar and his men steadily advanced. We saw some men climb the krantz on the left and shortly after one fell, landing heavily on some men gathered there below. The man's life was saved as his fall was broken but he remained a cripple for the rest of his life. His name was Muller, a watchmaker by trade. I saw him years after in Fryburg. Commandant Wippenaar was one of the men who climbed the krantz but was shot dead, as was his body servant, a Hottentot, and some others.

For a moment the advance wavered and then came a wild retreat back. Some men who had got up into the opening between the krantzes endeavoured to run but slipped and fell, falling one men on to the next, the whole became a terror-stricken, running, rolling crowd. Some of the wounded were left there and, if I remember aright, about eight or ten were killed. From our position, about 150 yards from the attacking party, we were able to aid the retreating men who then gained the loose rocks under cover of our fire.

14

In Commandant Wippenaar's death, the Free State lost one of her best officers. (It was said the Basutos ate the heart of Wippenaar. It was their custom to eat the hearts of brave enemies who fell in action.) Shortly after the second attack on Thaba Bosigo an envoy, Ried by name, was sent by the High Commissioner of the Cape with dispatches for Moshesh who, it appears, had asked for the intervention of the Imperial Government. Ried came to our *laager* [wagon camp] and from there went on to the mountain to interview the chief, Moshesh. I do not remember the results of the negotiations but at any rate they did not at once bring peace, but aided in the termination of the war some months later. I may add here that the war was brought about mainly by the frequent depredations and murders inflicted on the Boers who lived on the border sequent to the line made by Sir P. Wodehouse in 1864 that I have previously referred to.

Chapter 2

I should have stated in the earlier part of my narrative that the Orange Free State had become a British possession having been proclaimed the Orange Sovereignty by Sir Harry Smith in 1848. At the time it was described by a traveller as a 'howling dessert'. The Boers who had settled there to be free of the British yoke, rebelled, and under Commandant General Pretorius took up arms to oppose British rule. Sir Harry Smith entered the territory and met the Boers at Boomplaats where an engagement took place. This practically ended the war and Major Warren was appointed British Resident of the Sovereignty. He also encountered troubles with the Basutos and a British force under Sir George Cathcart was sent to punish them. Cathcart's experience of the wily Chief Moshesh, and his cattle on the Berea, was by no means an agreeable one, ending as it did, in a reverse to British arms. Moshesh sued for peace and the British tax payers became impatient. An appeal was made to the imperial authorities against the retaining of a 'useless possession' and in 1853 Sir George Clarke was sent to withdraw British authority from the territory. On 23rd February 1854 the country was formally handed back to the Voortrekkers and once again became the Free State, governed as a Republic as was the case in the past, but now under the guidance and wisdom of President Sir John Brand, one of the best and most able men of the period.

It was after the second attack that the Basutos, acting under the instructions from their chief, drove their cattle on to the Thaba Bosigo in vast numbers. The mountain plateau presented one moving mass of animals. Orders were given to lay siege to the mountain, and small camps were formed all round. We were on a plateau point which we named 'Mount Misery'. Our camp was a bare sandstone rock, with one bell tent for the use of the officers, a couple of small patrol tents and, for the rest, stone walls with a covering of anything obtainable. A lot of native mats and *karosses* [animal-skin garments] found under the overhanging walls of where we set up camp, were put to good use, but needless to say we all became full of vermin. What with short rations, bad clothing and filthy vermin, the place was worthy of the name we gave it. Day after day we exchanged shots and epitaphs – by no means of refined quality – with the enemy. The Basutos were adept at using bad language – as were many of our men!

The supply of water on Thaba Bosigo was limited, being scooped out of holes made in the sandstone and barely sufficient for the use of the Basutos themselves, much less for many thousands of cattle congregated on the mountain. The result was that they came to the edge of the krantzes and, smelling the water below, those behind pushed forward forcing those in front over the edge to fall to their deaths below. The stench arising from the many dead carcasses made our position unbearable.

One night we were attacked, the enemy got right in among us before resistance could be made. In a patrol tent on the outside of our encampment lay one of the rangers (Chatsfield), who on hearing a noise, got up and went to the tent of Captain Hanger shared by Adjutant Bert Owen. 'Mad Owen' as he was called, belonged to the Smithfield contingent but had attached himself to us. Chatsfield asked for matches but said nothing about having heard anything unusual. (He had been unmercifully chaffed before for timidity hence perhaps, the reason.) Having returned to his bed Chatsfield was fast asleep when the Basutos rushed the tent and stabbed him through it. If I remember right he had fourteen stabs but none fatal as his blankets saved him. George Hanger, David McMaster and myself were sleeping in one of these stone huts when the shouts of the enemy woke us. We were not expecting any attack and were not prepared; in short, there was mismanagement somewhere. Hanger seized his sword and shouted: 'You knaves.' (A favourite expression of his.) 'Give out the guns and ammunition and I will keep the door clear but quick.'

I handed him his gun and McMaster got his. We were not many seconds getting out. Just as I was crawling out, a man fell almost on top of me. He had been stabbed close to the heart as he had rushed towards the centre of our encampment. His name was Venter. Another, Bower by name, awoke, heard the noise outside and against the horizon saw figures which he took for our men and did not realise his mistake before the Basutos stabbed him. I found him later, after we had driven off the enemy, in a hut into which he had crawled. He was stabbed in nine places but recovered. His knuckles were skinned, for he had only his fists to defend himself, his gun having been wrenched from him by the Basutos. Our salvation was due to the efforts of about nine men who got together and succeeded in inspiring courage in others. Several of the enemy were left lifeless around our camp; and down around the rocks where they had made their hurried departure, were smears of blood. We had a narrow escape and precautions were taken to prevent a re-occurrence.

I did my best that night with some others but as I looked back I felt that we had had a very narrow shave indeed. One generally realises great danger when it has passed. Many, many have been narrow escapes I have had during my varied life both in action and during war, and on other occasions, but I often look back to Mount Misery and think how near we were to being wiped out on the night I have referred to.

Some time after the second attack our commando moved up to Molopos, one of the under chiefs of Moshesh, who ruled the northern portion of Basutoland. Shortly after setting up camp opposite the chief's kraal, a commando from the Transvaal under Commandant Mathinus Wessels Pretorius, who had once been President of the Transvaal, arrived and camped close by. Pretorius was accompanied by Assistant-Commandant General Paul Kruger and it was the first time that I met the man who later had so much to do with the destiny of South Africa.

We had been at Molopos about a week when orders were given to prepare for a five-day patrol. On the following morning before daybreak, we left our laager for the mountains and were shortly joined by the mounted portion of the Transvaal commando under Commandant General Kruger. We marched for about three hours through ravines and streams of beautiful clear water, often leading our horses up the steep sides of the many ravines we encountered. We then halted for breakfast and while off-saddled our scouts reported a large herd of cattle being driven towards the Malutis. We hastily saddled up and gave chase. Away, some miles ahead, we could see the herd being driven by some Basutos. Owing to the number of gorges and ravines that we had to cross our progress was slow but at last we reached the plateau the cattle were on. I was among the first to cross the final ravine and as I reached the summit I saw a man crossing our front at right angles followed by others staggering on behind him. The man I noticed rode a good strong horse. He was cloaked in a long drab dust overcoat and behind, bobbing up and down on his saddle,

I saw something which proved to be a long and heavy Colt revolver. I soon drew alongside him for I was riding a swift pony. '*Wie is jy?*' ('Who are you?'), he asked in short decisive tones.

I told him who I was and he replied '*En ek is Paul Kruger*' ('And I am Paul Kruger'), and away we galloped. I turned to the left and as I joined our men, and as we turned the cattle on the one side, Paul Kruger with a few men turned the other. He then threw himself off his horse and fired at the Basutos who had cleared off and abandoned the cattle. We also opened fire, and I watched the man I had so often heard spoken of, and was surprised to see, despite his clumsy build, that he was an exceedingly agile man. I saw a great deal of him on our expedition and was very much drawn towards him for he was undoubtedly brave, very active and with sound common sense. He had often been known to leap into the saddle with a heavy gun in his hand without touching a stirrup. In later years I got to know him intimately.

During this expedition we suffered many privations and the daily rain, without firewood, made our marching and camping a misery. On our return journey we camped with the enormous amount of loot that we had captured. The Basutos harassed us all the way along the mountains but eventually we reached the plateau below the mountain range, and on a good open spot. One day horses were grazing freely and we were resting against our saddles (It was not raining that afternoon) when I noticed one of the *brandwacht* [pickets] galloping towards our encampment. Immediately there was a rush for the horses as orders were given to catch and link them together, while a number of men were hastily told off to advance to the brow of the nearest ravine. I was among that number and on taking up our position we heard a peculiar sound; something like the rattle of assegais against shields. Zulus!, we thought and anxiously sat behind rocks waiting for the enemy to appear. Nearer and nearer came the sound until a horseman came in sight followed by about four hundred footmen of the Transvaal Commando.

A loud shout from us and bursts of laughter greeted the approach of this extraordinary-looking army. Men with wide brim straw hats, coats of all descriptions and leather trousers. These trousers had by constant exposure to all weathers become hard and shrunken, the bare legs – in colour practically the same tinge as the trousers themselves – protruded many inches below and the noise made by hundreds of the trouser legs rattling one against the other was the sound we had heard. Four hundred pairs of dry hard leather breeches rubbing together was enough to alarm any camp! We were unaware that these men had been sent for by Commandant Kruger. Many and often was the laugh we had about the four hundred leather breeches.

It was during this expedition that we came in contact with Lothordi, the present chief, son of Letsea and grandson of Moshesh. We had halted away in the mountains on the edge of a kloof in which were a large number of cattle. The rangers were ordered to go down and drive them out. We led our horses down the steep hillside to a level in front of the kloof. We then mounted and rode towards the entrance. The interior of the kloof was hidden from us by a ridge projecting on our right. As we walked our horses towards the ridge, shouts came from our men above and they started firing towards the kloof. We guessed, or rather our officers did, what was wrong and they gave the order to charge. We went for the ridge and on dismounting at the top we saw a force of Basutos galloping straight towards us led by a young chief. A volley from our rifles checked them and sent back many a riderless horse. We noticed the horse of the leader fall. He seized the bridle of a passing horse and bounding on to its back raced round in front of his men, halted them and brought them on again. But our fire was too heavy for them and they retired for a second time. We followed after them and brought out their cattle.

Their leader was Lothordi who seemed to bear a charmed life, for regardless of bullets he tried again and again to stay the retreat of his men but to no avail. Many acts of bravery were accredited to this young chief.

A short time after our return from this expedition, a deal of dis-satisfaction occurred among our men regarding the non-distribution of loot. It was well known that a certain official had already removed 800 of the best oxen and that others had also removed quantities of stock. Our captain then gave way to the repeated and urgent wishes of the men to have no more of it, and gave the order to pack our wagons for a return to Bloemfontein. Commandant General Fick, on being informed by Captain Hanger of our intention, had threatened to have us stopped by his burgers. However, we trekked off the next morning without any interference; in fact we knew that the feeling of dissatisfaction was general and doubted that had such an order been given to the burgers it would have met with no response from them. All were as dissatisfied as we were.

When near Thaba Nchu, George Hanger and myself left our party and rode straight across country for Moroko's Town. I took no further part in the war but went on to Aliwal North. I omitted to mention, regarding the store of Mr Webster's I was managing, that I met him in the laager at Thaba Bosigo.

'What!' he said. 'What are you doing here and what have you done with my store?'

I told him what I had done and that I had written to his manager to that effect.

'You young scoundrel,' he said, 'You have ruined me. I will institute an action against you.'

Then turning on his heel he walked away but presently turned and said:

'Come here you young devil. Give me your hand. I admire your pluck. Think nothing about what I have said because if I had been in you place I would no doubt have done the same.'

I was greatly relieved as 'Fighting Tom', as he was called, shook me heartily by the hand. He was ever after my friend and I often met him years afterwards in Kimberley.

On arriving at Aliwal North I met an old friend of my parents who had been the deacon of our church at Grahamstown, the Baptist Church of Settlers. Mr Stanger was his name. Well, Stanger engaged me to manage a business at Sandrift on the Orange River and to take charge of the pont there.

On the opposite side of the river in the Free State, lived a Mr Hoffman and it was there that I met my wife who had but shortly before arrived from Somerset West. She was the third daughter of Mr Hoffman and had been brought up in Somerset West by an aunt, Mrs David de Villiers, and on her mother's death had come to join her father. We were married in Aliwal North in 1867.

I conducted Mr Stanger's business for some months and then took it over from him but, owing to a disagreement with my father-in-law, I sold out in 1869 and moved to the Transvaal with my wife and first-born, then a babe in arms. I was accompanied by two young friends, Alfred John Osmond and Charles Kidwell. Together we took a quantity of goods from a business managed by Mr C. Kidwell's eldest brother, Alec, one of my oldest school friends and a thoroughly good chap. Well, away we went with our trek of four wagons. In those days the Free State flats were covered by thousands of game, black wildebeest, blesbok and springbok, which we often shot off our wagons. The horizons sometimes presented a moving mass of game; but now all but gone. The days of the hunter are past. With the advance of civilisation things have changed. The habits and customs of former days are changed and have we the same men as then? Civilisation has its many benefits and blessings, true, but have we the same good, honest, fearless men we had in those days? Before civilising influences became part as they are now, men trusted one another. A Boer did not want a man's promissory note; no, he wanted his word. I once bought some oxen from one Louw Erasmuss in the Transvaal and had agreed to pay him half and the other half in some months' time. When I paid him the cash I said:

'Give me some paper, pen and ink.'

'What do you want it for?' he asked.

'Why, I must give you a bill for the balance,' I said.

'No, cousin, I don't want your paper. If your word is no good, your paper is no good also, but come to me when the time is due, even if you cannot pay all, but I must see you.'

And so it was.

After a journey lasting over twenty-five days we reached Rustenburg. We left our wagon on a Sunday morning and rode into the village on horseback. I looked away down the other end of the town, across the square, but could not see a soul. A solitary dog crossed in front of me. I rode on across the square and on entering the street on the other side I saw a man come out from a house at the corner. I halted and spoke in English. He replied in the same language. He asked me who I was and where I came from.

'What!' he said. 'Are you one of the Dennisons of Cradock?'

'Yes,' I said. 'I suppose so for my father lived there.'

'Well,' he said. 'My name is MacDonald, I also come from Cradock.'

'I see this is a hotel,' I said, looking towards a signboard above the door under the verandah.

'Yes,' he replied, 'the place is mine, but come, you must off-saddle and dine with me as my guest.'

I thanked him for his hospitable offer while he called a boy to off-saddle my horse and forage it.

We went inside. I found that his father had lived in Cradock and that he had come up to a friend's farm when very young. He had then married a relative of that friend's wife and had settled in Rustenburg. Later I made enquiries about a house but found none empty except for a couple of rooms in an old building, two *erven* [plots] off, which we made use of when my wagon arrived the next morning. I shortly afterwards got a cottage which for Rustenburg was fairly decent; the town then, with few exceptions, being made up of small shanties with thatched roofs.

The situation of the village pleased me, lying as it did on a flat about two miles north of Mogaliesberg. An open stretch of fairly flat country stretched away north-east and west while along the base of the mountain range the path-like growth of boekenbond, wild syringa and other trees greatly added to the beauty of that semitropical part of the Transvaal.

Parallel for miles, running east and west, were a line of broken hills or *koppies*, called Zwaartkoppies, while the flat was referred to as 'Turf' or 'The Black Sea', as some preferred to call it, which I learned to know only too well ere we had been in Rustenburg for many months.

While dry, the 'Turf' was hard and fairly smooth, but when wet is was cruel to travel through and when drying it was worse: the stuff sometimes clogged the wheels so that an empty wagon would have all its wheels locked, as the clay packed on to such an extent as to cause them to lock against the duck-rails of the wagons. It frequently happened that it took a day to travel six or eight miles on the 'Black Sea'.

We soon settled down to work, having unpacked our goods against the walls of the first rooms we rented. With the aid of buck-sails, together with our wagons with poles, we made a fairly good shelter for our merchandise. Jock MacDonald helped us a lot and also introduced us to the Landrost, Piet van Staden, or Klein Piet, as he was called, for his father, Old Piet, was still alive and lived near the village. Van Staden was a totally uneducated man of no particular ability and how he came to be Landrost puzzled us. The office of Landrost and in fact everything was managed by his clerk Kroep, a Hollander, and a very good sort we found him. There were several young men in the place, one of whom became a fast friend namely John Wagner, then Sheriff of the Rustenburg District and who later practiced as a law agent.

Alfred Redhead, a blacksmith, was also a good sort and a good shot as was Waters who succeeded Wagner as sheriff before the war of 1881.

There was little or no cash in the Transvaal in 1869. All paper money, 'blue backs' and 'good for's' (printed cards) were used by everyone in all businesses of any kind whatsoever and were valued according to a man's standing. That is, if a man's position was good, his paper, or his card, was readily taken at face value; on the other hand it would be taken at a discount, or not at all. The value of government paper was about one-third of its face value. In those days we were all involved in little intricacies of primitive finance! Handling, or barter, was the principal mode of trade. The produce taken in exchange was grain, tobacco, *reims* [thongs], whips, *sjamboks* [African rawhide whips], soap, bacon, eggs, ostrich feathers and ivory. To carry on our trade effectively we had to make frequent trips into the district and away into the Waterberg, about 100 miles east of Rustenburg. Many pleasant trips did I have, trips that recall to my mind very many incidences of adventure – pleasant and otherwise.

The Boers, though kind and hospitable, were in most cases 'hard nails' to deal with and very suspicious of being 'Jewed'. Among a certain class, pilfering was very frequent. I must mention an occurrence that happened during a Nachtmaal time in Burgensdorp when I was living there. A Boer woman, noted for her proclivity for pocketing anything that came in her way when an opportunity offered, went into the store of Messrs. Goldman Brothers, and asked to be shown some ribbons. One of the clerks showed her several rolls from out of a glass case; but she was hard to please and at last turned and left without purchasing anything. But the clerk noticed a length of ribbon hanging from her dress pocket and dragging on the ground. He quickly jumped over the counter and placed his foot on it. The woman walked on, away along the *stoep* [verandah] she walked and the ribbon unwound from her pocket. Several young men were standing on the stoep of the Albert Bank (The district is called the Albert Drift District) and laughed loudly as the woman strolled on until the unwinding process had finished with the last of the ribbon from the reel. I have no doubt that the ribbon was paid for later as it was the custom in those days, if anyone was caught pilfering, to charge the article or articles at a good price. Very seldom were the articles disputed. On one occasion a saddle was missed from one of the stores. The owner charged the article to several different customers. The entry was disputed in all accounts but one who paid without a murmur and asked no questions. I knew in good time who could not be trusted while I was out on trading trips and if any article went missing, or the thief detected, I always charged those suspected and generally got payment in full.

The trading trips, especially those to the Waterberg, gave an opportunity of hunting for game which was fairly plentiful such as springbok, wildebeest, hartebeest and pallah. There was also game in profusion on the Springbok Flats near Waterberg. Birds such as guinea fowl, pheasant, partridge and wild ducks abounded in the pans during the rainy season. In those days, while travelling from farm to farm, we often heard but seldom saw lions. But we often heard of exciting experiences. One story I remember, told to me by one of the party concerned, Kornelius Botha, concerned an incident when he and his companions were travelling between Pretoria and Waterberg. It seems that they had sent their wagon on the day before and were following in a cart with a pair of horses. Having left Pretoria late in the afternoon, darkness came upon them ere they reached the wagon. They had a young kaffir boy with them who set his feet behind the splashboard. While travelling along in the dark the horses suddenly stopped and snorted and one commenced to plunge and struggle.

'What is it?' asked one of the men of the boy.

'A donkey is biting the horse, Baas,' was the reply.

But as they spoke they heard a lion growl and realised it was attacking one of the horses; then suddenly the horse was down: a crunch or two followed and then an expiring groan. The other horse, which had been violently plunging and had partly broken away from the cart, was also seized by the lion and in a short space of time it too was killed. Only the noise of the struggle and groans of the horses could be heard: it was too dark to see anything. The men had a loaded gun with them but no percussion caps with which to fire it. The front seat had, in the struggle of the horses, got shifted down off its resting ledge and the men and the boy were squatting in the bottom of the cart. One of them had a box of matches with which, at last, he succeeded in striking the gun, which exploded with a roar prompting the lion to display its fury by soaring over the men and catching the back of the cart with its teeth, tearing away a portion of it. The lion then again resumed eating the horses. The men tried no more matches that night. They sat still until the arrival of another wagon pulled by a team of oxen which scared the lion away. The cart was then hitched on to the back of the new wagon and their journey was resumed.

Chapter 3

The most attractive trading trips of those days were down the Crocodile River, for during the winter the Boers trekked from the Highveld, or Witwatersrand. This was the district where Johannesburg now stands in the centre of the greatest gold-mining area of the world. However, at that time it was an almost wild waste with here and there a few scattered impoverished farms which, with few exceptions, could be bought with the price of an ox-wagon.

As I have stated, the Boers from the Highveld used to trek down to their winter quarters on the Crocodile – the Bushveld as they called it –not only for the grazing but chiefly for hunting, for in those days game abounded in the bushveld: blue wildebeest, hartebeest of all kinds, sasabie, koodoo, pallah and ostriches, while up in the hills away to the north-east herds of buffalo were to be found. Lions were numerous and were heard every night. The nightly chorus of the jackal, hyena and lion, the hooting of owls interluded with notes of other night birds and chirping of insects, all helped to give the charm that has fascinated so many of our African travellers who, once having experienced nature in its varied quantity as we have it in Africa, would again and again want a taste of the wilds. For me it had great charm, the life in the veld (away from streets and houses) and the life of the bushveld amid nature. It satisfied me, and did not tire me mentally – though often physically. My spirits were ever buoyant in the veld, the never-to-be forgotten hunting veld of my young days in the Transvaal. Many, many pleasant days can I recall and many amusing instances that even now make me smile as they float o'er my memories of trading and hunting expeditions of former days. On one occasion while lying in wait for game at a waterhole some miles from the river, there were three Boers and three of us colonial English. Old shooting holes were occupied by us, holes made some years before for lying in wait. All dogs had been tied fast at our wagons before we started for the water. It was a bright moonlight night, and very still. Nothing disturbed the quiet except the chirping of an occasional insect and the distant bark of a jackal. We had been seated for some time in the holes. Not a word was spoken above a whisper and our ears alert to the slightest sound of game approaching when, suddenly my ears, always acute, caught the sound of something approaching from our rear. It was not the sound of any animal with hoofs. The quick pat-pat was that of a soft-footed animal, not a hyena I could detect from the evenness of the sound. It struck me that it was my dog Leo that had got loose and had followed our tracks down to the water. Next to me sat one of my colonial friends. I noticed that he had become uneasy and had turned his head towards the approaching animal. Suddenly Leo's big tawny frame loomed on the horizon above us, appearing bigger and double his size. The pent-up suspense of my friend overpowered him and, with one wild shout of 'Lion!', he rose and plunged forward into the muddy pool below us and emerged on the other side where he rushed up the bank, a bedraggled, muddy spectacle, followed by shouts of laughter as the terror-stricken chap tried in vain to scramble up a tree. To make it worse the dog ran around the pool towards him; he saw him coming and rushed into the bush screaming for help. We followed and by continual shouting brought him to his senses at last. To make things worse for him there were Boer families at the camp and the women and girls gave our friend a rough passage. For a long time the dog and the victim were a great source of amusement at the waterhole.

Many were the exciting chases we had after game in those days, often dangerous owing to the many pitfalls in the bush made by the natives to trap game. They would dig deep holes planting the bottom with sharp stakes which impaled animals that fell into the holes. These traps were generally in gaps left open here and there in long stretches of the bush fence. On one occasion while chasing a herd of wildebeest I noticed the leading animals scatter and leap, the others following their example as they reached a certain spot. As my horse galloped up to the spot I noticed a hole but I was too close and riding too hard to stop. The horse I rode was good and active, so tightening my grasp on the reins, I touched him with my spur and called his name: he rose in the air and landed well with his four feet beyond the trap which yawned beneath me like an immense grave. But for the space of a few seconds we hung there, his hind hoofs scrambling for a grip while I clung with my arms around his neck. Then with a supreme effort he drew himself out of the hole. I dismounted and looked down upon the sharp pointed stakes and saw what a terrible fate my horse and I had so narrowly escaped.

On one occasion while returning from a trading and hunting expedition down on the Crocodile River, I decided to go upstream through Vleigpoort, so called on account of its once being plagued by tsetse fly: however the place was now supposed to be free from infestation. It was a hot afternoon and I lay on top of some buffalo hides on the wagon, my rifle alongside me. Suddenly our kaffir boy held up his hand, halted my tired team and then pointed with his forefinger to the left. Looking, I saw a large warthog and I aimed and fired from the wagon. The pig dropped, then rose and staggered away into the bush. I jumped down and followed, but before doing so told the boys to outspan when they reached the river as the road seemed to be leading towards it. After walking some distance on the blood spoor of the pig, I gave up and turned back towards the road, which I crossed, and walked on down towards the river about a mile and a half away. On reaching it I thought that I would find my wagon below a ridge in front of me that ended at the river. The sun was by this time just going down. On reaching the ridge there was no wagon, in fact no road. I quickened my pace and walked up along the side of the ridge, concluding that the road had crossed it higher up. I had not gone far before I struck the road and walked leisurely along. By this time it was getting dark. Suddenly I heard a rustle in the long dry grass near the road and stood for an instant listening as the sound approached. It was the movement of a heavy animal, creeping softly, cautiously towards me. I stood up on the side of the road furthest from the approaching animal, my gun – a Snyder sporting rifle – held ready and cocked. Suddenly I made out the head of a lioness parting the grass very near the edge of the road. My gun went instinctively to my shoulder but it was too bad a light to see my sights clearly. The animal crouched ready to spring and I took aim at a spot between its eyes but dropped the muzzle a bit to about the throat and pulled the trigger. The lioness growled sharply and commenced tearing up the grass around her. I hastily put another cartridge into my gun and walked quickly away, about twenty or more paces. The lioness continued growling and tearing the bushes and grass around her. I left her after sending in a parting shot and went quickly along the road where I found my wagon outspanned by the river just beyond the ridge mentioned earlier. Had I gone about 200 yards up the river instead of turning and going obliquely back, I should have reached the outspan before reaching the wagon.

It was about eight o'clock when I finally got to the wagon where I found several of Ramakoek's natives, who were out hunting. I told them about the lioness and next morning got them to bring me the skin and claws but they were worthless, for the claws were worn down with age and the skin was mangy. 'Tis such lions that are dangerous to man as they are too old to catch game. Lions rarely attack humans unless they are noted man-eaters; or when they have killed an animal, and are approached; or when wounded or have been disturbed while eating.

Chapter 4

While in Rustenburg in 1871 we formed a local volunteer corps of which I was for a time Lieutenant and, later, Captain. In 1876, I was ordered to accompany President Thomas Burgers during the war with Secocoeni [Sekhukhune]. Burgers had become President of the Transvaal Republic in 1875; he was a cultured, clever man far in advance of his time and environment. The contrast between him and Vice-President Paul Kruger and other members of his government – excepting the Hollanders who were, of course, well educated – was remarkable. Many of the Boers believed themselves to be as Israelites of old, the Chosen of the Lord, and that Paul Kruger was as Moses, chosen by the Almighty to guide the people after their emancipation from the British yoke. Good folk, but the superstition of ignorance ruled them strongly.

Well, as I have stated, we formed a volunteer corps and to please our captain, who was a German, we called ourselves, at first, the Schutzen Corps. We did in fact follow some simple old German military customs and our duties consisted mainly of target shooting and a little quaint drill, etc. We had a uniform, of course, a green tunic with red facings, white drill trousers and a peak cap covered with white calico. We gathered once a year for feasting and dancing when everyone was invited. Rich and poor in those days were on a common footing. Our feast usually lasted about three days and they were pleasant days in many ways. But I realised I had often gone too far, for my life in Rustenburg was wasted time and was not spent to the advantage of my mental capacity or my morals. There were undoubtedly many happy days spent in Rustenburg but there was much done that brings sadness to my mind when I think of my life there.

During the year 1871 I accompanied Captain Diedricks [a German ex-officer], George Grimes, Mr Harmse and a party of Australian diggers, led by a man by the name of Lofty, to the Tati goldfields. Our convoy consisted of three tent wagons, one Australian dray, and one buck wagon. It was a very dry season and the only fodder for our cattle to be had down by the Crocodile River were the green reeds that grew along the river banks. In consequence, with our wagons being heavily loaded with meal, tobacco, and with dried fruit, our animals suffered severely. The diggings were then being worked on the site of some ancient shaft discovered by the late Mr Hartley, the hunter of the Transvaal. The site was under the management of Sir John Swinbourne of the London and Limpopo Company.

The country in those days abounded in game of different kinds so that we were always well supplied with meat. I was the only one of our party who had a horse; Bob was his name and he was a good sound stayer and fast. He was bred by George Palmer of Grahamstown, so that I was able to supply the whole party with meat. With the exception of Michael Harmse and myself, the rest of our companions were indifferent shots and poor hunters. Getting lost in the bush was a frequent occurrence to one or the other of them. On one occasion one of the Australians left the wagons while on the trek, lost his direction and was trapped by a lion and kept the whole night in a tree, managing to fasten himself some way or another in order to prevent himself falling during the night. He turned up about noon of the following day in an exhausted condition and never again went hunting alone. So frequently were our raw friends getting lost that finally, by common consent, it was agreed that none of them should go out hunting without a guide obtained from the local Vaalpens natives.

On leaving the Crocodile, at a place known as Wegdraai, we had a heavy sand ridge to cross by a narrow road, bushed on both sides with many windings making it difficult to work a long span of oxen. This consequently increased the difficulty of our progress, the tent wagons however managing to get along the best. My wagon was twenty foot long and built in Grahamstown. The result was that although we left the river late in the afternoon, intending to get through the sand ere the heat of the day became too oppressive, my wagon did not reach the camping place before darkness had fallen. My driver, Half Crown, (a Basuto boy I had brought up from the Cape Colony) gave up early in the day. Want of water was our chief cause as our supply had become exhausted.

Grimes' wagon and my own stuck together, or rather he stuck to me until I urged him to push on to the others and send back some water. We were all parched with thirst. All we had to drink was some peach brandy with which we wetted our lips from time to time but this made matters worse. And when Half Crown collapsed I had to drive the wagon. With a parched throat, I struggled on for a time after Grimes left me and, with my voice gone, at last fell down exhausted. Then all became oblivion until the following day when I came to my senses and found myself resting against Lofty who had me in his arms and was bathing my feverished and aching brow. It seems they had gone back to my assistance, bringing water with them, and had found the oxen lying down in the yoke with myself in an unconscious state on the ground. My driver was in a similar condition and the leader asleep in front of the oxen. As we were now at the Brak Water which, though bad, was better than nothing, we decided to rest at this spot for a couple of days. I soon pulled round thanks to the kindness and attention of my companions.

Several natives from Bamwangwato came to our wagons; most of them were very insolent. One went so far as to climb into Capt. Diedrick's wagon and demand gunpowder and lead. This was too much for our German friend – not so much the demand as the insolent manner of the native. Diedrick quickly drew a dagger from his sheath at his side and the native leapt from the wagon and bolted with Diedrick throwing the knife after him. It stuck into the trunk of a tree just missing the flying fellow and quivered there. The force of the cast was shown by the depth of the knife's penetration which was about two inches. Several natives, numbering in all about twenty, were about the wagon at the time, some armed with guns. A shout of defiance came from them and their actions indicated trouble. So, fourteen of us in all, quickly got out our guns and the natives gave us no more trouble that day.

In the afternoon of the third day after our arrival at Brak Water, we trekked on towards Bamwangwato, another long stretch without water being before us, but we hoped for rain as the clouds were showing up well all around. We trekked on for a couple of hours and then outspanned for an hour and then trekked on again. The night was bright and clear and the moon full. After about a three-hour pull we outspanned for three hours and then on again until just before sunrise when we outspanned until the afternoon. The next water was at Bamwangwato, still about twenty-five miles off. However there was a chance that water might be found at some pans about eighteen miles ahead. That night about 10 o'clock, I noticed my oxen seemed to be stepping out at a brisker pace; first one then another lifted their noses and sniffed the air. Before this I had great difficulty in getting any pace at all out of the weary and thirsty brutes. Shortly before this we had heard some of the oxen of the front wagons lowing.

'There's water in front Baas,' said Half Crown, my driver.

'Yes,' I replied. 'There's water or wet ground. We shall soon see.'

In the bright moon light I saw a bunch of tall trees away ahead and shortly after the croaking of frogs was heard. Soon we reached ground that was harder than the sandy stretch we had been on before. Faster went our eager oxen and yokes commenced to rattle against their horns. The damp smell and croaking of frogs was, and always will be to the thirsty, 'like news from a far country'. (I am thinking years ahead as I write this and I will make more applicable references to the text shortly.)

Loud shouts ahead came back to us on the gentle breeze. 'Whoa, whoa! Stop them Bill' was the shout we distinctly heard, and as we neared the trees the shouting and noise increased; and the best of all, we heard the splashing of water. Presently in the moonlight we could see the Australian dray [cart] and their oxen standing in a pond of water. Despite the Australians' continual efforts, they had failed to keep their oxen out of the water. Shouts of laughter pealed from every throat, white and black, as vain attempts were made to urge the thirsty animals on to dry land.

'Let them drink their fill first,' shouted Grimes, 'and then talk kindly to them, you bet they won't stay in there too long.'

With difficulty my span was unyoked and as each ox was freed it ran to the water to quench its thirst. Each one of the front wagons had had the same experience as they got near the water. The three tent wagons had been outspanned fully for an hour before us and a welcome drink of coffee awaited each one of us, and never before was a cup of coffee so much appreciated. It was on a Saturday night when we arrived at the welcome water and the next day, Sunday, we decided, as was our custom, to lie over. It was also decided that I should go and see Chief Machin at Old B'Mangwat. This I did after breakfast, and an hour's ride later I came in sight of the native town situated beneath the bare rocky hills which backed it to the west. On arriving at what appeared to be a store, I met Bill Finnaughty whom I had known in Grahamstown as a boy. I off-saddled and with Finnaughty went inside and found another Grahamstown boy in George Francis who is now the Market Master of Mafeking. I was warmly welcomed by all. The store was owned by a well-known firm of early interior traders, Messrs. Francis and Clarke. I enquired the way to the Chief's kraal and, on being directed, I was not long in finding it with the chief himself sitting on a chair inside a *scherm* [a protecting fence, usually in a semi-circle, made of thin sticks of the wild currant of Bechuanaland], in front of one of his huts. He insolently asked me where I came from and what I wanted. I told him I had come with the others with our wagons and we were on our way to the Tati goldfields and that our wagons were standing at the pan.

'Very well,' he said, 'but your wagons must come here. The road is through my town.'

Now we had been warned by some men who had been fleeced by this scoundrel to try and keep our wagons away from the kraal. So I said:

'The road we are travelling does not come here. This is not the way to Tati. Tomorrow, on outspanning, our wagons will stand at the point of the hill near the water.'

'If you do not come here with your wagons,' he replied in his former insolent manner, 'and pay me for coming into my country, I will send my men to bring them in.'

'No! You will not send your men to bring in our wagons; but you can send some men to the outspanning tomorrow and from each of our wagons a roll of tobacco will be sent to you.'

I then saluted him and walked away amid jeers and insults from his men who were standing around nearby. I felt pretty bad, and did not feel like taking it lying down.

I rode back to our wagons and reported to my companions the result of my mission. All agreed that we should inspan and trek very early the next morning at 2 o'clock, which we did. We then outspanned again before sunrise at a point in the hill opposite to where there were waterholes. We outspanned where I told Machin we should be.

We all agreed that we should stand firm in opposing any of the chief's blackmailing attempts. We had fourteen good men, all of whom were well-armed. At about 10 o'clock a headman, attended by a few followers, came on horseback and said the chief had sent him to demand £2 per wagon for the right to pass through his country. I acted as spokesman for our party and said:

'You can go back and tell Machin that his people pass freely through the white man's country but as I promised him a present of a roll of tobacco for each of our wagons, I will give you five rolls. You can see for yourselves that there are four wagons and a cart.'

The tobacco was placed on the ground nearby our servant. After a lot of talk the tobacco was taken by the headman. Before going he said:

'White man, the Chief is not a child. He will send his men to bring you and your wagons to his kraal.'

'Go,' I said, 'and tell your chief we also are not children and will not be driven like cattle. We do not seek for trouble and it will be wise for him not to seek it. Should any harm come to us in his country my Government will seek an explanation from him.'

Our firmness had the desired effect, for we were not troubled further and in the afternoon inspanned and trekked to Lemone Vlei where we had heard there was water. On our arrival there we found Elephant Phillips, George Weartveach and Argent Kirston, all on their way to Matabeleland which was then still under the rule of Moselekatse [Mzilikazi]. We told them of our little trouble with Machin, and were informed that our firmness saved us from being robbed as was Machin's custom whenever an opportunity offered.

'You chaps all come from the Transvaal,' said one of the trekkers, 'hence the reason why Machin did not press matters too far. However, a number of traders have been severely handled by Machin, but they came from the Cape Colony and besides were green at the game.'

'And does he not give you any trouble in your journeys up and down?' I asked.

'No,' they replied. 'We are under the protection of old Moselekatse [*sic*] some of whose people are with us and Machin dreads the Matabele.'

And so I found out later. Machin had been in the habit of blackmailing whenever an opportunity offered. He was, however, later superseded by Khama, the rightful chief and a man who has ever held the respect of all classes. A good Christian chief with ability to rule, gentle in manner but possessing a firmness suiting him to the position he has held long since; and also a warrior chief of no mean order as Lobengula, the successor of Mzilikazi, found out in his endeavours to root out the B'Mangwato. At one time during an attack upon Serowe Hill by the Matabele, it is said, Lobengula was shot through the neck by Khama, thus narrowly escaping with his life.

On arrival at Lemone Vley we decided to wait a day or so as long as the muddy water lasted, ere moving forward. On the first day of our arrival I had been round in search of game and not far away, among a cluster of

Mimosa trees, I found fresh giraffe spoor. So early the next morning I started on old Bob towards the same spot and sure enough, there were giraffe feeding high up among the top most branches with the long necks up-stretched. Bob did not feel himself, which I could tell by his languid manner. However, I pushed him forward as the giraffe made off but he responded with only a tired sort of gallop, yet I urged him on. He seemed to try to put on more speed but was incapable and instead of gaining on the giraffe lost ground whereas usually he was capable of carrying me in among them. The giraffe crossed the road some 500 yards ahead and just as I urged my poor horse on he came to a sudden stop. I hurriedly jumped off from the now-quivering animal and pulled off the saddle and bridle. It was a clear case of ordinary horse sickness and I had bought Bob as a salted horse. [A horse that had suffered horse sickness and survived, thus being immune to the disease.] 'Sold again!' I thought, for I had expected him to die. My two boys who had been following me came up. I left one with the horse and walked back along the road followed by the other carrying my bridle and saddle. I suddenly heard the crack of a whip and then noticed dust rising from the road in front. The sun was becoming obscured by heavy black clouds and the reason for our wagons moving on was a sudden dust storm. I sat down and waited, and shortly after the wagons arrived. Captain Diedricks' wagon was in front; he called out from where he was sitting:

'What's up Dennison? Where is your horse?'

I pointed back: 'There he stands'.

'What? Is he hurt?'

'No,' I said, 'a case of horse sickness.'

'But I thought you said he was salted.'

'Yes,' I said, 'I thought so too, for he was bought as such.'

Suffice to say I had Bob led on behind my wagon and he did not die but lived to carry me for many a long day thereafter. What should have killed him had in fact cured him; I have heard of one such case besides.

We had not gone far from where I had met the wagon when thunder commenced to roll from the west. Peal followed peal accompanied by vivid lightning flashes; big drops of rain commenced to fall.

'Push on! Push on!' was shouted by our German captain. 'Lets try and get through the river before it is full.'

Ahead of us, about a mile further on was a small river and all of us were eager to cross ere it was too late. Loud were our drivers' shouts and the constant noise of the whips roused our oxen to a brisk walk. The rain came down in torrents on the sandy veld and soon we were splashing several inches of water in the road. We just managed to cross. The last vehicle, the Australian cart, got through with its oxen all but swimming and barely had we outspanned in the welcome wet when the water rose above the river banks and flooded the flat ground. A typical bushveld storm. Our animals stood behind the bushes in the pelting rain while we sat in our wagons thankfully watching it all. Our water troubles were over, or rather I should say, our want for water was over.

After many little exciting episodes we reached the Tati goldfields. One incident I must mention which occurred to Grimes' wagon driver, a Dutch lad by the name of Ignatius du Plessis. We had outspanned beyond the Macloutsie River for the night. It was just about sundown when Du Plessis, hearing some guinea fowl in the bush, asked for Grimes' shotgun and went after them. Some hours later we heard a distant shot, then another, far away in the bush.

'That chap has lost himself,' shouted Harmse. 'The lions will eat him.'

'All right,' I called out, getting out of my blankets. 'Get your guns,' I continued, 'and we will go and find him.'

But no one would move. It was pitch dark and cloudy for the moon had not yet risen. I called to my Basuto boy, Half Crown, to come with me and gave him a gun and a lantern.

Away we went through the bush in the direction of the shots. It was hard work and not pleasant for lions were plentiful; and in parts the thorn bush worried us not a little, tearing our clothes and hands. An occasional shot still guided us and at last we heard the terror-stricken chap shouting away in front of us. As we got closer we could distinctly hear him calling: '*Kom haal my! Waar's die wagon? Waar's die wagon? O my Mama, kom help my. O my Mama, kom help my.*'

He was up a big tree. We got beneath it and I shouted:

'Ignatius, come down. Ignatius, come down.'

But he had lost his head and kept on shouting.

At last I fired a shot past him. He suddenly let go and fell from branch to branch until he hit the ground and then got up and tried to run off. With difficulty we held him and got him partly to his senses. We then retraced our steps towards the wagon with nothing to guide us in the black night. After walking for about two hours we struck the road and saw no wagon spoor, so we knew that our wagons were still further back. We followed the road and after a long walk we reached our companions. A fire was burning and my friends were sitting around it anxiously awaiting our coming with a kettle of coffee ready for us. For the rest of the trip Du Plessis could never be induced to leave the wagons alone.

On arriving at the Tati I went up to Sir J. Swinburne's hut, he being the manager, and offered him our loads. I found him hard to deal with and eventually sold the stuff elsewhere to some young Scotchmen who represented the Glasgow and Limpopo Company. We stayed two days at the Tati, saw the ancient workings and turned homewards. We had, on the whole, a fortunate trip and had little or no trouble with lions until we were near Lemone Vley when Phillips, Westbeach and party had an experience one night. We were all awakened by a shot close by. I and others got up and in the moonlight noticed several people standing talking near the wagons. We walked up to where they were and saw that they were examining a lioness which was lying dead. It seems that a Bushman servant, who had gone to sleep under his blankets near a fire with his gun alongside, was woken up by feeling something pressing heavily on his legs. It was a lion and he slowly and gently turned the muzzle of his gun towards the animal's head, pulled the trigger, and shot it dead. The little chap was quite cool about it but of course thought not a little of himself thereafter.

On Christmas Day of 1871 I arrived home in Rustenburg. The others had returned some days earlier as I had been delayed shooting some game along the Crocodile River. Three years later I went down from Rustenburg with my wife and children to Burgersdorp to meet and to bring up my mother and the rest of my family consisting of my three sisters and my only brother who had been with me for a time but had subsequently gone to Aliwal. My sisters later married, one J. H. Tennant, the other William Tennant, and the youngest married J. Batterson of Pretoria.

In 1875 I entered into partnership with my brother-in-law while a year later, in 1876, the war with Sekhekhune's people broke out. Prior to this I should mention that the Schutzen Corps had been appointed as a sort of Guard of Honour to the President, Thomas Burgers, and that we got arms and ammunition from the government. The President himself went to the front and we accompanied him as his guard. We joined the commando on the Olifants River opposite Matebe's Kop. My corps, the Rustenburg Rifles, numbered about thirty rank and file. On our arrival at the laager we ascertained that a futile attack had been made on Matebe's Kop. It was then decided that the President should accompany a reconnoitring party. The next day we started out at daylight and arriving within a mile of the rocks forming Matebe's Kop (This rock so named after the headman who ruled there, a subordinate of the Chief Sekhukhune). The natives fired at long range and shouted in defiance. After a thorough examination of the place with General Pretorius and Assistant-General Niklas Smit, the party including myself and the corps who had accompanied the President, returned to the laager. A council of war sat the next day, when an attack was decided upon two days hence.

Our force consisted of burger contingents from practically every district of the Transvaal besides two native contingents, one from Magaliesberg (Magoto and Magalies men) and another from Zoutpansberg. The number of white men totalled about 2,500. The Contingents from Magaliesberg and the Rustenburg Districts were commanded by Commandant W. Meyer and that of Zoutpansberg by Captain Dahl, who was a Dane. The Native Contingents numbered around about 1,300 men.

The Pretoria Artillery was also there with Colonel Weatherley who was accompanied by his wife and two sons, Paulett and Rupert. They had come over from Eersteling where the Colonel was Managing-Director of the Eersteling Goldfields Company. He had come down with his family as a spectator of the war.

About two o'clock on the third morning following our reconnoitring, we left camp to attack Matebe's stronghold. I got permission to accompany the attacking party with my small band leaving four men to accompany the President who, with Commandant General Pretorius, would be on a point of observation to the west of Matebe's with the artillery. All the men were on foot with the exception of some of the officers including myself, who were mounted. One of my men, W. Sargeant, also had a horse as he had hurt his foot. Assistant-General Smit led the party of about 600 burgers away round to attack from the east and we accompanied him.

Commanding Matebe's Kop, and about 150 yards from it, was a conical hill surmounted by an immense precipitous rock, around whose base lay huge rocks with bush growing thick in parts. Deep yawning crevices were visible in the crown rock. All this had been seen on the day we had reconnoitred. The President, observing the rock remarked: 'It wants but an ocean to make it another Gibraltar.'

Away we went quickly and quietly round to our point of attack. As we neared the rock top (kop) I heard enough from one and another of our Boer friends to satisfy myself that they would not attack while it was dark. My men walked in half-sections on the right of the commando and as we neared the kop I noticed that our leader kept away to the left as if to pass it. I quickly passed the word along to my men to edge off towards the kop which they readily did. We descended a low ridge into some flat ground, the kop looming up against the horizon. I halted my line of about twenty-five men and told them my plan. I wanted the honour of victory. So quickly I explained that when I gave the order, they were to advance quietly and quickly, and when I gave the signal they were to fire their volley and, with a wild shout, to charge. I knew enough of the natives to feel quite sure that they would make no stand when thus rudely and unexpectedly awakened. Not a sound was heard from the kop looming black against the morning skylight which was now breaking into day away in the east. When within about 150 yards of the black prominence I halted and fell back into line with my men.

'Be ready,' I said quietly, 'and fire when I give the word.'

In a few seconds I shouted: 'Fire and charge home Boys.'

The line of fire lit up the darkness for a minute as the report of our rifles rang out sharp in the keen morning air and went resounding from hill to hill being carried far and loud by the magnetic iron rocks which abounded in Sekhukhune's country.

Yells and screams came from the rocks in front as we rushed up among them. All the natives except a few on the top rock bolted and the fastness was ours without one man wounded – although several shots had been fired towards us.

I called to my men to scatter among the rocks at the base of the krantz and await daylight. Loud and incessant came the firing from the attacking party from the west side of Matebe's Kop which was returned with vigour by the enemy. As it became lighter, bullets commenced to whiz about us fired by the enemy to our front and above us. In a few hours it was all over. The few natives on the rock had got away except all but one whose body lay in a crevice of the rocks. Our flag fluttered in the breeze from a tree on the summit. We were in full view of the President where he stood with the guns next to Colonel Weatherley and his family. Our flag was plainly visible to all of them by the aid of glasses [telescopes]. Our success gained us the goodwill of all, for the position we took commanded Matebe's Kop and thus rendered the taking of the latter less difficult. A considerable number of the enemy were killed, and some were taken prisoners. The women and children were released straight away. We lost two men killed and several wounded. On our arrival in camp that evening we were warmly welcomed by President Burgers and Colonel Weatherley.

After the capture of Matebe's which, perhaps after all was only wasted time, we moved on to Masaleroomes above Fort Weeber. Cattle were reported in great numbers down by the Olifants River and the burger officers repeatedly asked President Burgers to sanction their capture, but he would not have it. He was, in fact, opposed to looting. By slow stages we moved down the Olifants, having daily scraps with the enemy, until we reached Olifants River Poort, later called Murder Poort from the fact that two natives were, to my mind, cruelly executed there: a patrol under Assistant Commandant General Niklas Smit, had gone forward into the mountains to our front where it was thought a large number of cattle were stowed away in the deep kloofs. The patrol, on reaching an ugly pass, had been suddenly fired upon killing one and wounding another. The guide was accused of treachery and, together with a young Zulu who had earlier been accused of complicity in the murder of a Boer farmer near Wakkerstroom, were put on trial. As martial law then ruled, both prisoners were tried by court martial and condemned to death by the assegai. They were handed over to our native levies and stabbed to death. Hence the name of Murder Poort.

We moved the next day, crossed the Olifants and skirted the Lulu Mountain towards Sekhukhune's stronghold. One Schlickman, who was with us at the time, nearly lost his life having being shot at by a young German who was part of the commando. The President had halted under the shade of a marula tree, for the sun was intensely hot. A few men were riding slowly along towards a stone koppie in their front when suddenly we saw the smoke of fire arms arising from the rock and the leading man, Badenhorst of Maquassie, fell from his horse. The koppie was quickly rushed.

I went through with some of my men but the burgers were already on top. A cluster of them were standing together and on going closer to investigate I heard a revolver shot and exclamations from the men: 'Out of this you drunken ass! What do you think you are doing? That was Von Schlickman you fired at!'

Von Schlickman had got down into a crevice and was dodging around a rock shooting at a kaffir inside when a young man came up, revolver in hand, and seeing something below, without asking any questions, suddenly fired at Von Schlickman. Fortunately the young man missed his mark and became the butt of our humour for a long time. Needless to say the lad was new to the game.

At last we arrived at Sekhekhune's Stadt (town). A council of war decided to attack the next morning before dawn. I cannot find dates, as my records were lost, so give only details and facts of that misconducted war of 1876. We moved out long before dawn and waited in the bitter cold. Delay after delay occurred until at last, about sunrise, we reached the point of attack. My corps was supposed to remain in camp with the president but he kindly released us saying:

'There will be quite enough of the sick, lame and lazy to protect the laager and myself. Go, Dennison, by all means and try to inspire some life in the Boers.'

Let me here explain that the whole commando was in a sad way; the men had been kept too long at the front, they were homesick and had no heart to fight. The officer commanding the attack had not noticed me or my men until it became quite light, then, as he was riding past, he turned and drew up beside me saying:

'Captain, you and your men should have stayed with the President.'

'The President thinks the same as I, that there are quite enough sick and others in the camp without me and my men,' I said.

'Well, promise me one thing,' he said, 'and that is that you will stay with the guns. You are too headstrong.'

'All right,' I replied, 'there will be plenty of work everywhere today.'

Under cover of the cannon fire, a futile attempt was made to take a koppie near the stadt, but the attack was half-hearted. The burgers were not for fighting: their longings were homewards. Having placed my men in position at different vantage points around the guns, I went to where General Pretorius was standing. On passing through a sluit I noticed a number of burgers hiding, which I reported to the General.

'Go!' he said, 'and drive them out.'

Then seizing a pick handle lying nearby he walked into the sluit and started belabouring the burgers, who scattered right and left but only to take cover elsewhere. Further up I found a field-cornet with twenty men. He was lying on his stomach groaning – though it struck me he had seen me coming and the pain had got worse for the nearer I got the louder and deeper were the groans. I knew him as a nephew of the late president, so calling him by name I asked if he had been hit by a bullet.

'No,' he replied, 'but my stomach is very bad.'

I noticed a giggle among the men nearby. 'Yes, your stomach and no doubt your pluck too,' I said, and caught hold of him by the foot. I dragged him a bit but he got worse, so I applied my boot but he got no better.

'The General's orders are that you are all to go forward,' I shouted.

One very bad man got up and shouted: 'Here come the kaffirs. They are storming us.'

That man knew how to cure stomach aches for no sooner had he said it than the late President's nephew got up and, not wasting any time, rushed forward. It was indeed a most sudden cure.

The men all laughed and made a pretence of going forward but they didn't go far so I returned to where the General stood and said:

'It is no use General. The men will not go forward. Some are so sick that "kaffirs" is the only remedy that seem to do them any good.' I then asked: 'Shall I go forward with my men? You have too many here to guard the cannon and perhaps some of them will follow me.'

'Yes, thank you and shame the cowards.'

I hastily sent and collected my small party and away we went towards the stadt. The firing came pretty thick but the kaffirs fired badly. Not one of my men was hit. I found the Assistant-General with a few men sitting behind an embankment under a large marula tree.

'Not this way! Not this way! You will draw the enemy fire upon us,' one of them shouted.

I halted my men for a few minutes to get back their breath and while doing so Niklas Smit called out to me, saying in Afrikaans: 'Fanie Roos and Nel are in the sluit with a few men.'

'All right,' I said and we ran forward and found Roos and Nel with thirteen men up on the edge of the stadt, sheltered behind a thick palisade of poles. The fire from the front and flanks was heavy. About seventy-five yards off was a long gulley from which the enemy kept up an incessant fire, while from the barricades on the mountain side, the fire was also very heavy; it seemed like one continual patter of bullets, some making most weird noises like stones with lead cast around them. Fortunately the barricade was good and decently set. One of my men, Adendorff by name, a plucky sort, in fact a regular daredevil, would have charged the barricade had I permitted it but the idea was a mad one for no man could live outside the barricade.

'All right, Captain,' said Adendorff, 'excuse me then for I'm going to sleep in this hut.'

He crept in whistling his favourite tune Nancy Barr. In fact, he whistled the tune so often he got the nickname of 'Nancy Barr'.

One of Nel's men named Horn, who was standing alongside of my brother Dan, was shot dead through the shoulders. Seeing we could do no good with a handful of men (we had about forty all told) I suggested to Commandant Nel that we should retire, especially as the Boers from our rear were also firing on us! He agreed, so we sent the men back to a deep gulley in our rear going in twos and threes at a time, while the others kept up a constant fire on the enemy's palisades. When all were gone but for Nel, three men and myself, we too ran for the gulley, but as I leapt into it I remembered Adendorff and quickly rushed back. He had just awakened as I called sharply to him and he met me at the door of the hut. We quickly put in a couple of shots on the advancing foe and gained the gulley and safety.

Horn's body was carried out by Daniels, Kirton and a couple of others, all Zeerust men.

We were able to keep the kaffirs in check by alternate covering parties and all got safely out and reached the guns with but the loss of Horn only. A general retreat was now on, regardless of order, while the enemy showed themselves in hundreds advancing among the rocks. My men had got scattered and it took me some minutes to get them together at the guns. One gun carriage was out of order so I called to some passing burgers to help me but no one responded. We were able to check the advancing kaffirs who were making a terrible noise shouting and blowing their horns. We hurriedly tied the gun carriage together with reams taken off the oxen harness until one case of shells remained. Each of the men and myself carried one shell each and got out, but were very nearly surrounded. Had it not been for the cool pluck of my Rustenburg boys we could never have got clear. When we got through a deep sluit in our front, Commandant General Smit with some men came to our assistance. The enemy were driven back with loss and we reached the camp about 9 p.m. tired, hungry and disgusted. Thus ended the attempt to take Sekhekhune's stronghold in 1876.

Although the President had been eager to try again and a council of war, held the following day, had decided to make a second attempt, the attitude of the commando made it impossible to do so. In open rebellion, the burgers commenced dragging out their wagons: home they wanted to go and home they would go at all costs. Colonel Weatherley advised turning the guns on them but instead their commandant called another council of war and later sent a deputation offering to contribute £10 per farm to enable the government to raise a paid force. The people crowded around the council tent to hear the result of the deputation. The President thereupon decided to talk to them and got up on to the back of a wagon and spoke, but it was useless.

Shouts of defiance came from the mass of men around. One man, an officer into the bargain, shouted: 'You can talk as much as you like,' and continued in Afrikaans, 'we will go home! Home! Home men!' It was a unanimous cry.

Mr Burgers then got off the wagon, disheartened and disgusted, and went to the council tent again. The proposal of the delegation was considered and adopted pro temme [*sic*] to be made law later by a special meeting of the Volkstadt.

The majority of the commando turned back that day and our laager was broken up. The President accompanied by about 300 men, including my corps and myself, went round via Styl Poort to Lydenburg. The others returned via the road by which we had come, via Olifants River.

We lost several men on our way, one of mine whom I had given to the President as a driver, was shot on the wagon while trekking along.

On arrival at the Styl Poorts River we built a fort and christened it Fort Burgers. We then continued on to Lydenburg and from there to Pretoria. At Middelburg we were met by Mr Phillip Watermeyer, a friend of the President's, who drove us in a carriage and four to Pretoria. I accompanied them at the President's request and on arriving at Pretoria remained at his house as his guest until my men turned up a few days later. On arrival the men were paraded in front of Mr Burgers' house, where he addressed them, and gave the officers a copy of his photo. Mine I still have. He thanked us for what we had done and said it was a source of great gratification to him to be able to say that his bodyguard had done their duty faithfully and well. I felt that I now had a friend in the President; Colonel Weatherley also became a firm friend. The President and myself corresponded until shortly before his death.

Chapter 5

Shortly after the arrival of President Burgers, a special session of the Volksraad was called regarding the levying of £10 per farm being confirmed. Then the trouble began. The men of the commandos who had been at Sekhekhune's Mountain had offered, and faithfully promised to pay, £10 per farm rather than fight. Now, away from the menace of kaffir arms, they indignantly refused to pay up – even in face of the fact that a force of volunteers was being enrolled under Von Schelkman to do the work they had refused to do, and such at their own suggestion. Groot Adriaan De la Rey was one of the ringleaders and threatened to shoot the sheriff, Walters, who came to him with a summons. It was mainly owing to the interference of Jerry Jennings of Hek Poort that he did not fire on Walters.

The position of the Transvaal Government was pitiable: nothing in the treasury and the country in a state of anarchy. Petitions were made for annexation to the British Empire through the Government of the Transvaal. Sir Theophilus Shepstone was sent with twenty-five policemen from Natal and the country was annexed by the Crown. I will not enter into details fully but should recommend reading of a little work called *Boers and Little Englanders* by John Proctor. This gives a fairly accurate account of the true state of affairs in the Transvaal at the time and deals with the annexation and causes which led up to it.

The Boers were satisfied with the annexation. Shepstone understood them and knew exactly how to treat them, and as long as he remained the possibility of trouble seemed remote. But he was recalled and when Major Lanyon became Administrator of the Transvaal the position of affairs changed. Lanyon was an autocrat, and treated the people with abruptness; and no courtesy was shown to them as was not the case with Shepstone who had furthermore promised the Boer leaders a constitution. A promise that was later confirmed by Sir Bartle Frere, the then High Commissioner. However, month followed month and nothing was done that showed any intention on the part of the British Government of carrying out the promises that had been made. Dissatisfaction spread, fanned by the action of several Hollanders and the want of a conciliatory policy by the Administrator. Since Shepstone had to go for some reason or the other – probably because he was too honest – had a man been sent who knew the Boers and how to treat them, the probabilities are that the subsequent war of 1880–81 would never have been. The ultimate bloodshed can be traced to this and to the unfulfilled promises on the part of the Crown representatives.

The Boers were grim, obstinate folk, both men and women, for the latter shared all the dangers and though a woman personally did not carry a gun, she could load and fire one when needed – at times a most helpful accomplishment. Their religion was entirely in accordance with their views derived from the study of the Old Testament; the New Testament being to them, practically a 'sealed book'.

Proctor is correct in the main in his latter remarks regarding the New Testament but this did not apply to all by any means. There were very many exceptions. Proctor goes on to say that on two points the Boers were united – this is after referring to dissensions among them – first, hostility towards the Englishmen and secondly their desire to subjugate the kaffir. And on these two issues their energies were invariably concentrated.

It will be easily understood that owing to the stress of the times the Boers were only too pleased to have the protection of any powerful authority. Yet the fostered hatred of generations was by no means dispelled and the actions of our imperial agents provided a reason, which was eagerly grasped by the Hollanders and others and made the most of by them, resulting in a war that might have been avoided.

Previous to annexation by Shepstone and the subsequent trouble caused by the natives of Zoutpansberg, Colonel Weatherley had been authorised to raise a volunteer force for border protection [named the Border Horse] between the farmers and the natives of Zoutpansberg of which Moqato was the principal chief. Colonel Weatherley, who had previously spoken to me about the probability of his raising a force and had hinted that he wanted me, met me in Pretoria in 1878 and offered me the post of his second-in-command of the corps he was raising. I accepted and went to Pretoria to assume my duties. The first troop was raised and was soon under marching orders for Eersteling, near Marabastad. I should have taken command of this troop as far as its destination but, the day previous to our departure, I received a letter from Rustenburg informing me that my wife was seriously ill.

I left that night and rode the thirty-six miles home. About noon the following day a rider from our corps brought a dispatch recalling me at once as all available men were wanted for Zululand. This was shortly after the disaster of Isandlwana. I still have in my possession the old order book in which appears the following order:

'Regimental orders. Pretoria January 30th 1879. According to instructions received, B Troop will parade at 10.30 a.m. in full marching order for active service and will proceed to Luneburg to join the Transvaal Column.'

On the 30th January 1879 we left Pretoria for Zululand with about sixty-six rank-and-file. The following officers were detailed: Lt. Col. Weatherley, Capt. C. G. Dennison, Lt. Palmer [*sic* – he means Parminter], Lt. Lys, Lt. Poole and the colonel's youngest son, Rupert, a boy of thirteen who was later attached as a supernumerary lieutenant. Nothing particular happened on our march down; training our men in cavalry movements while on the march was our daily work. Our colonel had been an officer in the Inniskilling Dragoons and took great interest in the training of his officers and men.

On arrival at Luneburg, a German village, we joined Colonel Rowlands who was in command of the column with Captain Harvey as his chief staff officer. Colonel Schermbrucker, later of Cape Parliament fame, was also there in command of the Kaffrarian Rifles – a fine good-natured piece of peculiarity. A really good officer he afterwards proved to be despite his oddities. While at Luneburg one of our men, Archer, who is at present an overseer of the divisional council of Vryburg, was sent with a dispatch to Wakkerstroom and on his return had a narrow escape: the Zulus waylaid him but he dashed through them and escaped. He got a bullet through his hat which his comrades chaffed him about saying it was he who had made a target of his hat, etc., etc.

We had been about a week at Luneburg when orders came for the Border Horse and the Kaffrarian Rifles to march to Kambula forty miles off. Kambula was the headquarters of General Sir Evelyn Wood's column [at the time Wood's rank was that of Lt. Colonel and he was yet to receive his knighthood]. We arrived there a day after leaving Luneburg. We found Kambula Camp situated on an open rise immediately above the head waters of the White Umvolosi River. As a defence camp it was well placed. We found many we knew among the officers of the 13th and 80th Regiments and Raaff's Rangers, under Pieter Raaf, whom I had known as a small boy, in the Free State. Baker's Horse was also there with Capt. Parminter, brother of Sub. Lt. Parminter, who had joined us on our march from Pretoria. The present secretary of De Beers, Mr Pickering, was also an officer in Baker's Horse.

Buller's Frontier Light Horse was also there together with a Basuto mounted contingent and other native forces. Three regiments of regular infantry, or portions thereof, were also present: the old 13th, 80th and 96th [the author is incorrect, the 96th was not present]. All in all a strong force, with several guns including a Hotchkiss mounted on a fort on a mound overlooking the base camp. A cattle laager adjoined our camp, or nearly so there being about twenty paces between us. Commandant P. Uys, with about forty men, was also at Kambula.

A few days after our arrival news came of the almost total annihilation of a portion of the men that comprised the guard of a convoy of wagons on their way to Luneburg. The convoy was under the command of Colonel [*sic*, he was Captain] Moriarty, who at the time was laagered on the banks of the Entombu [Ntombi] River. There was evident carelessness in guarding, for it appears the Zulus had actually got into the camp without warning and assegaied some of the men through their blankets as they slept. The attackers had helped themselves to what supplies they could carry away, destroyed all they could of the balance, and had driven off all the animals. Some men managed to escape. One, Lieutenant [*sic*, he was Sergeant] Booth, with a few men got out and away into a farm house close by and managed there to hold his own. Others (a few) got into the river and lay under the water. A man called 'Fat Jones' of Kimberley was one. He told the story of how he lay on his back in a pool half hidden by some rushes and how the Zulus came along the river bank prodding with their assegais and saying: 'Come out Johnny, come out Johnny.' He told how nervous he felt as he laid submerged for he was bulky and it took some water to cover him. He thought his breadbasket might be seen above the water. However, he got off Scot-free but not so others who were found and killed in the water.

Umbeleni was the Induna or chief who with his men wiped out the convoy. It was stated that Umbeleni was living, or had moved, on to the Hlobane Mountain, and it appeared that Col. Wood, although instructed by Lord Chelmsford to act purely on the defensive, allowed himself to be persuaded by Col. Buller and Commandant Uys, to attack Umbeleni. Uys had a bitter score to settle against the Zulus for in earlier days he had lost many friends by Zulu treachery. In addition to this his father and two brothers had all been killed by the Zulus. His tent was next to mine in the Kambula camp and shortly after our arrival he told me how he had joined the column, not for love of the English, but rather for an opportunity to avenge those of his family and friends he had lost by the assegais of the Zulu. It would have been better for him had he remained on his farm.

As I have stated, Col. Wood was persuaded to attack Umbeleni at Hlobane and here again is the instruction as given in the regimental orders, and signed by our Acting Adjutant B. H. Lys.

March 26th 1879
EXTRACT FROM BRIGADE ORDERS
All available men of the Frontier Horse, Border Horse and Bakers' Horse will parade at 8 a.m. for patrol.
Each man will carry seventy rounds of ammunition, a blanket and two days' rations, one day to be of preserved meat.
Spare ammunition to be carried by the corps.

The time mentioned for parade was the day previous to our marching for camp, for we left on the morning of the 27th March. Raaff's Rangers were included in our Horse but not in brigade orders, why I never knew. Well, I do remember that morning, foggy, as was usual at that time of the year. In fact the fog was so dense that men in front were only visible at a short distance. All hands were cheerful and looked forward to a brush with the enemy with feelings of eagerness.

It was known that Hlobane Mountain was our destination. We were the last of the force to leave camp and after marching for about three hours we came upon Col. Buller off-saddled near a *spruit* [stream]. The sun was now shining brightly, dispelling the fog. As we neared Col. Buller he called to Col. Weatherley who rode towards him, saying distinctly:

'Weatherley, you had better veer away to the right and off-saddle; you will be freer from the crowd.'

I turned to the right with the men and we off-saddled near a running stream of water. I omitted to mention that Col. Buller added: 'and I will send you word when to move on.'

We had our breakfast. The men were lying idly about resting except those who were guarding the horses. The colonel and Rupert lay against their saddles on my right. Hours passed. Noon passed, in fact it was about four o'clock in the afternoon when I faintly heard the sound of a bugle.

'Boot and saddle, sir,' I said, turning to the colonel, who appeared to be half-asleep.

'Does not matter Dennison,' he replied. 'Buller said he would send me orders when to move on and I shall not move until I receive the order to do so.'

Shortly after I saw a horseman ride by, then others, and away moving over the rise on our left was the main body. Our total strength of mounted men, I must here add, was about 350 aided by a strong native contingent who were away on the left. Schermbrucker's Horse also formed part of the force but they, with the native contingent and others, were to attack at a different point thus they were marching separately some distance from us.

I spoke again to the colonel and said:

'The whole crowd are off, Sir, Colonel Buller has forgotten us.'

'Well then here I stay,' replied Col. Weatherley. ''Tis Buller in command, not me.'

The sun was near setting and the men were growling. They were by no means cautious in what they said; murmers were in fact growing into loud plain talk when I again turned to Col. Weatherley and said:

'We must move, sir, or we will be left behind.'

Our Colonel was to blame for it was quite evident to me that Col. Buller had acted purely with kind intent which I could judge from the manner in which he spoke. He assumed Col. Weatherley might be out of sight and hearing when orders for marching were given but found later, as he must have done, that we were only a few hundred yards off and could see and hear the orders of march. He thus presumed that Col. Weatherley would know what to do remembering that he was an officer of long service and considerable experience.

'Well, all right, order the men to saddle up,' said our colonel.

I gave the order and it was quickly carried out. As the sun disappeared down west we moved on following the tracks of the main body. After crossing the first ridge and gaining the top of the second, mist and rain commenced. Away in our distant front we saw the light of camp-fires, for which we made a bee-line, but on gaining the next ridge the fires had disappeared. We at once guessed the reason, for Col. Buller had many old hands with him: to mislead the enemy, who might be contemplating an attack, camp fires were lit and left burning while the troops moved off to another spot that had been chosen earlier in the evening. This was a ruse adopted in the early days when night attacks were probable. We marched on in the dark and drizzling rain for about two hours when suddenly, on gaining the top of one of the ridges, we saw away on our right what appeared to be stars in the distance. I was riding alongside of our colonel at the time.

'The weather is evidently breaking,' he remarked.

'No, sir,' I replied. 'Those are not stars, they are fires, and if I mistake not 'tis the fires of a Zulu impi camped on the sides of the kloof below us.'

'Then halt,' said the colonel, 'and send scouts forward to reconnoitre.'

'Very good, sir,' I replied, and added, 'and I think it would be wise to form a ring camp and let the men hold their horses individually. I will with your permission go forward myself with two men on foot and find out what it is we can see.'

The colonel agreed and I passed word for Louis Bernard and Barth, two German colonials of British Kaffraria, two good, keen and trusty men, on whom I could fully rely. Leaving our horses and arms we went forward on foot, down the grassy slope of the mountain side towards the fires to our front, feeling our way down the rain-sodden decline. We reached a ledge behind which the light of many fires lit the sky, while away on both sides of the wide deep kloof, and glimmering away far down like distant stars, we could see the many fires of the Zulu impi. The hum of numerous voices broke the silence of the night.

'Twas a weird scene we looked upon as scarce breathing, noiselessly we advanced step by step to the edge of the krantz below. When within a few yards from the edge I touched one of the men and whispered: 'Wait here both of you.' Then, cautiously feeling my way, I reached the edge and, looking gently and quietly over, I saw below me groups of Zulus squatting around their fires. So close were they that with an extended rifle I thought I might have reached their bald-ringed heads. Though not knowing much of the Zulu tongue, I heard enough to gather that they were bound for our camp at Kambula. I quietly withdrew and with my two followers returned to where we had left the colonel and our men. I found Col. Weatherley and Rupert lying wrapped in their cloaks, the boy asleep, while the men lay in a circle around them, each man holding his horse. I reported what I had seen to the colonel and suggested remaining as we were until we could get our direction right to Hlobane. To this he agreed and so we lay. Needless to say I did not sleep but kept watch away from the group where I placed a couple of guards to warn us on any movement by the enemy. No movement was made by them nor did we expect it until towards sunrise for we knew the Zulus would not likely march in the drizzling rain which prevailed throughout the whole night. About three o'clock in the morning I saw distant flashes away to the north, which we judged was the flashing of firearms on Hlobane. I quickly woke the colonel and had such men as were asleep awakened. We then mounted and as silently as possible we moved away in the direction of the flashes of light. As we advanced the flashes became more incessant giving continuous light which guided us. Our progress was slow owing to the darkness and the dongas that we had to cross.

As the light of the dawning day broke gradually around us we could see Hlobane Mountain looming through the mist to our front while loud and continuous firing could be heard. As we crossed the last marsh, it was by then quite light and we saw a party of horse men galloping across our front. We caught them up at the foot of the mountain: 'twas Col. Sir Evelyn Wood, the officer commanding our column, with some of the mounted infantry. Lt. Syrus Fowler [Fowler was a private, not an officer, but would shortly be awarded the Victoria Cross] and some others I recognised, among them Capt. Campbell and Col. Wood's interpreter, a Natal man [Lt. Llewellyn Lloyd].

'What's the matter Weatherley, where do you come from?' asked Col. Wood as we rode up. The position was explained and Col. Weatherley told Col. Wood about the Zulu impi.

'Nonsense,' was the retort. 'I have had my men out yesterday, there is no Zulu impi about.'

I then replied: 'But I saw them, sir, I was in fact almost within touching distance of them and judged them to be a strong force.'

'Can't be, Dennison. You are mistaken,' said Col. Wood.

I made no response but when the opportunity arose I rode to Col. Weatherley's side and said: 'Don't you think sir, we should place a picket on that hill', pointing to a semi-conical hill to our east, 'and leave our horses here and to advance up the hill on foot until we gain the summit? Then we can bring the horses all the way up.'

'No, no,' said Col. Wood who overheard the latter part of my suggestion. 'The others in advance have gone up with their horses, you can do the same.'

I saw the folly of such a course for one could plainly see that we should have to fight our way up the mountain, and to do so leading our horses appeared to my mind – untutored though I was in military tactics – to be wrong. However, up we went doing the best we could, with Col. Wood and his party accompanying us. I was leading with my men close behind making straight for the path showing red on the summit. Up among the rocks we had already seeing Zulus taking up their positions.

'Keep to the left,' came the order from Col. Wood. So to the left we turned, only to face a horse-shoe krantz of great height, at the base of which lay numerous boulders intermingled with bush. Heavy fire rained down upon us from the horse-shoe and it was evident that the enemy were in force among the rocks. A large number of cattle were in a kraal we could plainly see, and whether or not it was they that gave rise to the order to veer to our left I cannot say.

Here and there a dead body marked the course of our main advance which had been led by Buller. Several of our men were struck down including my two faithful followers Bernard and Barth. Both were shot dead near me. Several were wounded, including my batman, Cameron by name, and Sgt. Fisher. There were others whose names I now forget, but as I am giving the casualty list later, all names will show.

We were working from rock to rock, when word was passed on to me from Col. Weatherley, that he wanted to see me. I returned to where he stood near some rocks, with Rupert his son sitting near him under cover of a boulder. Col. Wood was nearby and close to him was the body of his servant and interpreter, Lloyd [Lloyd was not his servant, merely his interpreter].

'Col. Wood says you must charge, Dennison,' Col. Weatherley said to me.

I look amazed at such an order when men could only advance in baboon-fashion to make progress.

As I was turning to rejoin my men, Capt. Campbell who was with Col. Wood, rushed forward calling: 'Forward boys!' A few minutes later he was lifted back a lifeless corpse. The top of his skull had been blown off. My men lifted his body over the rocks with Lysons and Fowler assisting for which they were each awarded the VC.

I know that Col. Wood stated in his report that the Border Horse hesitated, hence the reason Capt. Campbell rushed forward. What I have stated is the simple truth. The Border Horse never deserved a slur in this action and Col. Wood was mistaken.

Immediately Capt. Campbell fell, Col. Wood left us with his mounted infantry and retired. I was standing alongside Col. Weatherley when Col. Wood left. He gave no order to my knowledge or I must have heard it. He took with him one of our wounded, a young man named Andrew Hammond, whose name I found years later on a monument to some of the slain of Rhodesia which stands near the Shangaan River. We were in a tight spot, and by means of alternat[iv]e cover I got the men out and on to the red foot path to the summit of the mountain. Here Col. Weatherley left us with the order to remain where we were. He was going to find Col. Buller for orders. He had only been gone a very short time when a youth without a hat rode up hastily and asked:

'Where is Col. Weatherley?'

'Gone to look for Col. Buller,' I replied, 'but if you have any orders, give them to me.'

The youth replied: 'Col. Buller's orders are that the Border Horse are to return to camp at once, we are surrounded by a large Zulu impi.'

The young Frontier Light Horseman then left and a few minutes later Col. Weatherley returned and I gave him the message.

We retired fighting our way down again and suffered no further casualties. We took one of our wounded men, Sgt. Fisher, down with us and while halted at the foot of the mountain, made a stretcher for him. Then Capt. Barton of the Coldstream Guards arrived leading a troop of Buller's Horse. As he passed us he shouted:

'Don't delay Col. Weatherley, the mountain is surrounded.'

We tied Fisher on a horse and followed Capt. Barton round the point of the mountain. He was about 500 yards ahead of us when we rounded the point. Then we saw to our left a portion of the Zulu army holding the ridge all along the south of the donga, which was between us and them, while on our right was Hlobane Mountain. We saw Capt. Barton and his men gallop into a passage between two stone kraals. A heavy fire was poured into them at point blank range by Zulus waiting hidden behind the kraal walls. Confusion resulted and some riderless horses scattered away in a terror-stricken gallop. How many men fell there I never knew but the rest retreated towards our party advancing from their rear. Capt. Barton's men soon steadied down under his command for he was a brave and cool officer.

We halted and then all retired together making for a nek to the east of Hlobane. Our horses had been under saddle since the previous evening and it was now about 11 o'clock in the fore noon. They were 'blown' and many of them weak. Col. Weatherley rode behind the men with myself and Lts. Poole and Parminster. We cut the blanket straps of the men as we reached them and ordered all possible weight to be cast off. Behind us the enemy advanced in swarms, faster than we could move. We helped the men on all we could but several were caught and dispatched by the enemy. We saw one man, Riley, our trumpeter, dismount from his knocked-up horse and fire on the close advancing foe. Then turning the rifle to his head he shot himself. The most important fact was that but few of our men had any ammunition left or we might have made a stand at times and saved some of those who fell in the retreat. All was done that under the circumstances could be done, for such who had ammunition left, kept up a dropping fire on the enemy which did little to check their advance.

[The following description, in italics is exactly as given by Dennison. Despite the confusion that the wording introduces, the editors decided that it should be repeated exactly as originally written]:

As we neared the nek dividing Hlobane from the continuous ridge, or rather which formed a low nek on our side was on the facing north, one continuous precipitous mountain ridge way high on the west forming Hlobane whose table top was rimmed by krantzes.

As we neared the top of the nek up the gentle slope of which we galloped, Capt. Barton suggested making a stand, which, as I have stated, would have been useless owing to the want of ammunition. As such Col. Weatherley considered that to stand without means of defence was giving our lives to the enemy for naught. So the idea was not for a moment entertained. Lts. Pool and Parminster were riding near me. We saw Zulus from the mountain clustered on the heights on either side of the nek.

'We're enclosed Captain,' said Parminster, a favourite expression of his.

'I'm sorry for you,' said Poole to me, 'for you have a wife and family whereas we are single men and our lives will not be much of a loss.'

'It may not be as so bad as all that, all is not lost yet,' I replied.

Suddenly the men in front hesitated, then scattered. The reason was soon apparent to us for there was no gentle decline on the other side, rather a steep and high precipitous mountain with krantzes and loose rocks leading down to a level plateau far beneath us.

The hope gave way, brave men now defenceless became panic-stricken, death faced us behind and our retreat to all appearances cut off in front. For the moment we drew rein and looked aghast at the prospect before us, the yelling from a thousand enemies' throats became more distinct. Right and left our men disappeared while about twenty obeyed an ordered given to keep together. We bore away to the right riding against the hillside on the right of the nek and then on along a ledge. We cantered till a sudden halt in front brought us to a standstill. I pushed forward to see what the cause was, and found that the ledge we were on joined another but higher one above. A waterfall with loose rocks and brambles about five yards below seemed to block further progress.

'Make way,' I called out. 'Let me give you a lead,' for I knew if any horse would try the jump, my horse Beaufort would. I walked into the edge and spoke to him while I patted his neck, then backed him and with a touch from my spurs with tightened rein, loudly calling his name, I trotted my noble horse forward again. A touch with the spurs again, his name, and without any hesitation my noble animal leapt away forward and down alighting on an open patch just over the brambles: quickly one and then another followed. Some, however, refused. Hurriedly we led our horses down on foot, they seeming to realise the danger behind and followed at a trot. Capt. Barton with four men and myself were close together. I heard a Zulu shout behind, and looking back saw the enemy leaping down the ledge above us. Col. Weatherley was leading his horse with bridle rein linked in his arm while with the other hand he helped his cripple son. His drawn sword was in his left hand. He was but a short distance from us perhaps not more than twenty-five or thirty paces. Others were leading their horses down the hillside scattered about, each finding his way as best he could down the ledges and through the rocks. We were by this time not far from the foot of the mountain. I turned, leading my horse and, with two other men, turned back to aid the colonel. My idea was to get Rupert on to my horse. We were, however, too late. The Zulus had caught them and I saw the sword of Col. Weatherley flash in the sunshine as he used it to protect himself and his son. 'Twas but a moment and we were surrounded. The colonel was down and Rupert, with a piercing cry, fell dead from a spear thrust on to his father's body. I struck out right and left with the butt end of my carbine. I hit one of the Zulu warriors fairly above the top of his head as he stabbed one of my men, and he sank lifeless on the ground. Another I hit in the face and as the man fell it gave me an opening. I was young and active, and with a few bounds I reached my horse and was on his back in an instant. I saw one of the other men stabbed behind as he tried to mount his horse. Capt. Barton mounted at the same time and then came a race dodging the Zulus to our front. Two ran towards me, one from either side with their shields covering their bodies and up-raised assegais. The stock of my carbine was cracked but I was still able to use it as I galloped along. I fired at a Zulu and he dropped on my left; another halted and cast his assegai but missed. I crossed a small stream and caught up with about twenty-seven men, mainly of Capt. Barton's troop of the Frontier Light Horse, with a Sgt. Winterfeldt, a German, who was urging the men on for all he knew. A few of my men were also there, including Archer and Sgt. Brown, eight in all. One was killed later, a trooper Martin by name. I helped him out a long way but he lost his head and was killed. Brown and Archer rendered me great assistance. On one occasion after passing some mealie lands, we heard a shout, and looking back saw a white man running towards us pursued by Zulus. I called to Brown and Archer and they turned. I covered them by firing a couple of shots from my scanty supply of ammunition. They succeeded in reaching the man, one of the FLH, and saved his life. I saw many, very many, daring acts of bravery that memorable day, the 29th March 1879, combined with actions also that were of no credit to men, but so we always find. As we rode on towards Blood River, the number of the enemy following lessened until we neared Potter's Store, named after a trader of that name who before the war carried on a business there. Three Zulus only were seen following us persistently. These were waylaid and shot. A drenching rain set in just before sundown which wetted us all to the skin. But the camp fires of Kambula were now visible and we could ride straight for the camp. After being delayed by the outer circle of guards, we at last reached camp, stiff, weary and worn-out both physically and mentally.

Aided by one of the men who had remained in camp I removed my drenched clothing and got under my blankets. A hot drink was brought to me by our mess cook, an Indian coolie, followed by some supper. I ate well and tried to sleep but the scenes of the past day rose too vividly before me. Again I saw poor Parminster as he called to me from the ledge above: 'Dennison, for God's sake show me the path.' I had waved with my hand to indicate the path where the pathway was but he was stabbed ere he could reach it. The colonel falling so near me with Rupert his son, whose dying wail still lingered in my ears. Many of my brother officers and comrades-in-arms were now dead. One does not realise these things in the heat and excitement of battle but only afterwards. So it was with me as I saw it all again. The reaction drove sleep from my eyes for the greater part of the night, fitful snatches only, till morning broke at last. The cook told me breakfast was ready about eight o'clock. I walked into the mess tent with one plate, one knife and fork and one cup. I turned and went out saying: 'Bring my breakfast to my tent.' I could not sit alone at the mess table when last time we all sat together.

After finishing my breakfast I went into the colonel's tent and with the aid of one of my non-commissioned officers, was making out a casualty return when Col. Buller entered the tent. I had not yet reported myself at headquarters, intending to go over later. He shook hands with me and congratulated me on my escape.

'Tell me,' he said, 'how it fared with you and then come with me, the OC wants to see you.' He then asked: 'What are you writing?' and I told him it was a casualty list.

'Don't worry yourself Dennison,' he replied. 'Get all the rest you can for you will want it ere the day is gone. We expect Cetshwayo's impi here around about noon. Some of Oham's men were among them last night and have brought tidings. Had we but known of that impi in time yesterday, the chances are all our fellows who fell yesterday might have been saved.'

'But we knew it, Col. Buller,' I replied, and then gave him in detail what I had seen and had reported to Col. Wood.

He turned sharply towards me for an instant and looked me square in the eyes:

'I believe you Dennison, what a sad mistake, but say nothing for the present, lay low.'

We walked over to the staff tent. Col. Wood met us at the door of the tent and shook hands.

'I am glad to see you out of it Dennison, come and sit down and tell me all.'

Col. Buller had left us at the tent door and I told my story to Col. Wood commencing from the time he had left us on the previous day.

'But why had Col. Weatherley not returned to camp as I ordered him when I had left?' Col. Wood asked.

'I did not hear your order sir, nor do I think Col. Weatherley did, or he certainly would have carried it out.'

I doubt that Col. Wood gave the order, he may have intended doing so but had forgotten for I knew he was very much upset at the death of Capt. Campbell. Had Col. Weatherley got such an order he most certainly would have carried it out in which case most, if not nearly all our men and officers would probably have been saved. Col. Wood, I could see, was uneasy. He knew that Col. Weatherley had done his duty. Col. Wood had been warned about the Zulu impi but discredited the word of a colonial officer. I made reference to it:

'I was right, you see, sir, about the Zulu impi.'

He did not reply, and after give me some orders allowed me to leave. Perhaps had credence been given to the report of colonial officers the disaster would never have happened. Similar things in the last war (1889–1902) happened and many such instance in formal wars. Perhaps a great deal of cramming at Sandhurst or other military schools gave the officers a prejudiced and false idea of their superiority over men with no Sandhurst training. A lifelong practical experience of colonial officers was ignored. 'Oh he is only a colonial!' was too often heard from the lips of men whose position should have placed them above such petty thought. The empty-headed exclamation 'Ah don't you know Ah?' of such characters were as a rule treated with the contempt they deserved, but insults from superior officers were very deeply felt. Bitter enemies were made of men who would have sacrificed much had they been treated better.

Preparations were now in full swing to give the Zulus a warm welcome. Col. Wood had on his arrival back in camp the day before prepared the camp in a fair position of defence. Earthworks were thrown up along under the wagons while sandbags were placed on the wagons thus completing two tiers of defence, one above and one below the wagons. I must here add that Col. Wood narrowly escaped on his retreat from Hlobane the day before, his horse being shot under him. Fortunately he remounted another and reached the camp in safety. Tents were all struck at about 11 a.m. quickly and in a most orderly way. There was no hurry or excitement but rather an eagerness showing clearly on the features of most men. An eagerness to wipe out the reverse of yesterday and to avenge the deaths of the many who had fallen victims to Zulu spears. Just about quarter past twelve (noon) I heard a shout of 'Here they come, as thick as bees,' and looking eastwards I saw a column of the enemy advancing towards our left flank from Zinguin's Nek [usually Zunguin]. Another column advanced straight towards our fort. The bugle call of 'Boot and Saddle' sounded and quietly a body of horsemen lined up outside our camp near the fort. Then, mounted and in half sections galloped away left towards the advancing Zulus. The guns had now opened fire and we could plainly see gaps in the advancing Zulus as the shells struck among them, not to burst as we found out later but to bury themselves deep in the soft sodden earth.

Capt. Baker-Russell [this is incorrect – the officer concerned was Lt. Col. Cecil Russell] was sent out in command of all the mounted men [also incorrect – Lt. Col. Redvers Buller was in overall command of the mounted foray]. The idea was to bring on the attack and to prevent the flanks from encircling us. Other Zulu regiments had already reached the White Umfolozi River below our camp. We watched the cavalry attack the Zulu regiment in front of the camp drawing them on. Soon the cavalry regained the camp with the enemy following close behind. The Zulus now opened fire, the fire being returned from our fort, guns and small arms. Cases of ammunition had been opened all round our camp and the officers ensured the troops were sufficiently supplied.

Loud and continuous was the din of battle, interluded with the deep hoarse bass and weird battle cry added to the rattling of many thousands of shields of the Zulus, as they made successive charges on one or other side of our camp. A sudden cry attracted the attention of an officer of the 96th [*sic*, actually the 90th] and myself to our left, and as we looked we saw some soldiers leap down from wagons on to the ground. Then shields and heads of Zulus appeared climbing up. The soldiers stood with bayonets fixed and pointed at an angle to meet the foe, should they get over. We rushed up to help with some men of our party. Captain Parminster and others then assisted in repelling the Zulu attack. Had a few of them got over it would have caused trouble and perhaps disaster for so much attention would in all probability have been attracted to them, that it might have provided an opening for a Zulu charge.

The Zulus then got possession of the cattle laager adjoining our camp. A company of soldiers had been left to hold the laager as long as possible, and then to fall back on the main camp. This was done as they could not possibly stand against the determined rush of the Zulus, and they retired as ordered. A company of the 13th and one of the 80th [*sic* – 90th], then made an attempt to dislodge them, but were unsuccessful. Again an attempt was made, this time aided by Commandant Raaff and his men, and the Zulus were finally driven out. A most determined rush was made on our side by the foe but they were mown down by our rifle fire. An *induna* [headman], riddled with bullets came on, only to fall with his face to his foes within twenty-five paces of our wagons. The guns from the fort and the rocket too did terrible execution among the enemy as did the small arms. Fierce but vain was the onslaught of the brave Zulus who dauntlessly rushed our camp only to fall dead or wounded which was the fate of nearly all of them. Their attempts from the north were soon given up for our mounted Basutos, [the Natal Native Horse] who had refused to come into the camp, constantly harassed the enemy from the rear as they stormed us from the open country side. Splendid service was done by the Basutos which perhaps was never properly appreciated. The hospital tents were near our lines and were ere long after the attack commenced in full use. The surgeons and assistants were kept busy. Groans, and now and then loud shouts of agony, were heard perhaps during operations or movements of the wounded. One man, an Irishman was carried past on a stretcher after his leg had been removed: 'And how's the leg Murphy?' asked one of the soldiers as the man was carried by. 'Lost a lig but a pension for life I'll be havin', that's better than any lig or the two for the matter of that,' replied the wounded man. Poor chap, the prospect of rest and ease with one leg was not something to look forward to, thus a small pension was some little silver lining to his perhaps long clouded life, for he appeared to be a man of over fifty years. No doubt many others were maimed for life that day, but had at least of gleam of light in the prospect of a pension even if it were a pittance.

Five hours the attack continued, but our advantage of arms and position gained the day and between five and six that evening, the news was quickly passed that the enemy were retiring. During the fight I have omitted to mention that one of the officers came to me and said:

'Dennison, one of your men is supplying drink to my men, where does it come from?'

Now in the colonel's tent stood a cask of rum.

'Is that so?' I replied. 'I think I know where it comes from.'

We went together to the tent now lying struck and on lifting the side on which the cask was I smelt the liquor and saw where it had trickled down from the taps and was still dripping. The thief was known and immediately placed under arrest. However he escaped with our horsemen when they followed the retreating Zulus. He did good service and so the matter was overlooked.

Away to Zinguin's Nek the horsemen followed, shooting down the retreating Zulus who seldom offered resistance. On one side of the camp the men leapt over the barriers and I say it now with the feeling of shame, dispatched the wounded lying around ere it could be stopped. To try and stop the men from leaving their positions appeared useless as far as the irregulars were concerned. Tommy, however, impatiently awaited the order which came at last, when all, officers and men, left the laager. Enemy dead and wounded lay thick around. With two other officers I walked to the edge of the steep decline bordering the Imvolosi [Mfolozi River] down the sides of which our men were advancing, firing on the retreating Zulus who had hung back, no doubt, for the purpose of aiding wounded friends. One warrior who apparently hid in the river growth sprung up with assegai and shield and rushed a soldier who with his bayonet parried the thrust (his rifle evidently not being loaded). For some minutes the hand-to-hand combat lasted while our men stood watching until it became clear that the active Zulu was more than a match for Tommy. Then, one of the onlookers shot the noble Zulu Brave. It seemed a cruel and dishonourable act but such things do happen in most civilised warfare, if there is such a thing.

It took three days with five mule-wagons to bury the dead Zulus whose bodies, if I remember rightly, numbered 2,500. Impis that attacked us was supposed to number from 25,000 to 30,000 of Cetshwayo's army and the defeat at Kambula no doubt broke the spirit of the Zulu Army and saved our Col. Wood from trouble.

I believe Col. Wood had orders from Lord Chelmsford to act purely on the defence, but owing to the pressure brought to bear upon him by Col. Buller, Commandant Uys and others, following the affair of Moriarty's on the Entombe [Ntombe] River, he gave way and attacked Hlobane which ended in a disaster but dovetailed all right with the result of the next day coupled with the fact that nothing succeeds like success – even if gained at the expense of an order. I do not consider that Col. Wood was to blame but acted as no doubt half the generals in the British Army would have done under the same circumstances. [Col. Wood was, in fact, ordered by Lord Chelmsford to make a demonstration that would distract the Zulus while he, Lord Chelmsford, attempted to relieve Eshowe.]

The excitement of battle was soon past, and the men got together to recount the circumstances of the past few days. Tales of bravery, and deeds of heroism were many. The names of fallen comrades or missing were counted and it was only the day after the Kambula fight that we really knew what our losses were at Hlobane as well as at Kambula. A full account of the struggle at the west end of Hlobane was given to me by Commandant Pieter Raaff. How men died fighting bravely against odds while vainly trying to escape down the rock-capped Hlobane. How the dauntless Piet Uys fell as he rushed single-handed on to the Zulus in search of his son. As this was told to me I thought of what he had said to me when first we met: 'I am not fighting with the English because I love them, oh no! I have lost a father and brothers by the assegai of the Zulu and this gives me an opportunity. I am fighting to avenge the deaths of those I loved. Some fell through treachery with Retief at Dingaan's kraal and some at Blood River. We have many lives to avenge, very many,' said Piet Uys with a sigh as he stroked his long beard.

Raaff told me of good old Schermbruiker [*sic* – Schermbrucker], how when he called to his men to follow him to help those on the rocks above [at the top of Devil's Pass], his superior officer countermanded the order and said: 'You must fall back.'

To which Schermbruiker replied: 'You can order my men to run away but you don't order me,' and he galloped away followed by his men to help those struggling on the mountain tops. I must here state that Schermbruiker and his men formed part of a contingent that were in action from the west point of Hlobane.

Many were the tales we told and heard told after Kambula. Much remains fresh in my memory today of those days, the 28th and 29th of March 1879. Many also are the tales told today if any of the old hands meet; seldom now, for many are dead and gone, while those alive are scattered far and wide.

After the battle of Kambula the late Piet Uys's son-in-law, I forget his name, came to me and asked about a little six-year old boy of Trooper Bernhardt who fell at Hlobane. He said he would like to adopt the child. I referred him to GOC Col. Wood, who later sent for me and the matter was temporarily arranged pending confirmation by the civil authorities.

While sitting in the mess tent talking to Uys's son-in-law, we spoke about the old warrior and his death and about the early Dutch pioneers and their hardships, their sufferings, the innocent blood spilt different places and the treachery of Dingaan that resulted in the massacre of Retief and his burgers at Dingaan's kraal. As the young man spoke, I felt, as I had often done before, that the Boers as a people had been misrepresented in many ways and that their hatred of the British flag had just cause due to the treatment meted out to them in earlier days. In latter days this had perhaps been carried out to an unjustifiable degree to answer selfish ends.

The next day, after the Kambula fight, came the burial of the dead. Long deep trenches were made in which we buried our dead. The burials continued for three days as we followed, to the sad strains of The Death March in Saul Fallen – To The Last Resting Place. It saddened and softened the hearts of the most hardened among us.

The usual routine followed after the battle was that casualty returns and etc. was made up and sent to Headquarters. The following is a copy of mine as I have it in my old order book. It is of those who fell at Hlobane on 28th March '79:

Lt. Col. Weatherley	Trooper Martin
Adjt. Lys	Trooper Thompson
Lt. Poole	Trooper King
Sub. Lt. Weatherley	Trooper Underwood
Sub. Lt. Parminster [Parminter]	Trooper Ried
Regimental Sgt. Major Brown	Trooper Evans
Sgt. Major Fisher	Trooper Craig
Qr. Master Sgt. Russell	Trooper Jefferies
Sgt. Stewart	Trooper Brooks
Corp. Porter	Trooper Barth
Corp. Ford	Trooper Meillot
Corp. Blackmore	Trooper Muller
Corp. Coetzee	Trooper Mellma
Pay Sergt. Johnson	Trooper Miller
Farrier Major Frieze	Trooper Van der Westhuizen
Trumpeter Meridith	Trooper Dary
Trooper Wynnan	Trooper Farquarson
Trooper Shepherd	Lance Corp. Bernhardt
Trooper Mann	Trumpeter Rielly
Trooper Hartman	Trooper Williams
Trooper Cameron	

Forty out of fifty-five of the Border Horse alone. Of the other corps, I am not sure, but I think I am correct in saying about eighty. These were the casualties of Hlobane alone. I forget the number who fell at Kambula. If I remember correctly these were over one hundred.

One of the Border Horse, our rough rider, a Frenchman, Grandier by name, was, it appears, found hidden away on Hlobane after the fight by some Zulu women. He was taken to the headman Mbeline, who sent him on to Cetshwayo. Cetshwayo then sent him back again in charge of two Zulus to Mbeline. They halted on the way and one of the guards went to cut some sweet cane. The other left in charge of the prisoner carelessly lay down his assegai and gun. Grandier seized the assegai and killed his guard. The other Zulu saw what had happened and that Grandier was now armed and so made off. Grandier knew the direction of Kambula so, footsore and bereft of all his clothes but for his shirt, (for the Zulus had robbed him of all else) he made his way towards our camp and was picked up by one our patrols. He had a narrow escape and a most exciting time. I shall have need to refer to him again later on in my narrative.

Chapter 6

A few days after the Kambula fight, I got orders to return to Pretoria and report to the OC. So accompanied by one man as a servant, I started on horseback. A packhorse carried our blankets and rations and after six days travelling I reached Pretoria and reported to Col. Rowlands. Meanwhile, Captains Sanctuary and Daniels, who had been sent to Kimberley to recruit, had during our absence arrived with 120 men and were encamped above the town. I left our horses on the lines of our corps and on seeing Col. Rowlands and Capt. Harvey (his staff officer), I was informed that I was recognised as the OC Border Horse in place of the late Col. Weatherley. Both these officers, as did all others, treated me with the greatest kindness. I then applied for leave to proceed to Rustenburg to see my family, this was on a Saturday. My leave was granted on condition that I did not go until after the following Monday as Sir Bartle Frere, the Governor and High Commissioner, would that day be holding a reception and wished me to be present. I stayed over and met His Excellency who greeted me most cordially and said:

'I wish you to remain as my guest for a week. I must know all the details of Hlobane and Kambula as far as you can give them to me and that will give ample time for you to tell me.'

'Your Excellency,' I replied, 'I must thank you for the honour you are doing me, but I am on leave from tomorrow and am anxious to spend the time with my family at Rustenburg.'

His Excellency replied:

'Under the circumstances I must excuse you but would like you to send me a written report.'

I promised that I would and shook hands again with the good, kind and genial gentleman. I circulated, accompanied by an officer, among the crowd in the garden grounds of Government House where I met many I knew. Numerous were the handshakes and many the congratulations on my escape, however I was glad when it was all over.

The following day I left for my home in Rustenburg, where a reunion with my family was a source of great joy to me. I had been reported among the fallen on two occasions, hence the readers can imagine that ours was a touching family reunion. Our family circle consisted of my wife and seven children, my mother and three sisters, brother-in-laws J. H. and W. H. Tennant and my brother D. J. Dennison, to whom I had to recount my adventures as well as to many friends. By an inscrutable will of Providence I had again and again been spared, and not because I deserve such mercy, far from it. How often we who least deserve it are spared and blessed while so many who could ill be spared are taken. We do not know; we cannot say; and we dare not judge why it pleases the Almighty that it should be so.

My eight days were over and I returned to Pretoria, taking command of our corps. About this time, thirteen young Englishmen joined our force and proved a most valuable addition. Mr Arthur Mayers, of the Grootfontein in the Kuruman District was one of them. For some time we were encamped on Erasmus Spruit, at Redhouse Kraal, and thereafter we moved back to Pretoria. Later we marched to Fort Weeber in Sekhukhune's country where one troop under the command of my cousin Capt. H. E. Dennison, was stationed with other mounted units under Maj. F. Carrington.

Our marching orders came and on the church square a banner, made by the ladies of the town, was presented to the Border Horse by Maj. Lanyon, the Administrator, as a gift from the citizens of Pretoria. This banner is still in my possession it having hung for a time in the English church, Pretoria [as at the time of writing the banner resides in the care of the National Cultural History Museum, Pretoria]. Some time later it was sent to Rustenburg but when the church fell into disuse, the banner was sent to me at Vryburg. It has been in my possession ever since. It was a memorable day for the Border Horse. We were honoured that day of 1879 (I forget the month) with a big march past of all the troops in Pretoria, led by two military bands. At the first march past the saluting point the banner was received by my youngest subaltern.

Our wagons had gone on ahead and we followed escorted by several of our friends, officers of the 80th and 13th Regiments, who rode with us for a mile or so then bade us farewell. After marching about an hour, the transport officer, Capt. Edgerton, caught us up and addressing me said:

'Don't proceed too far as there are a number of wagons you will have to escort down to Fort Weeber.'

'Very good,' I replied, 'I will halt at Gray's farm until they turn up.'

On arrival at Gray's farm (this was a Saturday, I remember), we formed camp and on the day following, Grandier, the Frenchman who I have alluded to in earlier pages and who was now one of my troopers, arrived with a note from Capt. Sanctuary, my Adjutant, requesting me if possible, to return as the men left at Kambula had arrived and required their pay and I had all the books. I then heard from Grandier, from his own lips, of his escape from the Zulus as I have recounted in former pages.

I immediately had my horse saddled, and accompanied by Grandier and an orderly, rode back that evening to Pretoria. I stayed the night at a hotel and the next morning, about sunrise, went up to the Border Horse lines. I found Capt. Sanctuary with Maj. Clarke – 'one-arm Clarke', as he was called owing to his having lost an arm in action. Major Clarke was a fine old soldier, rough in manner but of a friendly disposition. An honest and true man who was later appointed Native Commissioner of Basutoland but resigned that position to take up that of Imperial Commissioner of Southern Rhodesia. He and Sanctuary were examining the horses in the lines and I shook hands with them and Clarke asked:

'What are you doing here Dennison? I thought you were miles away marching on to Fort Weeber.'

'Yes Major,' I replied, 'so I should have been but I am kept waiting for wagons from the Transport depot which have not yet arrived. I am camped on Gray's Farm and yesterday got a note from Sanctuary which brought me back here.'

'You had better be sharp about it,' Clarke replied, 'and get back to your command, or there will be a row if Lanyon hears of your return.'

'I must see Major Lanyon,' I answered. 'What time should I go to Government House?', for I knew Lanyon had been appointed Staff Officer to the Administrator and also acting GOC Volunteers.

'You had better keep away from Government House,' said Major Clarke, 'unless you want to get into trouble.'

'I have done no wrong and I am here on duty,' I replied. 'Major Lanyon can hardly be unreasonable when he hears what I have to say.'

'Well of course, if you will go, be there at a quarter past nine.'

So at the appointed time I walked around the corner of Government House and met Major Clarke.

'Oh, you have come,' he said. 'I was hoping you had thought better of it. Anyhow, come along and brace your nerves for a row.'

'All right,' I replied, laughing, and followed him into the building.

He showed me in to the reception room and then went to inform Major Lanyon.

I remained sitting for about ten minutes until Major Lanyon came out. I rose and saluted him but he took no notice of my salutation, but instead started ranting me very roughly for being away from my command. I endeavoured to explain but he would not listen to me.

'Silence sir! I don't want to hear your excuses,' he said.

'Very well, Major Lanyon,' I replied. 'I am a volunteer officer and as such won't be treated like this by you or any officer of the British Army. Give me ten minutes and you shall have my resignation.'

'I take the resignation of officers or dismiss them when I think fit and not when they choose to resign,' he retorted, and then added: 'What did you come here for?'

'You would not allow me to inform you,' I replied, 'but this was the principal reason that brought me here,' and I handed him the note of Sanctuary's.

'I wish to see you concerning my march to Fort Weeber.'

'Why did you not say so before?' he replied.

'Because you would not allow me to speak,' I said, 'and Good Morning to you, sir,' I said, and saluted and left him standing looking daggers at me.

I acted wrongly, I admit, but I had stood more from the man than my temper would take. As I got off the stoep Major Clarke met me and took me by the arm and said:

'Come along, you hotheaded devil, you have made an enemy of Lanyon, he will never forgive you, but I admire your pluck. Come, let us go and see Saunders.'

Captain Saunders of the 80th, was the officer who dealt with all volunteer forces. We went to Captain Saunders' office. I knew him well. Major Clarke told him all about what had occurred with the Administrator. We had a good laugh over it, and some chaff at my expense occurred, but on the whole I do not think I suffered for my action. No doubt Major Lanyon, on calming down, saw that he had acted hastily. I heard nothing more about the affair but left the same afternoon, accompanied by Grandier, for my camp on Gray's Farm. The wagons I was waiting for arrived and we moved on. After about six days, if I remember right, we arrived close to Fort Weeber, where we were met by Major Carrington, the OC of Cavalry in Sekhekhune's country, accompanied by all the mounted men from the camp. They consisted mainly of Ferreira's Horse, commanded by Commandant Ferreira in person, together with the troop of the Border Horse which had been sent to Eersteling under command of my cousin H. E. Dennison. There were in addition other details, all of whom had come to meet us. I felt we were well received and appreciated the mark very much. Major Carrington and Commandant Ferreira rode at the head of the troops with me and conversed chiefly about Zululand and the narrow escapes, etc.

On our arrival at Fort Weeber, my officers and myself were entertained at a Mess spread in Major Carrington's Mess room. All the officers of Fort Weeber were present. After dinner Major Carrington asked Ferreira and myself to accompany him to his tent, which we did. After being seated he said:

'I have asked you both to come here so that we may talk of the possibility of attacking a position that for some time has been a great source of annoyance to our patrols. As you, Dennison, may not know the position, I have drawn a rough sketch. I want you and Ferreira to arrange an attack, the date of which I will later give in orders, after seeing you again.'

I examined the sketch and found that it was near where Commandant Piet Raaff's camp had formerly stood. It was near Magnet Heights (so named on account of the rocks on that range being chiefly magnetic iron stone).

'Well Major,' I said, 'as Commandant Ferreira knows this spot better than I do, I think we should allow him the honour of attacking.'

'Oh no,' Ferreira replied. 'Your men are better trained and more fitted in every way to attack, you undertake that part of the work and I will support.'

'Very well,' I said. 'Either support or attack will suit me.'

After arranging further details we retired for the night.

The next morning I walked round the camp before sunrise. I was an early riser and always enjoyed a walk in the cool morning air. That was the best part of the day in summer and autumn and if people only knew or could realise what they are losing of life, they would quickly change their bed-loving habits and become early risers. I believe it would save many a doctor's bill and add to life's length as it does to its pleasure.

Fort Weeber is situated about two miles north of Maseleroomes Kop, so named after Sekhekhune's headman who once lived there. A sod wall forming a square surrounded the camp which consisted of tents and huts built of clay and sods and thatched with grass. Away north were loose ironstone koppies about three or four miles off, while in the distance were the black peaks of the Lulu Mountains. Behind them was Sekhekhune's Stadt or town at the foot of the range, which I got to know well, as events will later show. A few days after my arrival Major Carrington received orders from Headquarters, Pretoria, to occupy old Fort Olifant, of the river of that name. This fort had been built by Captain Moriarty who fell on the Entomba [*sic* – Ntombi] River in Zululand , and had not been used since he left it.

Major Carrington decided to send Ferreira and his men to occupy it.

'How will the day after tomorrow suit you both?' he asked.

We agreed, and so the next morning on parade the marching orders were read. We were to start at two o'clock in the morning.

Ferreira's Horse, the Border Horse, and the Rustenburg Native Contingent, with one of our artillery guns, were to form the attacking force. At two o'clock, or thereabouts, all the Horse had fallen in and was ready outside the camp. Shortly after we started, long lines of horsemen in half sections with the natives bringing up the rear, the guns, with its guard of mounted men were immediately behind the horsemen. Easily and quickly, we marched along as it was our intention to make the attack before daylight and we had a good many miles to cover. We arrived near the spot in good time, dawn not yet showing when we halted. Major Carrington was trying to get the Native Contingent, who had passed us on halting, to ascend a steep hill, the name of which I found later to be Mamalube. The idea was that the hills on either side should be held by the Native Contingent while the attacking force went forward to burn down the kraals, secure the stock and return before the enemy could arrive in any force.

Some renegade Swazis who lived a few miles further back, were especially to be avoided if possible. They were said to be some two hundred or more strong and would prove a formidable foe in the narrow pass we had to get through to attack the kraal situated away up in the Lulu range. (Mamalube was the name of the place we were to attack which I had previously forgotten.) A move was made at last by the Native Contingent but only when some of the white force went forward to lead them. But scarcely had they commenced to ascend the hill above us when, to our intense disgust, they opened fire. I immediately ordered my men forward at a trot up the mountain side following the path that led to the kraal above. Then Major Carrington joined us, our position having being sorely tried by waiting, until, as I have said the unexpected fire was commenced by our stupid and timid natives.

'The whole game is spoiled,' said Carrington, 'by those cursed niggers, you will have the Swazis on you.'

'Never mind Major,' I replied. 'Let Ferreira back me with his men and we'll manage all right,' for I knew my officers and men were good.

We hurried on as fast the rough ascent would allow. The day by this time had broken and ere we reached the top 'twas quite light. Away to our left was the kraal and over a distant deck were a herd of cattle being driven. I sent one of my officers, Capt. Daniell, a colonial with dash and courage, to stop them. He required no urging but sped away at full gallop while I pushed on with the rest of the force. After collecting what stock remained, we set light to the huts and fell back. As we did so I saw Daniell returning with the cattle he had gone to collect. Meanwhile firing had commenced from the rocky heights around us. I saw a body of kaffirs coming down the hillside to our left who we judged to be Swazis. They were making for the path with the idea of intercepting us, but I had taken the precaution of leaving some men there under Lt. Blencoe, together with another party lower down, under Lt. Rikman. This saved us, for as the Swazis neared Blencoe's position, he opened fire on them and drove them back. The same thing happened with Rikman; these young officers, with their handful of men, had saved us from the enemy, for had they gained the path our chances of getting out would have been small.

Commandant Ferreira had not backed us as I had expected. On reaching the exit from the basin above, I made my men dismount and link their horses' reins through the stirrup leathers over the saddles and they were driven down with the cattle. This allowed more freedom of action, for my men were not hampered by their horses. Suffice to say we got safely out without loss with three men hit or slightly hit. It was a narrow shave for if the enemy had got possession of the path it would have given them time for a force to come over behind us and we should have been entrapped. With such officers as Capt. Sanctuary, Daniells, Dennison and others, and a force of good tried men, I could dare much and it was owing to their bravery and ability that I owed our success on that day and on other occasions later. We reached camp without any further resistance and shortly after Ferreira moved down to Fort Olifant.

Chapter 7

One morning about nine o'clock I was called from my hut by an orderly; Major Carrington wanted me at the Orderly Office. I went at once and found two or three natives standing outside.

Major Carrington said:

'Sekhekhune has sent these men over with this man whom I recognised as one of Ferreira's, a German named Ricka by name' (I must here state that we had gone the previous week down the Olifants River on a cattle raid, when some four or five of Ferreira's men had got lost. All of them eventually turned up save Ricka, whom it was presumed had been killed.) 'He tells a queer story but the story is confirmed by a Swazi, a boy named Jim. Ricka, it seems, got lost in a gallop pursuing some cattle. The bush was thick and he at last after riding for some time approached Sekhekhune's main kraal where he was caught and taken to the chief who detained him for some days, then gave him ten half sovereigns and sent him out to Fort Weeber with Jim and two others.'

The story seemed incredible but true.

'Sekhekhune evidently wants peace,' I remarked.

'I'll send him a present,' said Major Carrington. 'Will you write him a letter in Dutch, Dennison, thanking him for his kindness to Ricka?' (It would be possible for the chief to have someone translate a letter written in Dutch but I doubt if they would be able to read anything in English.)

I wrote the Dutch letter and the next morning the natives returned with it and a present for Sekhekhune.

The week following Jim again turned up, this time accompanied by the chief's son and one of the natives who had accompanied him before. Major Carrington again sent for me and on my entering his office said:

'Dennison, Sekhekhune it seems has no one who can read your letter and wants me to send someone to read it for him. What do you think?'

'I think Major, you should let me go in. I believe that the chief has no one who can read the letter. I also think that the information I can gain as to the strength of the position may be useful to us later should we attack him.'

As the natives were sitting some distance off, we could speak freely, for Jim, having worked on the diamond fields for some time, would understand and speak a little English.

'No,' replied Major Carrington, 'I shall not let you go as this may only be a ruse to get an officer there to hold as hostage against demands.'

I, however, persisted, pointing out that Sekhekhune's whole actions proved an inclination to use for peace. Thus the Major at last gave way.

Capt. Wools Sampson of Ferreira's Horse had arrived at our camp the day before and was standing nearby while the conversation between Carrington and myself took place. As I turned to go he met me and said:

'Let me go with you.'

I replied:

'Sampson, I will take one of my own officers.'

However, on second thoughts I agreed for it struck me that it would be of greater advantage to also have an officer of Ferreira's to see Sekhekhune's stronghold.

So, after making all the necessary arrangements we started the next morning on horseback accompanied by Sekhekhune's men and, from my lines, a native servant. We slept the first night at a deserted hut near Mamalube and the next afternoon reached Sekhekhune's kraal where we were conducted to a hut belonging to one of the chief's counsellors while our horses were taken away to be cared for. A goat was sent by the chief to be killed for our use and in fact, the whole attitude of the natives was friendly. We supped and inclined on our blankets in the *scherm* (a protection, usually a light fence composed of thin sticks, or reeds, supported by poles and lathes). This was after having being told that Sekhekhune would see us the next day.

All went well until after midnight when we were awakened by a terrible noise outside accompanied by shouts, yells and the galloping of horses past our hut. The wooden slab forming the door of our abode was pushed aside and the native counsellor entered.

'What is the matter?' I asked in Dutch which I knew he spoke fairly well.

'Myn Heer, Ferreira is killing our people on the Olifants River and the chief now wants to kill you both.'

76

I turned to Sampson and said:

'Carrington has failed to send word to Ferreira, which he promised to do, and now we are in for it.'

(I must here mention that Major Carrington had ordered Ferreira to go down the Olifant and raid the kraals for grain. However, he had promised to send a messenger to Fort Olifant to countermand the order. Ferreira may, however, have left ere he got the countermand. But the fact remained we were in a critical position and both of us realised it. My companion was a brave cool young man and this helped me much outwardly. We perhaps showed no signs of fear but what I felt was another thing and no doubt this applied to my companion as well.

After drinking some coffee, made by our servant, we went out and as it became light, crowds of youths, women and children came round the corner shouting and calling us all the disgusting names they were capable of in their language, their vocabulary being unlimited. We kept very still and talked about possibilities. I smoked but my companion did not. Presently Jim, our Swazi friend, came by and told us the council of Sekhekhune would shortly meet when our case would be heard, but we would not be allowed to be present.

Shortly afterwards we heard that the council had gathered and that our case was being investigated. We were informed from time to time, as the long anxious hours of the day wore on, how we were to be disposed of according to the different, and various ideas of our swarthy judges. Some, 'twas said, wished to burn us alive. Others to skin us and torture us with ants or hot ashes or tied to a post as a target for the youth to shoot at. Alternatively, handed over to the women who had lost their husbands, to dispose of us as they thought fit. We sat through it all listening again and again in dreadful suspense to the different proposals our servant brought to us. What we mentally suffered during that long day in Sekhekhune's kraal, I can never forget, nor I am sure, can my companion Sampson (later Sir Audrey Wools-Sampson of Johannesburg).

Before us under the eaves of an adjoining hut hung an assegai with a large long blade. I saw that my companion was observing it, but neither of us said anything. My idea was to seize it if possible at the last moment as some means of defence. Sampson had the same idea. While sitting thus after several hours of waiting, a native came in a wild frenzy with an assegai in his hand and a leopard skin over his shoulders. He glared at us for a time but we sat still, his object being intimidation. We saw it and instantly recognised it. Later Sekhekhune's son came crouching down with his hand over his mouth expressing sorrow. He sighed and left. We thought our time was near at hand. At last towards evening our counsellor friend came to our hut and said:

'Sekhekhune says you must go. Your horses are coming, get ready.'

I thought he looked sorrowful. We left soon after returning by the same way as we had entered along a slippery path with rocky sides. It had rained during the night and there was the spoor of natives on the path.

'What do these spoors mean?' asked Sampson of Jim in the Zulu tongue.

'They are the spoors of the men who are to kill you, the witchdoctor said it would bring a curse on the kraal to kill you there, so the chief has sent his men to kill you at the hut where we last slept, but I will help you.'

We rode on in silence across the mountain top and down the decline on the other side. In the distance we could see the hut and some natives near it.

When we reached the valley below, now out of sight of the hut, Jim pointed to another path to our right and said: 'Go, ride fast.'

We did so, trotting our horses down the path that led past Mamalube and got out without seeing anything more of our enemies, and pushed on down and across the turfy flats beyond, arriving at Fort Weeber about eleven o'clock that night.

We had returned in far less time than our outward journey. After handing our horses over to our men and receiving a friendly welcome from my officers, I reported to Major Carrington who was sitting before a fire in the corner of his room. He jumped up excitedly and warmly welcomed us.

'Thank God,' he said, 'you are safely back. ''Twas all a mistake, Ferreira leaving. He should not have gone but my messenger was too late.'

We sat down and I told him what we had gone through. When I had finished he said:

'Dennison, send me a written report.'

This I promised to do and left to get some sleep for I was tired out and so was Sampson. Thus ended another of my varied and many escapades.

It might naturally be argued that as Sekhekhune had sent for us and his intentions were bona fide, there should have been no danger as far as we were concerned, even though a fault had been committed by Carrington or Ferreira. Such argument from our standpoint would be right and reasonable, but the native in his simple mind, without regard to reason or justice, 'the white men are killing our people and here we have two of them so let us kill them'. The fact was 'here is an opportunity for revenge, let us make use of it.' But thanks to the noble Jim, the Swazi, their designs on us were frustrated. I know that it was said at Headquarters that an exaggerated report had been made, but I have given simple facts in detail as far as my memory serves me, and should Col. Sampson ever read these pages he will bear me out in my statement and no doubt could add to the details that I may have forgotten.

Orders came from Pretoria that one of the corps, (either Ferreira's or my Border Horse) was to proceed to Zululand to join the main column there under the General Officer commanding, Sir Garnet Wolseley. I read the order which stated that Major Carrington was not to send the Border Horse if it could be avoided, because we had suffered so severely in Zululand. However my officers and men were all eager to go and I told Major Carrington that we surely had a prior claim, but he would not hear of it.

'No! Dennison, I want you and your men here. You will have to take Ferreira's place in command of Fort Olifant.'

Ferreira went to Zululand with his men and I moved down and took command of Fort Olifant, where, acting on Major Carrington's orders, we, as well as the men of Fort Weeber, were simply to act on the defensive till the arrival of Sir Garnet Wolseley. We did so passing the time in hunting and sport. On one occasion two men deserted from my force and were traced to Marabastadt in Zoutpansberg District.

Being anxious for a change I left Capt. Sanctuary in charge and went off accompanied by my cousin, Capt. H. E. Dennison, and four men to try and affect the arrest of the deserters. We arrived at Marabastadt but were unsuccessful in our mission as the men had already left. They had in their possession government horses and full equipment, together with rifles and ammunition. It was thought that they had gone off to the low country. We returned after staying a day at Marabastadt. Shortly after my arrival back in camp, Major Carrington came down accompanied by Capt. Campbell, the officer who led the Turks at Shipkah Pass in the Russian-Turkish War.

The next morning the major asked me to show him to my Orderly tent. I did so and left him there. It was not long before he came out and handed me a letter addressed to myself. It contained two questions: the one was, 'Why had I left my command and proceeded to Marabastadt?' And the other alluded to a hunt in which, accompanied by some of my men, I crossed the borders into a friendly chief's country and did some game shooting thus frightening the natives.

I smiled and took the document back into the Orderly tent where I replied to the queries. I then gave it back to Major Carrington who was still waiting outside. He opened it and after reading my answers to his questions, smiled and said:

'You hot-headed devil, you will be getting both yourself and me into hot water.'

I never heard anything more of the affair but shortly afterwards was promoted to the rank of Commandant, whereas, hitherto, I only held the rank of Captain commanding the Border Horse. Thus I lost nothing for doing what I thought to be my duty or for the accidental crossing of a boundary.

At last, in October 1879, Sir Garnet Wolseley arrived with his troops among which were the 21st Scots Fusiliers, or portion of that regiment. Marching orders came at last, to attack Sekhekhune. Ferreira's Horse were sent on ahead to the lower drift of the Olifants River, there to await the arrival of the main column and to guard a commissariat base. The main depot nearer Sekhekhune's kraal, was about eighteen miles further east on to which the main guard advanced. On the arrival of our column at Fort Olifant we camped across the river with orders to march at 4 a.m. the next morning.

Major Carrington and myself sat up late that night and as we parted he said:

'Of course you will be awake and have all hands in order to march at 4 o'clock?'

'Yes,' I replied. 'The guard has been warned to wake me.'

Now, as a rule I could wake up about any time I wanted, but fate was against me on this particular occasion and I lay in a deep sleep dreaming I could hear the most beautiful music. It came nearer and nearer, till at least I woke to find the Scots Fusiliers marching past me scarcely six feet away. My trumpeter lay asleep near my feet and I raised him with my foot.

'Boots and saddle' rang out at once in the cool morning air and in ten minutes I was off with some of the men to gain our position in the advance as the Fusiliers gained the bush ahead which consisted chiefly of *swart haak* [black hook thorn through which, lacking a road, it would be most difficult to get through].

We galloped past and barely gained the front in time, greeted by curses from the OC Fusiliers as stragglers deterred his march.

The music that in my dreams sounded so sweet that twain would I lie

80

down to hear it again under other circumstances, was the much condemned bagpipes. I was always told that I had an ear for music; perhaps so, my readers can judge if they so wish, but the fact remains that no sweeter strains ever fell upon my ear than those of the pipes on that memorable morning of years ago.

Many of the men who could not gain the path in time were in a sad way with torn clothes, hands and faces scratched and full of blood. Some looked a sorry sight, but all turned up in time. Carrington and his men were blessed by the colonel commanding the 21st Scots, but all were soon passed and no one much worse except those who came in contact with the swart haak. We camped for some time on the Olifants River from whence the Border Horse conveyed troops and wagons to Sekhekhune's or rather to a camp formed near a hill about two miles from the chief's town or kraal. It was while conveying thus that I got to know Capt. Herbert Stewart, of Sir Garnet's staff. He twice rode with me and was a pleasant kindly gentleman and a good officer. He fell later on the Nile after having been part of the force sent to relieve Khartoum and General Gordon. He was also well-known in South Africa and was once British Resident of Basutoland. Capt. Stewart, as well as Col. Brackenbury, Chief Staff Officer to the General, were friends throughout this campaign.

All the troops and necessary commissariat at last arrived at the camping ground and on the evening of 27th November 1879, orders for the attack on Sekhekhune's stronghold were read out at a special parade. Ferreira's Horse was to attack the right of the kraal, the Regulars the centre or the Fighting Kop [head] as it was called, while the Native Contingents of the Zoutpansberg and Rustenberg together with Macaulay's Cape Mounted Corps and the Border Horse, were to attack the mountain to the left. Sekhekhune's Kraal was situated at the foot of the Lulu Mountains that form an impressive curve in the range of the foothills of which are a natural fort. It was the same place we had attacked three years earlier. After the orders were read the men dispersed and preparations were made for the morrow. Ammunition was issued as were provisions for the day. I had occasion to go to the Commissariat tent and there found Mr Longlands, my Quartermaster, together with the Quartermaster Sgt. McLeod. Longlands was shaving and as I came in I heard McLeod say:

'May I use your razor, Mr Longlands, when you have finished?'

'Why do you wish to shave tonight?' I asked. 'You will have plenty of time tomorrow, McLeod.'

'Why am I going, sir? Surely I need not stay in the camp and you promised me I should go out the next time,' replied McLeod.

'Oh did I? Well if so, then of course you may go,' I said, 'and your assistant must take charge.'

Well did I remember our conversation the next day as I gazed down on his lifeless form. It was not only he of my men who met his end the next day; just before I went I retired for the night I noticed Macaulay lying beneath the tree on his blankets with his face upturned fast asleep. He too slept his last sleep on earth that night.

At about 2 o'clock the next morning we moved out across the camp in pitch dark crossing over a sluit. We passed masses of assembled men on foot, plus the Regulars, the Infantry. We, however, were all mounted and we advanced for a mile and then halted awaiting a signal to continue. On our left were Macaulay's men and next to them, and slightly in advance, lay the Native Contingents. We could but dimly discern them. After waiting for some time the signal was given and our native allies advanced to break away the fences, but as the fire from the enemy had commenced, they all faced about and cleared off. Macaulay was then ordered to advance and the Cape boys surged forward led by their captain. 'Twas light now and everything could be plainly seen. They reached the huts, but our own heavy fire stopped them; they wavered and took cover.

'Are your men ready, Dennison?' asked Major Carrington as I returned to him after inspecting my line.

'Yes,' I replied, 'quite so.'

'Then Forward the Border Horse for all your worth,' he ordered.

I gave the word and away we went, on foot of course, because our horses had all been sent back to the rear. We ran on under a heavy fire through the lines accompanied by some mounted infantry, also on foot, whom I had forgotten were with us. As we got through the huts the Cape boys rallied and, led by Capt. Macaulay, charged on our left.

The enemy remained in their *schanse* [barricades] to our front until we got within about seventy-five yards of them. They were firing, but all high, and would not risk their head above the breastworks. We were getting close when they rose and bolted further into their barricades higher up. Some fell and as the last of them leapt over the walls my men were up on them. Poor young McLeod was among the first and as he reached the wall a kaffir placed his gun against the lad's chest and fired. He fell instantly and his men lifted him up and carried him to one side under the rocks. As they laid him down he said:

'Write to my mother,' and died.

I felt very sad for I liked the boy. He was in fact a general favourite.

The kaffirs were nearly all killed in that barricade. Only a few escaped. Then we got on to the first spur of the mountain above with one tier of schanses taken. While resting there, some of us sitting on the stones, others lying about, I noted Capt. Macaulay sitting smoking on a rock near Major Carrington. A minute later he laid dead beside the stone on which he had been sitting, with a bullet through his brain. The bullet came from no one knew where. It is true that an odd shot was fired from time to time from above us, and no doubt his death was due to one of these stray shots. I thought of his calm face the night before as he lay sleeping beneath the tree near my tent. He lay calm now, but it was the sleep of the dead. Several others had fallen dead and wounded but our losses were by no means heavy. After a short rest we again advanced up the black rocky mountain, and drove the enemy from schanse to schanse. We were, however, suddenly recalled – or rather word was passed from the rear that Major Carrington wanted me. I went back and found that my men were wanted to assist the native allies who were being driven back by the enemy. I got some of the men back and checked the enemy's advance. Our natives then gained courage, wheeled and drove their assailants back. Then, suddenly, we heard a wailing sound coming over the mountain spur to our left, accompanied by heavy firing. The enemy in scattered numbers then went flying, terror-stricken, towards the mountain top pursued by some of our Swazi contingents who although delayed, now came over the spur in pursuit of the enemy. 9,000 Swazis were now along the mountainside driving all before them. The wail we had heard in the distance was the war song of the Swazis.

It was a cruel sight. Have you, reader, seen dogs scatter about among rocks hunting out an exhausted hidden hare? Well, such was being enacted all along the mountainside. Victims would suddenly rise and run, but to be stabbed down by the Swazis. 'Twas indeed a cruel sight. They, the Swazis, were stopped at last before a cave and several of them were shot down. We had just reached some huge rocks near the cave entrance when we saw the Swazis driven back. One of their indunas came up and asked for some white men to lead them in. I turned to Major Carrington and told him of the Swazis' request.

'No, tell him no, Dennison. They can go into the hole without us. I

83

don't want my men mixed up with them, for these fellows will kill friend and foe when heated,' Carrington replied.

One of my sergeants, Mitchell by name, was several paces away and, knowing the Swazi language, he called out to them to follow and dashed forward only to fall dead. However, it gave the Swazis a lead, and away they went on and into the cave opening. The climbed the rocks around, searching every hole and crevice. Shrieks and shouts came from the mouth of the cave, and it was said that the Swazis left nothing there alive, not even a cat or dog. Why the Swazis were asked to aid us I know not for they were not needed and our arms derived no luster through their aid. We would have been far better without them. While standing behind some huge rocks watching the Swazis hunt, for we could do naught else, we saw a native with a leopard skin around his shoulders break cover and run towards a gap between the rocks. He was at once fired upon by my men and fell just as he gained the gap. He, we found out later, was Sekhekhune's brother, the man who had tried to intimidate Sampson and I on a former occasion while we had been his prisoners.

A flag was seen away on the top of the topmost krantz and was recognised as that carried by Capt. Campbell, who commanded a portion of the Swazi Contingent. Strange to say that officer was seen to ascend to the top of the mountain but disappeared and was never heard of again not was his body ever found. For some days a search was carried out but nothing discovered. It was Campbell who led the Turks at Shikpah Pass during the Russian-Turkish War.

About 4 o'clock in the afternoon, we were ordered to retire as our work was complete. Below us the Irregulars had still not taken the hill, the 'fighting koppie'. We watched them for some time and could not understand why the place was not taken. We descended and on gaining the sluit below the mountain, and about 300 yards from the koppie, we rested under the shade of the banks, for the sun was intensely hot. Presently an order came for us to get to our horses and mount. So we moved down the sluit, got to our horses and mounted in good order. Major Carrington at last came up and I rode to meet him saying:

'What are we to do now, sir?'

'You are to get round to the back of the fighting koppie and with your troops make a simultaneous attack. Ferreira will attack from the West,' he replied.

'Oh then, the Imperial troops were only keeping the enemy engaged while waiting for us to tackle the enemy,' I said.

'I suppose so,' was the reply, 'but Dennison, your men and officers can be on top first – Show them that you can do it.'

We quietly rode up the sluit and got into position behind the koppie. A signal was given and my men with a wild cheer, rushed forward led by their officers. The first to gain the top was Lt. Paulett Weatherley, our late colonel's eldest son. We were soon on top and met Col. Baker Russell who was the first from his side. The koppie was taken, or rather our troops were on it. Why this was not done before seemed to me curious.

Orders were then given to retire on to the plateau. The hollow rocks below, served as a shelter for hundreds of the enemy; women and children were there too, besides goats and sheep. In fact while standing on top it was as if one were standing on an immense beehive, for a continual humming sound came from beneath. The natives were again and again called upon to come out. None would do so. At last dynamite and gun cotton were resorted to and on each explosion clouds of smoke and dust accompanied by shrieks from inside took place. Cruel expedient, I thought. Some poor wretches initially came out then, at last, a great many did so and we were ordered back to camp. When we arrived we found the Swazis encamped opposite us across the sluit.

The next morning, on returning from an early morning patrol, I came upon a company of Regulars escorting a bunch of prisoners down to our camping ground. As we neared the Swazi camp and knowing their blood-thirsty nature, I divided my men so as to ride on either side of the soldiers who had fixed bayonets and had the prisoners marching side-a-square. As we neared the Swazis a loud yell greeted us and they rushed wildly on to us trying by every means to reach and kill the prisoners. It was with great difficulty that we kept them off until their indunas regained control. On arrival at my camp I heard that a considerable number of the enemy, men, women and children, had been cruelly butchered by the Swazis. Bishop Colenso of Natal took the matter up after the Sekhekhune affair was over, and enquiries were made by him as to what he stated to be the unnecessary use of dynamite and gun cotton at the fighting kop, and the butchering of Sekhekhune's men by the Swazi. Drastic measures are often necessary in war but I do think that undue cruelty should be avoided at all times, when possible.

The afternoon of the same day of the Swazi trouble saw the burial of our dead. Our losses were not heavy: the soldiers in their attack on the fighting kop suffered most. Again the solemn, oft heard strains of the 'Death March in Saul' was heard, and its echoes filled the calm solemn air, resounding from rock to rock in wavering cadences falling one on the other in its solemn grandeur. Finally the 'Last Post' and all was over.

The following day Headquarters sent for me and informed me that after returning from patrol the next morning I should, with my corps, accompany Sir Garnet Wolseley with the troops back to Pretoria. Commandant Ferreira would remain to collect the cattle. We left during the first week in December, and on arriving at the Olifants River I first met that grand old soldier, Col. Baker Russell. It was raining as we crossed the river. I saw a tent pitched among the trees near the road and as we were in the act of riding past, I was called by name. It was by the Colonel who came out of his tent. I turned towards him and saluted.

'Get off, Dennison, and come inside out of the rain, let your men camp over there, and pitch their tents,' said the Colonel, indicating a spot a hundred yards off.

I gave my horse to my man, and said:

'Tell the Adjutant to let the men pitch their tents if they like but we are only halting for a couple of hours.'

A cup-full of hot coffee and some biscuits were handed to me which, needless to say I enjoyed very much. We sat talking for a while when Col. Baker Russell got up and stood before the tent. Then turning to me said:

'Why, Dennison, your men have not pitched their tents. You will have them all down as hospital tenants before many days are over.'

'Oh no Colonel, it is all right. They don't feel inclined to go to the trouble; a little wetting won't harm them. They are used to it,' I said.

The order I gave was an optional one and at the time I doubted that they would bother.

Baker Russell remained silent for a few minutes and then said:

'Your volunteers are worth a lot more than British soldiers. For this work, they are as hard as nails.'

However, nevertheless, we did camp there that night and moved on the next morning. As my Quartermaster, Mr Longlands, was unwell, I decided to ride on to Fort Olifant to make arrangements about rations. I saw Col. Brackenbury, CSO [Chief Staff Officer], who approved of my decision. My cousin, Henry Dennison, was left in command during my absence. So taking a couple of men and my servant, I left the column and rode forward. On passing through Murder Poort, I met a rider from Fort Weeber with dispatches for the General who informed me of the threat among the Transvaal burgers, that mass meetings had been held and that trouble was looming. I arranged all that could be done at Fort Olifant in the way of supplies and slept there intending to proceed to Fort Weeber at dawn the next morning, there to make final arrangements. During the night, or rather towards dawn, someone came into the tent. I was immediately awakened and saw that it was Col. Brackenbury.

'Don't get up, Dennison,' he said. 'I hurried on to catch you here, fearing you might have left for Fort Weeber, to tell you that your marching orders are changed. You are to proceed tomorrow for Middleburg to assist Capt. Thompson, of the King's Dragoon Guards, who is garrisoned there. It is expected we may have trouble with the Boers.'

'But Colonel,' I replied, 'this is placing me in an awkward position, many of my men are burgers [citizens] of the State, they were engaged to fight against the kaffirs; you cannot expect them to take up arms against their fellow burgers. Nor will they ever do so.'

'Never mind Dennison, don't disobey orders. Your corps stands high in the esteem of Sir Garnet. You have a number of Britishers; when you get to Middleburg be guided by circumstances and if necessary let all your men who are burgers of the Transvaal take their discharge. But I do not think anything serious will happen soon and if not you will no doubt get orders at Middleburg to discharge your men.'

I saw the sense of this remark and hesitated no longer.

The column arrived early and encamped west of the river whereas Fort Olifant was situated on the east side. I reported to Sir Garnet Wolseley immediately and was instructed by him to get my orders from the chief staff officer which were in fact what Col. Brackenbury had told me. I was treated with kindness and consideration by Sir Garnet Wolseley, who shook hands with me and wished me luck. Without any further delay we mounted our horses and moved on from Fort Olifant to Fort Weeber. Then, after replenishing our supplies, we rode on to Middleburg. The day before our arrival at the latter place I paraded the men and warned them that I would give no leave before my camp was pitched and that then half the men would be allowed out and the following day the remaining half. I knew the characters I had to deal with. Fearless in danger, good soldiers away from the temptation of drink, but demons when they got within range of it. All appeared willing to abide by the order.

The next morning at about 11 a.m., we arrived at the camp of the King's Dragoon Guards, under Capt. Thompson, and started to fix up our camp near his. All went well for a short time, but while sitting at lunch in Capt. Thompson's tent, my Sergeant-Major reported that the men were quietly slipping away to the village.

'Will you have enough to finish fixing up the camp?' I asked him.

'I think so, sir. The few men left with the NCO will manage, but the trouble will be tonight on the horse-lines.'

Well, to cut it short, after lunch the officers had to assist and that night we barely had enough men for ordinary guard duty and the following day our mule-wagons were on duty carrying in drunken men who lay scattered all over the village. For several days the few sober men left did all the duty. I had expected trouble, for the men had been several months away from so-called civilisation, but little did I expect to have it to such an extent. Men who were placed in the guard-tent to sleep off the effects, woke during the night and made off once more. After a great deal of trouble we managed to get matters a bit straight. One man, an Irishman who was generally disliked for his all-round bad qualities, one of which was thieving, was particularly bad, but I must say that he was an exception to the rule, for all the Irishmen who have served with me, before and since were favourites among their comrades. But this particular Irishman was, of all my men, an out-and-outer. He was put in the guard-tent again and again, was punished, but to no avail. He sold nearly all his belongings to obtain drink and then stole from his comrades. I was loathe to go to extremes for the man had one redeeming quality and that was his pluck in danger. I was driven at last to get rid of him. He had been stealing, and the men were exasperated. As punishment he was made to run the gauntlet and then to be discharged in disgrace. A troop of men were drawn up in half-sections in open order about four paces apart, they faced inward, thus facing one-another. Each man arrived with his belt in his hand ready. The culprit was forced to take off his boots and tunic and made to run between the lines of men who struck at him with their belts. His boots and tunic were then returned and he was paid-off and discharged. A short time after, while sitting in my tent with Lieutenants Boswell and Davies, and Capt. Dennison, (my cousin), I was informed our Irish friend wanted to speak to me.

'Very well,' I said. 'Let him come in to the tent.'

He came and after saluting he said:

'Commandant Dennison, O'id foller yer ter hell in action, but you're a b— in camp!'

He left and I never saw him again.

Chapter 8

After remaining at Middleburg for about three weeks following the incident mentioned in the foregoing chapter, I got orders to pay off the men, and return to Pretoria. Such of our men as wished were to have free passage in our mule-wagons travelling thither. Thus ended our campaign under Sir Garnet Wolseley. We got credit for the part we took in storming Sekhekhune's and there is no doubt the Border Horse did their duty. The men were, without doubt, good, but we owed our success mainly to our officers and our NCOs, of whom I had the best; among them were my cousin Capt. H.E. Dennison, Lieutenants Boswell, Davies, and Paulett Weatherley. Sgt. Maj. Constable and others whose names owing to the lapse of many years, and having no record, I cannot place.

We reached Pretoria, and while at the old Edinburgh Hotel, I was invited to dine with Sir Garnet, but owing to some offensive wrong done to me I did not go and was not over-polite in refusing the kind invitation. For this I was to suffer later, for Commandants Ferreira and Roof [Raaff] got the CMG, I did not and the only reason I could imagine was the refusal of Sir Garnet's invitation. The General may live to read these lines and will no doubt remember. I was wrong, wholly wrong, and did an injustice to my corps by my foolish act. When Col. Brackenbury spoke to me at Fort Olifant (alluded to in a previous chapter) he said:

'What do you intend doing after this is over, Dennison?'

'I wish to get an appointment in the Civil Service in this country,' I replied.

'Very good,' he said. 'Make your application through Carrington, your OC, and it will receive the support of Sir Garnet and staff.'

My application was made from Rustenburg, my home, through Major Carrington, for a post as Inspector of Natives for the District of

Rustenburg. Month after month passed and I heard nothing and in the meantime I had started a business at Wolhuter's Kop. One Sunday morning while my cousin H. E. Dennison and George de Pass were spending the day with me on their way from Rustenburg to Pretoria, I was writing in my office when I heard a horseman ride up and De Pass say:

'Hello – Where are you off to?'

'I am going to Rustenburg. I am appointed provisionally as Inspector of Natives for this District,' came the reply.

I got up and to my surprise saw it was one of my ex-troopers, a relative of Hudson, the Colonial Secretary of Pretoria. This trooper had been an NCO and reduced to the ranks on account of drunkenness.

'What?' I said. 'Are you appointed for this district?'

'Yes,' he replied, 'by Mr Hudson.

'Oh, that is the little game, is it?' I remarked and went inside.

The next evening, accompanied by De Pass and Dennison, I went to Pretoria to the Colonial Office, saw Mr Hudson and spoke to him about the appointment. He professed ignorance saying he was not aware that I was down for a post. I left him and went to the inner office where Fritz Simons, (a young man I knew well) was working.

'Fritz,' said I, 'Let me see the Register of Applications.'

He showed it to me and turned to the page on which my application was registered with the recommendations of Major Carrington and Col. Brackenbury, Chief Staff Officer to Sir Garnet.

The man appointed went to Rustenburg, got on the spree and was duly discharged. So much for 'faith in princes'.

This occurred shortly before the fires of war commenced to burn at Potchefstroom. Meetings had been held at different parts of the State [Transvaal] by the Boer leaders: British promises were held up to ridicule – and was this without cause? On one occasion, being in Pretoria, I was sent for by Major Lanyon, and on meeting him at Government House, he said:

'Dennison, what do these Boers mean?'

'They mean to fight,' I replied, 'and if you are not careful, sir, they will have the best of you.'

'Nonsense,' he said. 'You know they can't fight for you were with them at Sekhekhune's; it's all bunkum, they are trying to frighten us into granting them all they want. You are wrong Dennison, they can't fight and they won't.'

'Very well, sir,' I said, 'but I think ere long you will find I was right.'
I then left.

About a month later Commandant Meyer and myself came to Pretoria from the Rustenburg District. The administrator wished to see us at Government House. We met Major Lanyon. He addressed Meyer, saying:

'Dennison has told me the Boers are going to fight, what is your opinion?'

'If Captain Dennison told you the Boers are going to fight, he told you right. He knows them better than myself, but I say also they are going to fight,' replied Meyer.

'Oh nonsense,' said Lanyon, 'you are all alike, you see danger where there is none.'

Well, so it was. Is it not more than probable that the liberal government of England was misled by the dispatches emanating from minds like those of Lanyon's who failed to grasp the true position and gravity of affairs? The then Prime Minister of this Liberal government of England, Mr Gladstone, was often blamed for what occurred. That he deserved such blame is doubtful under these circumstances. We who lived among the people, knew the intensity of the feeling that existed. We knew the vain attempts the Boer leaders had made to obtain what had been promised them. The result, after many meetings, the climax being the great meeting at Paardekraal on the 8th December 1880, settled the matter. It was to be war. Women in my hearing said to their husbands, who in some cases were not eager to go to the front, 'If you don't want to go and fight the Englishmen, give me your gun and ammunition and I will go and fight; you can stay at home and mind the children.'

Seeing that war was imminent, I rode out to see Paul Kruger, who was then living on his farm Boekenhoutfontein, about twelve miles west of Rustenburg. He was fortunately at home. After off-saddling I went inside and having had the usual cup of coffee, I said:

'Commandant, I have come to see you about myself, you know I am a burger of this State and as such I am supposed to fight against its enemies, but you know also that I am an Englishman. War is on the eve of breaking out against the British flag. I cannot fight against the flag of my fathers and my flag. And no more can I fight against the Transvaal.'

He looked at me for a moment or two when I had finished and then getting up from his chair, he came forward holding out his hand and said:

'You have done the right thing in coming to see me and speaking as you have done. Go home and remain quiet. I will see that no harm befalls you.'

I omitted to mention that troops had been stationed throughout the Transvaal after the annexation, and at Rustenburg there was a detachment of the 21st Royal Scots Fusiliers stationed under a Capt. Aunchlick. This officer had frequently been my guest: we were in fact on the most intimate terms. He had hinted that in the event of war, he expected me to join him with the corps I commanded in the defence of the fort.

I had said:

'No, I cannot do that. I'm going to resign my commission' (which I shortly afterwards did). 'And besides most of my men, like myself, are burgers of the former Republic. I do not wish to take part in the war should it occur. In any case I should be of more use to you outside the fort. I shall in all probability take no active part but time will show what I may do.'

This conversation was prior to my seeing Commandant Paul Kruger.

Chapter 9

Some time previous to the incidents mentioned in the foregoing chapter, I had been on a trading trip to Waterburg, and left a lot of goods there at Willem Pretorius's, an old friend of mine, who was also to collect certain debts owing to me consisting of reims, whips and sjamboks, etc. So away I went from Wolhuter's Kop where I had a business of my own, having discovered my former connections. I was accompanied by Jack Strike, a young friend who was residing out there for a time with Morris my manager. We arrived at Zacharias de Beer's farm, near the hot springs at Waterburg. I outspanned on the same spot as before and went up to the house. No one came to meet me. This struck me as unusual for these people had always treated me most kindly. Strike accompanied me to the house. On knocking Mrs De Beer opened the door and said in Dutch:

'Come in.' At the same time she pointed towards the garden in front of the house and said: 'Here comes my husband.'

I instantly turned and went to meet him. He shook hands coolly and said:

'Look here Carl,' (for I was always called thus by the Boers of the Transvaal, being Dutch for my first name) 'today I greet you as a friend; tomorrow, we are enemies for war has broken out between your people and mine; do you not know it?'

'No,' I said, 'I did not expect it so soon but in any case why should we be enemies, this is no personal matter.'

'Yes,' he said, 'it is a personal matter, for all the enemies of the Transvaal are also my enemies.'

I knew the man well, so said nothing further. We went into the house and had a meal, then we inspanned having decided to push on to Willem Pretorius' place. We reached there early the next morning and were warmly welcomed by the man and his family.

There we first heard of the disaster to Col. Anstruther and his men at Bronkhorst-spruit, and that every available Boer was commandeered for the front. [A heavily armed Boer commando had ambushed a convoy of the 94th Regiment, marching and strolling at ease, at a place called Bronkhorstspruit. This immediately created a state of war between the Transvaal and Britain. The convoy, under the command of Lt. Col. Phillip Anstruther had consisted of thirty-three wagons, two hundred and fifty-four infantry plus a number of civilians including a few women and children. Within fifteen minutes sixty-nine had been killed, including Col. Phillip Anstruther, and a further eighty-three wounded for the loss of seven Boer casualties].

'You have no time to lose, Neef Carl,' old William said to me, 'You must load and get away as soon as you can and take all your stuff with you, and be careful least the commandos leaving Waterburg do not come upon you.'

It took us the whole day, practically, to load and get away. We succeeded at last in trekking back through a poort, the name of which I have forgotten. It was the shortest way, but the road, although bad, would prevent us from the possibility of meeting any commandos. We bade farewell to the good people and trekked away about sunset. We pushed hard through the night, ('twas moonlight) and reached a farm outside the hills before sunrise. A native and his family were the only occupants: they lived in huts near the dwelling house of the farm and it was at this farm that the roads joined together. The native came to my wagon and said:

'Baas, you must not stay, you must inspan and trek for the Boer commando is coming. My son has just come from them and he says they were near Nylstroom when he left them last night, and that they would trek on at daybreak.'

We quickly inspanned and hardly had we gone two hundred yards into the bush, for we kept out of sight of the road, when, looking back, I could see the white tents of wagons approaching about five miles off. So I turned further into the bush and pushed on. Fortunately, I had a good strong and quick team of oxen. After trekking about two hours, we outspanned. We saw nothing further of the Boers or their wagons and reached Wolhuter's Kop about four days later. On arriving at my store, the news of Col. Anstruther's disaster and death was confirmed. War had commenced in real earnest. Shortly afterwards, news came to us of the siege of Potchefstroom where the troops in the open camp had to dig trenches and fortify themselves under fire from the enemy. We heard that several loyal families from the town had also gone into the camp. The sufferings, trials, and deaths have all been recorded long ago. Let it suffice to say a brave defence was made. I returned to Rustenburg and joined my family there and again met Capt. Aunchlick who tried hard to get me to enter the camp offering to give me one of the best marquees for my wife and children. I again refused saying that I should be of more use to him outside which later proved to be the case. The week following, a Boer commando under Commandant Van der Walt, took possession of the town and commenced firing on the fort. This was hotly returned by the men who only had small arms. The Boers also had no cannon but brought an old ship's gun from Potchefstroom. The morning following I was talking to my neighbour, Mr M. C. Genis, the Resident Magistrate, when a field-cornet accompanied by some men arrived with a message from the commandant who demanded the keys of the court house. This, Mr Genis refused saying:

'I give my keys only on an order from my Government.'

Resistance was however pointless and he was forced to capitulate. Although badly treated, and subsequently dying – the details of which I will relate later, he was ever loyal to the British flag.

All Loyals were ordered to collect at the courthouse the same day and this order was complied with. I went with the rest.

Groot Adrian de la Rey and others were standing not far from us, for we were collected under the trees on the opposite side of the street to the courthouse awaiting events, when we noticed de la Rey beckon to a powerful-looking young Dutchman, one of our guards, and spoke to him on the side. The man returned, put down his rifle and approached Walters, the Deputy-Sheriff from behind. He struck him a terrible blow behind the ear with his fist. Walters staggered to one side and sat down dazed as blood poured down his face. We all closed round him and objected strongly to the commandant who then had the fellow placed under arrest. Walters, it will be remembered, served a summons on de la Rey at an earlier date. I must give the Boers credit for resenting the action of de la Rey and his minion and I heard later that he was punished for this cowardly act. We were kept for some hours waiting and at last called in to appear before the council. We were advised to remain silent and then let go.

The fire from the town on the fort continued daily from morning to night and was returned at intervals from the fort. My house was on the outside of the village nearest the fort and about 900 yards from it. The Boers had taken cover behind the mud wall on my property and this drew fire from the fort to my house. This became so bad that I was forced to move my family away to a farm outside the town as all the local houses were occupied by the Boers.

During a lull in the firing, people, including women and children, would walk the street or go shopping as usual. When the firing started again, all would hasten to get behind cover. The officer commanding the fort used the utmost case in returning the fire and it was only when necessity demanded that the fire was returned on the town. Van der Walt, the Commandant, was by no means an unkind man but was hardly fitted for the position he held. He was of a suspicious nature and lacked judgment.

On one occasion my manager's wife, Mrs Morris, reported to me at sundown that she had been insulted by a Boer. Now we had been warned not to be out after sundown so I went to where some wagons were standing in front of the courthouse and approached a young man I knew well, Fritz Pistorius by name, and asked him to accompany me.

He said:

'Yes, but wait until my brother arrives. He is on guard and will shortly be here, I can then go with you.'

Hardly had he spoken when Commandant van der Walt approached the wagon and saw me.

'What are you doing here?' he asked. 'The sun is down and you as an officer, should obey orders. How can others be expected to do so if men like yourself will not?'

Then turning to a man standing near him he said:

'Field-Cornet, take him prisoner and keep him under guard all night.'

I tried to explain but it was in vain, van der Walt would not listen to reason. Pistorius said nothing although I also appealed to him. He made me a sign as I turned away from the Field-Cornet which I understood to mean 'It's all right'. I was taken to the front of the courthouse where a bucksail was spread on the ground. I was told I could camp in it. I asked one of the men I knew to go over and tell my wife, which he did, and my supper was sent to me by her. By nine o'clock as I was lying on my stomach half asleep, I was suddenly and violently trampled upon and I heard a man say in Dutch:

'I wish I could tramp the life out of you!'

I heard a blow and then saw the man who had been trampling on me sprawling on the ground. He was mobbed by several of the guards and had a bad time of it for some minutes. When eventually one of their officers intervened he was released. He crawled away in a sorry plight. I could see it all for it was bright moonlight. The assailant's name was Du Plessis, a miller who lived on the Hex River near the town. This man had the fashion of taking more of the meal than he was entitled to. Millers in those days took what they called the 'kop', literally meaning 'head'. It was the last one from the stones after the grain was removed from the hopper. This usually meant about three pounds' weight or more according to the miller's greed. Well, this man Du Plessis had ground many loads of corn for me and I had found out that the 'kop' he stole was abnormal, in fact ran to fifteen to twenty pounds from each two hundred pounds of corn. I challenged him about it but he denied the charge. So I awaited my opportunity and some time later, before sending a load of wheat to the mill, I had the lot weighed in the presence of witnesses who put a very small mark on each bag to identify the sacks. On receiving it from the mill it was weighed on the same scale, witnessed by the same men and found to be considerably short of the weight. Du Plessis was prosecuted and fined £2 sterling for the theft and swore to get even with me one day.

I gave him an opportunity some time after, when he abused me in a most vile manner that resulted in me knocking him into a muddy water sluit. He made no retaliation beyond abuse and dire threats of vengeance, hence his reason that evening for trampling on me. I must here add that on the day the firing opened on the fort, I was leaning over the front half of my door looking towards the fort when bullets struck up dust in the street in front of me. However the corner of my house protected me. My wife was standing behind me in the passage begging me to come away, and then burst out crying. I turned towards her and as I did so a bullet struck above the door and buried itself into the passage wall. Had I not turned at the instant I must have got the ball through my chest. I have ever suspected that it was Du Plessis firing at me.

The next morning after being made prisoner at Pretorius' wagon, I was standing near the corner of the courthouse when he came to me and said I was accused of trying to steal a horse from his wagon.

'You need have no fear,' he said, 'I shall give my evidence and two of the Krygsraad members to whom I have spoken, will see that justice is done.'

At ten o'clock I was told to go to the courthouse, which I did. I was charged with disobeying orders and being found in their laager under suspicious circumstances. It was believed I wanted a horse wherewith to make my escape from Rustenburg. I explained the position and ridiculed the idea of wanting to escape. What for? And besides I had two good horses in my stables. Commandant Pretorius and another spoke in my favour and after Pretorius, whom I called as a witness, had given his evidence, I was released with a solemn warning. I found out afterwards that some of the Boer leaders wanted me away from the area as I might be a source of danger to them hence the trumped-up charge. In fact, although released, with a warning, I was told my case would be submitted to the Triumvirate, consisting of Paul Kruger, Joubert and Pretorius. I heard later that the leaders of Rustenburg got severely sat upon by the Government Trio. I saw Kruger's hand in this. The following day Van der Walt sent for me and while sitting talking to him in the courthouse I found that he had been with us at Mount Misery in Basutoland in 1865. When I confirmed this and described the death of Venter together with other details, he kept me talking. Suddenly a man rushed into the courthouse and said:

'Commandant de Lange is shot near the cannon outside the town.'

Van der Walt quickly arose, took his bandolier and gun, and walked out calling as he did to the field-cornet to collect their men and to meet at the cannon. There was, however, no response and the Boers crept away behind the wagons. No amount of persuasion could get them out. So, turning to me, the commandant said:

'You must take a white flag and go out while my men bring in De Lange.'

I hesitated but gave way and hastily placing a white flag on a stick I went.

Van der Walt added:

'You are not to speak to any one who may come out from the fort.'

To which I replied:

'Then you will have to explain to them or they will doubt me.'

De Lange, who was alleged to have been shot, was one of my men during the Sekhekhune Campaign and I knew him to be a brave youth. I moved close to a deserted house, in which the Boers had foolishly dragged their cannon the night before: there I remained until the body of De Lange was carried around the corner of Wagener's Store. I noticed before

I turned, an officer coming from the camp towards me. I turned again and looked towards him. He hesitated, and then walked back to the fort. I halted with the white flag raised until I saw him safely disappear within the fort entrance, then walked slowly back and returned straight home, both disgusted and down-hearted. My intentions were pure, but what will my friends think of me in the fort? I had been barely home for a few minutes when I was sent for again by the Commandant. I found him in the courthouse, surrounded by members of the Krygsrsraad. I was offered a seat.

'We have sent for you,' said the Commandant, 'to ask you if we have done wrong in sending you with the white flag and not allowing you to speak to the officer who came out to meet you?'

'Yes,' I said. 'I consider that the officer was insulted. I could have explained the situation to him.'

'What do you consider should be done?' asked the Commandant.

'Write to the Officer-Commanding [Capt. Aunchlick] a letter,' I said, 'explaining your action and I must ask you to make my position clear to him.'

After conferring with the others, it was agreed that my suggestion would be acted upon. That they ever explained my case I doubt, judging by Capt. Aunchlick's actions towards me later.

All the Boer attempts to take the fort at Rustenburg were futile, and it was only owing to the kindheartedness of the Officer-Commanding that many of the Boers who repeatedly showed themselves in the open were not shot. Aunchlick was loathe to shed blood unless absolutely necessary.

Chapter 10

Capt. van der Walt was superseded by Sarel Eloff, a brother-in-law of Paul Kruger. This man was noted for his hatred of the English. Very shortly after his assuming command he issued an order to commandeer sums of money from the loyal pro-British community, mainly from the poor. Messrs S. V. K. du Toit, John G. Wagner and Walters went up to speak to him on behalf of the Loyals. On hearing them he said:

'It is you causing people to resist my orders. I will have you all driven up to the fort, there to starve in that hole with your friends.'

Forty-two Boers were ordered to saddle up and under a white flag escorted Du Toit, Wagner and Walters to the fort. Needless to say they were warmly welcomed there, especially Walters who was an excellent shot. Were they starving in the fort? Oh, No. They had plenty of food, for during the time that friendly guards were on duty, supplies – even a slaughtered oxen – were sent in. One young man, Gladhast by name, a young German, who was the son of the new miller of that name, entered the fort several times carrying in pockets of sugar and other items. He was a powerful lad not wanting in courage. After the war Capt. Aunchlick presented him with a revolver, this being the only recognition Gladhast ever got. Others received nothing, not even a word of recognition with the exception of myself who, years after received letters from Colonel Sir W. Bellairs, and A. A. Churchill, but of this later on.

After several applications to Sarel Eloff I was at last allowed to move out with my wife and family to where I had my store at Wolhuter's Kop. Besides myself and my family of six children, there were John Weatherley, brother of the late Col. Weatherley, Morris, my manager, Jack Strike, and a bastard – who was a blacksmith – together with several native servants.

Before my arrival at Wolhuter's Kop, the Boers had been there to collect arms, but I had previously on my return from Waterburg, buried all my good rifles and two cases, containing a thousand cartridges each. The guns were placed in a strong iron trunk and the ammunition cases were well protected being as usual in zinc-lined boxes. We also tarred them to keep the ants from destroying the cases. They were buried in my garden.

Parties of Boers from Rustenburg were continually passing my house on their way to the Front to intercept the troops coming from Natal. Others brought news of the disasters to the British at Schuinshoogte and Laings Nek, and how the British were shot down in their hundreds. And how they marched in quarter column to attack.

'Your English soldiers are very brave but they are also very stupid,' it was said. 'They come on in bunched in groups; why are they not taught to fight as we do?'

Ridicule and sarcasm were often cast at us and it was a bitter pill to swallow. We silently mourned the needless waste of life and the folly of the British officers who should have been guided by those who knew the enemy, their customs and their mode of guerilla warfare. Then, as it was said in the last war: 'Tinkers presume to teach blacksmiths their trade'. The 'Tinkers', so-called proved to the 'blacksmiths' that they could well accept a lesson or two from them.

The isolated activity, while others were fighting, became almost intolerable. We were shut off from all news from the front excepting what was told to us by the Boers, so I determined to gain some information. I sent to Frederick Mahalies' kraal for an old trusted servant, David by name, and arranged with him to get through to Pretoria, now besieged by the Boers, to obtain news. One night, shortly after, he left accompanied by another servant, with a letter from me to Col. Bellairs, the officer commanding. They got through the border guard safely and returned four days later with a huge dispatch written, in the ordinary way, addressed to the garrison OC of Rustenburg and another to myself, thanking me and requesting me to keep up the correspondence and to forward the dispatch to Capt. Aunchlick at Rustenburg. I did so through Magato, a native chief living near Rustenburg to whom I sent news by Mahalies' messenger. The next time the trusted boys went to Pretoria, I warned the OC there not to send anything other than cipher messages, which was done, and continued to be done up to the time of the armistice prior to peace. At my own request, I received only verbal messages until Jack Strike got there, he having gone with the messengers on one of their perilous trips. We arranged a code and several communications passed between us whereby I received a deal of information. One of the requests I received was that I should get as many of the Boer Government Gazettes, which were printed at Heidelburg, the headquarters of the Triumvirate forming the government, that consisted, as previously stated, of Paul Kruger, Gen. Joubert and M. W. Pretorius, former President of the Transvaal. This I was able to do from a Mr van Manen, formerly schoolmaster of Rustenburg, who got them from his son-in-law, I. Brink, then in the service of the assumed Transvaal Government. The gazettes were lent to me and some time later Van Manen asked for them to be returned but I made some excuse, he asking for them again and again. At last, one day, I said:

'Well, Mr van Manen, you profess to be loyal to the British and I will therefore place my life in your hands. I have sent your gazettes to Pretoria.'

'Why did you not say so before?' he replied. 'I would have had no objection to your doing so at all.'

'Well now you know and as I have told you, my life is in your hands, for if the Boer leaders hear what I have done my life will not be worth much.'

'You are quite safe,' he replied, 'I shall not tell anyone.'

But the news leaked out, and one morning shortly after I heard from a friendly Boer that I must get away for I was to be arrested and shot for sending the gazettes to Pretoria. After a great deal of persuasion from my wife and Fanie van Staden, a loyal Boer and my nearest neighbour, I agreed to go up into the mountain Magaliesburg. Van Staden went with me the next morning ere it was light for it was on that day that I was to be arrested. We remained all day in the mountain from whence we had a good view of my house and surroundings for miles, but no Boers came and after dark we returned to our homes. I sent to Magalie and arranged for sentries to warn me if our enemies should approach during the night. My faithful natives did so, but the night passed by peacefully and I saddled one of my horses after breakfast and rode over to Marthinius Barnard's, at Sterkstroom. I found him at home. He came forward as I dismounted and on shaking hands said:

'So, they have not got you yet? If Marthinius Barnard had not been here it would have gone hard with you,' he continued, 'Let us go into the house and have some coffee.'

We did so. He gave me the particulars of how his assistant Field-Cornet de Beer arrived with twenty-five men with written orders to capture me dead or alive. Barnard then told De Beer that I was well-armed and a known good shot and how this had frightened the Field-cornet who at last said:

'Well, my orders are not to lose any of my men. I will go back for further orders.' – Hence the reason why I was not molested.

I have always remembered good old Marthinus for his kindly action. On my return that day to Wolhuter's Kop I made arrangements to defend myself by loop-holing my stable. We had four good rifles and four good shotguns to use, and natives to warn us of any hostile approach. I was, however, never molested. Marthinus Barnard was not the only friendly and loyal Boer by any means, Oh no!, there were many. About 400 were at this time encamped in the Zwart Ruggers, in a fortified camp, who would take no part in the war. There were also a number at Hartebeestfontein, near Klerksdorp. Eloff, the Commandant of Rustenburg asked Paul Kruger, late President of the Transvaal, for instructions regarding the Loyals at Zwart Ruggers. Paul's reply was:

'Leave them alone, we have enough enemies to deal with for the present. We will deal with them later.'

And thanks to a Liberal government, wiped away any bitterness and all were forgiven. The following example will bear out what I say. One Saturday morning my wife and family were awakened by a tapping at our bedroom window. I got up and asked who it was.

'It is I, David, sir.' was the reply.

I hastily dressed and went out.

'What is it?' I asked.

'Magalie has sent me to you with a message.'

'Come into the kitchen,' I replied.

He then told me as near as I can remember:

'Magalie had a meeting with other chiefs and headmen, and sent me to tell you that the white men wants them to rise on Monday night next and burn all the houses under Magaliesburg belonging to the Boers. They are not to kill only burn. The white men said Magalie or any of the others must not tell you for you would try to stop it, but the chief at their meeting decided that you should know and that they would be guided by your decision. If you agree then you must pack all your things and be ready to move on Monday morning at daybreak, as all the people who are for the Government are to gather at Beathany (a German mission station near the Crocodile River) until the soldiers come.'

'Who has instigated this thing, David?' I asked. 'Who is to bring ruin on black tribes of this country?'

He replied:

'The white man is responsible. I will not mention names, suffice it to say that they are English and loyal Dutch.'

'Go,' I said, 'and tell Frederick Magalie and Cobus to come to me today. They must meet me at my stable.'

He left and while we ate breakfast on the Sunday morning, I was told that the chiefs had arrived and were waiting for me in my stable. I went to them and after they had greeted me and I said:

'You sent David to me with a message, please explain what it means.'

They responded and told me how certain white men had come to them and told them that on the night of this Sunday they were to rise up against the Boers. Magatos and all the other tribes living about would also rise up simultaneously on the same night and burn all the Boer farms along the Magaliesburg but not kill the families, for when the men on commando heard of the burnings they would no longer remain on the Drakensberg to stop the English, but would return to protect their families. The troops of Her Majesty the Queen would then come over and conquer the Boers.

I was astounded by what they said and could hardly credit it; but what had been said was confirmed when a warning came that two horsemen were approaching my house. Shortly after, John Weatherley came in and said:

'Two men are here to see you.'

Knowing they were so-called Loyals, I asked Weatherley to send them to the stable. They came back and shook hands with me, one saying as he did so:

''Tis all right, I can see you are with us.'

I felt disgusted with the fellow and replied:

'Go and talk to my wife. You people are mad. You do not know what you are doing and be thankful that the natives have confided and fore-warned me.'

They left without a word and I then said to the chiefs:

'You have done well to come to me. What were you told to do when this war commenced? What did the English Government tell you in the letter I read to you? What did Paul (meaning the late President of the Transvaal) tell you?'

The spokesman for the natives replied:

'The letter said we were to remain quiet and not to take any part of the war. Paul said we were to supply drivers and leaders for the commando wagons but were not to fight, as it was a white man's war.'

To this I retorted:

'If you do as these foolish men are advising you, don't you see that you will be making enemies of both the English and the Boers?'

'Yes,' replied Cobus Mahalie, 'we have thought of these things and that is why we decided to tell you so that you may advise what to do.'

In reply I said:

'I will write a letter to the Government in Pretoria under your name. Whatever the General there instructs you, you must obey. Are you willing to do that?'

They conferred among themselves and then confirmed:

'Yes, we are willing.'

They then left and I went to my house where I met the two white men who had returned. Speaking frankly I said:

'I cannot conceive how white men such as you could have participated in such a plot that was both cruel and cowardly.'

They remained quiet for a few minutes and then one said:

'Our lives are in it. Our lives are in your hands Dennison, do not give us away.'

'I will not do so though you deserve to suffer. Go and warn all the others. I have arranged for runners to go to all the other tribes and to stop any action on their part.'

After a while they left, but before doing so one of them said:

'Dennison, if the Boers knew what you have this day done for them they would carry you on their shoulders and I shall ever be grateful to you for opening our eyes.'

A few days later I received a reply from Pretoria, a dispatch for the chiefs and one for myself requesting me to read the letter to them and to use my influence to stop any native uprising. I had pointed out in my letter, as strongly as I could, what would result, for I knew the kaffirs would not stop at house burning, and that a dreadful massacre of women and children would follow once their barbaric act of burning homesteads had influenced them. David meanwhile had left for Pretoria the same Sunday night of our meeting. It was about three o'clock in the morning that the trusty boy arrived back at Wolhuter's Kop with the Pretoria dispatches. I had a horse saddled and shortly after rode down to the German missionary, and as the day was breaking we read the letter from Pretoria to his flock. This action saved the situation and also the misguided men who might, acting under a mistaken loyalty to the British cause, have sacrificed much innocent blood as well as branding themselves murderers. I knew they all realised this later.

The danger was passed and their dreadful secret remained safe in my keeping. I gained no distinction in any way for what I had done but I have felt ever thankful that I was the means under Providence of averting a dreadful calamity.

On one occasion a dispatch was sent to me for forwarding to Fort Rustenburg which also contained a note to myself. I sent it on in the usual way and the next day rode into Rustenburg. On my arrival I heard that Magato's messenger, while attempting during the night to reach our fort by creeping along down the watercourse, which passed near the fort, was captured by the Boers and the dispatch was in their hands. I had for various reasons not gone to stay at my brother-in-law's, but was at the hotel overlooking the church square with the Boer camp located opposite the courthouse. A friend of mine, an officer in the Boer commando then came over to me and informed me about the capture. He suspected that I might have had something to do with the dispatch and told me that I had for some time been suspected of communicating with Pretoria.

'If your name is mentioned in the dispatch it will go hard with you,' he said, 'but I will give you timely warning in order that you may escape. They have no horses here that can outrun your horse, Kambula.'

So I had my horse saddled and ready in the yard, and after waiting and watching from the upper window of the hotel for an hour or more after my friend Hans Bodenstein left, I got a message through the hotelkeeper that all was well. This was explained by Bodenstein who returned shortly and said:

'The dispatch is written in cipher and we have not got a key so you are safe, but do not delay here. Get back to Wolhuter's Kop.'

I thanked him, and after conversing with him for a short time, he departed.

I hastily went and saw my mother and Mrs Tennant with whom my mother was living. Then after several warnings from my brother-in-law, who had heard that I was a suspect, I bid them all farewell and returned to the hotel. Shortly after I mounted my horse and rode back to Wolhuter's Kop.

Chapter 11

No doubt some of those who read these pages may have heard of the cannon made by the Boers during the war of 1881. Well, two of these cannons were made about four miles from Wolhuter's Kop in Marthinus Ras' farm. It was he who manufactured them, assisted by others. I went up one morning to see him at work, but was only allowed a glance and told in no uncertain terms to clear out. The guns were manufactured out of wrought iron plates welded together to form a tube. Then successive layers of iron bands were bound over them. The first gun was fired not far from my house. The breach blew out, which was subsequently repaired. This gun, and another made later, were used against the fort at Rustenburg. I last saw it in the Pretoria Museum before the last war. [Presumably this would have been the Great War of 1914–1918.] It was this gun that threw its improvised balls of iron and lead at the fort at Rustenburg, one of which struck the hospital tent beneath the mattress on which a sick man was lying. It tossed him up, but other did no further damage. An old friend of mine, Michael Colley, owed his life to his height that day. If I remember correctly, two of the same balls that struck the hospital tent went over his head as he was short of stature. An inch taller, I was told, and he would have being counted among the fallen heroes of 1881!

Constant were the reports brought by passing Boers of the events at the Front. Nowhere, according to reports, were our armies successful, while the contents of the dispatches from Pretoria were the reverse, full of hopeful expectations. One evening, John Weatherley and myself sat in the stall (my wife had gone to Rustenburg with the children to get some necessities left there) when we heard a distant 'Coee'. This was repeated frequently.

''Tis Jack Strike's voice,' I said, and replied to the call which was repeated again and again.

'Peace at last,' he called as a mule cart came driving up with Jack Strike and another who was introduced to us as Lt. Rider of the 60th Rifles who had come from Pretoria and also from Amajuba [Majuba].

A hearty greeting was immediately given and soon questions and answers flowed. We heard of Amajuba and of Gen. Colley's state and the many who fell besides. Again the result of a fateful blunder, I thought. Will the pages of blunder, written in blood be ever repeated? The blood of thousands, the nation's best, sacrificed through blunder. Rider shared my room with me that night. He told me everything and praised the Boers who had done all they could to save the British wounded on that fateful day for as on previous occasions, our men had been left wounded and dying on the field of battle. He told me how he had ridden with dispatches from headquarters to Pretoria and now to Rustenburg, giving notice of an armistice. How well thought of President Brand was in involving himself in the cause of peace and etc. and that he, Rider, was disgusted with events and would resign his commission when the war was over.

The next morning I drove him to Rustenburg, and as we neared the village we met parties of Boers arriving. The leaders had heard of the armistice and had dismissed the majority of their men. They galloped past, wildly shouting that the English had given in and that the Boers had won, etc., etc. A few stopped to thanks us for the news. We told them of the armistice and that there was no doubt that there would be no more fighting. They were very civil and rode on after shaking hands.

On our arrival at the village, we drove on to the hotel where we were soon surrounded by many of my friends, both Boers and English, all eager to hear the news. The Boer leaders had got the information the day before and had told all they knew. Rider went up to the fort with his dispatches, and I went down to my brother-in-law's. My mother was no longer there as she had died a short time before. I did not manage to see her while she lay dying nor was I able to be at her funeral, something that I have ever regretted.

I had been warned by my friends to stay away from Rustenburg and being influenced by them did not go but it was mainly for the sake of my wife and children that I had kept clear of the village. The next morning after our arrival at Rustenburg I went up to the hotel to enquire about my horses, noticing a group of citizens and two officers standing before the courthouse. I went up, and on offering to shake hands with Capt.

Aunchlick, he drew back and refused my hand. I turned away and left, feeling aggrieved and deeply sore at heart. I had gone but a few yards when I heard my name called; I went back and the matter of the refusal to shake hands was explained but I never felt satisfied. I felt that I had been misunderstood and was distrusted, God knows I deserved it not. On my return to Wolhuter's Kop the morning following the meeting in the square, I was told that Slim Hermanus Engelbrecht and Marthinus Ras had been to see me and that the matter was urgent. They left a message with my wife that I was to go up to Ras's farm at once as they had some important private information for me. I rode up the following morning and was told by Ras and Engelbrecht that I was in danger and they advised me to leave the Transvaal until peace was finally concluded. They had found out there was a plot to do away with me. I could not believe it. However I loaded my wagons with what provisions I had and left for the diamond fields, leaving my wife and family at Rustenburg. My friend, John Weatherley, promised to look after them.

I cannot blame my Transvaal friends for feeling bitter towards me for no doubt they had relied on me remaining neutral. I took no active or aggressive part in the war, it was true, but I gave our garrison in Pretoria all the information possible for which I gained no credit. I also had the satisfaction of knowing I had been the means of saving at least the burning of the Boer houses. Furthermore, I only give some of the details of what was done to advance the British cause and for doing it, I lost heavily, and was awarded, when the Royal Commission sat to investigate claims, about £60, or approximately 6 % of my actual losses. If I did not get as much in lucre or honours, I must blame myself for being such a poor sycophant! I could never pander or creep to the powers that be and no doubt have failed to do so. I tried to do my duty and nothing more. I never sought for loot or favour, and so I suppose must ever be satisfied that I got neither, except honours in medals and the DSO [Distinguished Service Order] which of course I value as some little recognition of what I tried to do or have done, but enough, for I am digressing; I have stated that during the armistice in the Transvaal between the British troops and the Boers, I left for the diamond fields. A friend, W. Wagner accompanied me. I remember when we crossed the Witwatersrand we stood and looked back on the Magaliesburg with mixed feeling of sorrow and joy. Sorrow at leaving a country where we had both spent many happy years, and joy that we were leaving a country where dissension and strife always ruled. On our arrival at the Kimberley diamond fields, I sold my produce and employed my wagons, of which I had three, in wood – riding from Pokwani to Kimberley market. Wood was fetching at this time, from £20 to £30 a wagon-load, and I should have done well but for my unsettled state of mind and bad luck. The work of cutting down the camel trees was laborious and owing to the scarcity of water for our cattle, it meant sawing and chopping at night. As soon as a wagon was loaded, it was sent down to Moir and Drakes' store on the Hartz River by double-spans, due to the sand and extreme weight of the load, for as much as the wagon could hold was piled high. We paid a percentage per load to Gasibone, then Chief of the Pokwani, there being no limit to weight, and wood was plentiful. We had occasional news from the Transvaal and from my family I received two letters. Contradictory reports were frequent about the peace.

News came at last that the war was over and from my wife I had a letter stating that my family was starting for the diamond fields. About a month after, I met them at Christiana and took them down to Barkley-West, where I had succeeded in renting a house. At Barkley I continued wood-riding. The river diggings were at this time in full-swing, especially at Priel and Barkley, besides places down the river. I will pass over a period that was fraught with the results of disappointments. I became careless and dissolute in my habits, which to a great extent had hold of me for many years afterwards. I do not think I was naturally bad, but was weak and gave way to disappointments . . . but enough.

After I had settled my family in Barkley-West, I continued wood-riding assisted by my eldest son, then a little boy, but who was most willing, truthful and obedient.

After carrying on wood-riding for some time I gave it up and went trading into Gasibones country, Pokwani. This was during the war between Moukarane, the Botlapin chief of Taungs and Masaouw, the chief of the Koranna tribe at Mamusa, now Schweizer Reneke in the Transvaal, which became part of that Republic by the Convention of February 1884 but of which I will allude to later on. One occasion while trading at Gasibones with my goods unpacked on the ground, I was warned that the Boers were coming. So I hurriedly commenced loading, thinking to get out of the way, but hardly had I with the assistance of my boys, got my wagon half-packed, when I heard shouts and on looking out of the wagon I saw a party of about 300 horsemen galloping up. They surrounded my wagon. I at once got off and to my surprise met some of my old troopers and others I had known in the Transvaal in former wars. I was greeted in the most friendly manner and invited up to the laager. So it was arranged I was to go up to their laager on their return for, they were on a cattle raiding expedition, but would not tell me where they were going. Had I found out I could have given the people, one of whom was Jack O'Riley of Thomong, an acquaintance of mine of many years past, notice in time for them to get their stock across to the Cape Colony, for many of them were close to the border-line dividing the Cape from Bechuanaland.

I must here digress from my story and give my readers a little insight into this native war I have alluded to. Well, it was brought about in 1882 chiefly by stock theft and trespass on both sides. Well fanned by white men, ever eager to create war that might reap the benefits of blood and rapine. Morokani had his white men to aid him in his war. So Massow did the same and had a force raised of 400 men, chiefly burgers of the Transvaal, including as I have stated many I knew and the result of meeting them was that I went to their laager, sold all my goods and, eventually after much persuasion, became one of them being a force of white men. We became easy victors, took a large number of stock and a big slice of Morokani's country, which we called Stellaland. This was ruled as a Republic for some time and a President was elected, Gert van Niekerk by name and a Bestuur, or Executive Committee, and a Volksraad, with the usual paraphernalia accruing to a Government. We had our Landdros court, our Registrar of Deeds and other offices. We also had our flag, with its single star on a green background, and our paper currency. We were a cosmopolitan population among whom the families of De la Reys were prominent with Groot Adrian by no means the least of them. He was a man of contradictory traits of character, kind and hospitable to an extreme to all classes who came to his house on the Witwatersrand – even the hungry native never asked for food in vain, but at the same time he thought little of the value of human life. We had Long Adriaan, father of Groot Adrian, Cobus and Ignatius. One of the youngest, Ignatius, was unfortunately shot by accident and died at Vryburg. Cobus, of Jacobus, was the General of that name during the last Boer War [1891–1892] and a man much respected. 'Free Booters' we were called, and counted but few friends among the outside world. Whatever we were called, or were thought to be, the fact remains we burnt no huts and we interfered with no women or children. All such acts were strictly prohibited by our leaders. We did as the British did during the Russia-Turkish War; they assisted the Turks, we assisted the natives. It was Morokani who was under British protection but the experience of the war of 1881 was fresh in the minds of many of us. How some of us were treated by the Royal Commission we well knew. We had experienced the treatment, felt bitter and were reckless of consequences. I personally had always been loyal and had ever done my best for the old flag and, I ask, was the treatment I got a fair reward for my services and sacrifices? We were not fighting against the old flag, oh no! But the treatment meted out to us was unacceptable, we drew the line at that. I will pass over the many details that occurred during the war up to the finale, when the British envoy, Mr Hudson, from Pretoria came to our camp above Taungs. Through his services peace was brought about and a republican government formed. Then came the convention of 1884, whereby the country we had conquered [Stellaland] was shared between the Transvaal and the Imperial Government. The old line, called Warrens Line, running from Koppie Enkel, in a line running north-west to east of Mamusa, and west of Lichtenburg on to the Zeerust border was shifted to below the Pudumoe Fountain along west of the Morokane Range, giving the Transvaal, a large and valuable slice of country that we, the 'Free Booters' of Massow had taken from Morokani. Our actions were condemned but had resulted in being the means of opening the road to the north and adding to the Empire a valuable stretch of country.

Chapter 12

No doubt many will remember the Bechuanaland Rebellion of 1896–97 and the murder of Blum, another white man, and a coloured man by the natives of Pokwani. The remains of these murdered men were dug out of an old well at the back of the dwelling house on the farm Pokwani. Piet Gasibone, a son of the old chief of that name, was killed in an engagement with the Cape police near the present railway station a day or so previous to the murder and it was presumed that the murder was committed to avenge the death of Piet Gasibone. Gasibone, who became chief subsequent to old Gasibone's death, and after a long term of imprisonment for being implicated in the earlier murder of Mr Thompson of Conforth Hill, District of Barkley-West, was the ruling power when the events of this narrative took place. To make it clear I must state that owing to the ravages of rinderpest among the cattle of Bechuanaland, infected herds were, by the order of the Government, being destroyed. This order being carried out in Gasibone's country to which the natives strongly objected. Influence was brought to bear with the ruling powers of the Cape, with the result that the shooting of native cattle was discontinued on the condition that they kept all their stock within the limits of their own country; but in this they failed. Some of the cattle of Gasibone's people crossed the line at Border Siding and were destroyed by the police. This gave rise to the rebellion which was encouraged by some white men living in the Transvaal, who promised to assist Galishwe with men and arms, etc. The result was an attack on Pokwani by the Cape forces, including the Kimberley Rifles under the command of Col. Harris. All the native huts were burnt excepting one or two near the late Canon Bevan's church. The exhuming of the bodies of the murdered men caused a feeling among those present of bitterness and a desire to avenge the

These, the Albany Mounted Volunteers, or Albany Rangers, approximately twenty-five in number, were the type of unit that would have fought alongside Dennison's contingent during the war in Basutoland.

A hot engagement during the Basuto War. Note the quivers of throwing-spears on the horsemens' backs.

Campaign conditions in Basutoland were tough.
This engraving illustrates how primitive they were.

Colonel Frederick
Augustus Weatherley, who
raised the Border Horse
and appointed Dennison
his second-in-command.

Colonel Evelyn Wood (later Field Marshall
Sir Evelyn Wood) most likely at a time
prior to the Anglo Zulu War. Wood was
responsible for the debacle of Hlobane and
was the commander of the Flying Column.

Commandant Frederick Xavier
Schermbrucker trekked up from the
Cape with forty volunteers to join
Wood's Column. Many of his men
were German ex-soldiers who had
seen service elsewhere before joining
Schermbrucker's Kaffrarian Rifles.

Prior to the Battles of Hlobane and Kambula, Wood's irregular horsemen constantly raided into Zululand.

The banner of the Border Horse was made by the ladies of Pretoria and presented to the unit after the Sekhukhune Campaign, then commanded by Dennison. Nevertheless, the deceased Colonel Weatherley's family crest and motto 'Be Vigilant' was used as the centrepiece.

A contemporary sketch of the Hlobane Plateau and the curtain of cliffs that confined access and egress to one or two steep tracts.

Lieutenant Arthur Bigge of the Royal Artillery was a great friend of the Prince Imperial. Bigge, with eleven men, commanded a rocket-tube at Hlobane and also fought at Kambula.

Lt. Col. Redvers Buller, rescuing a wounded man and winning the Victoria Cross. Captain Walter Stafford of the Natal Native Horse later remarked: 'An award not popular amongst the rank and file who were of the opinion that there were more deserving cases amongst the lower ranks.'

The view from the Hlobane plateau looking west towards Kambula.

The massive boulders that cover the narrow pass at the western end of the Hlobane plateau.

Major Frederick Carrington, a seconded officer of the 1/24th Regiment, had command of Wolseley's mounted troops during the Sekhukhune campaign.

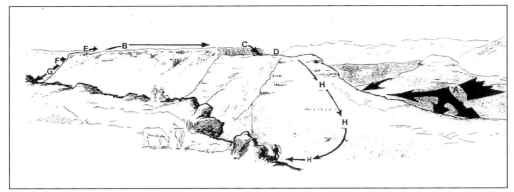

The Battlefield of Hlobane Mountain adapted from a contemporary drawing by Colonel John Crealock. Key: A) The approaching Zulu army. B) Buller's Column ascended the mountain followed later by Weatherley's Border Horse. C) The western descent later named Devil's Pass. E) Position of Buller's rear guard. F) Approximate position of Ityenika Plateau where Colonel Weatherley and many of his troopers met their deaths. G) Dennison's escape route. H) The escape route towards Kambula for the few who managed to descend Devil's Pass.

A rather lurid and fanciful sketch of Trooper Grandier of Weatherley's Border Horse, the only white man known to have been captured alive. He was taken to King Cetshwayo but subsequently escaped and, as Dennison relates, rejoined his unit.

Colonel Weatherley with his young crippled son, Rupert, dies swinging his sabre amid a flurry of flying spears. The view from the Hlobane plateau looking west towards Kambula.

ILLUSTRATED · PAPER
AND · ILLUSTRATED · TIMES

BRIGⁿ GENˡ EVELYN WOOD V.C.

ZULU SURPRISE AT THE HLOBANE MOUNTAIN: COL. WEATHERLEY'S FIGHT FOR LIFE

The Royal Artillery guns, firing shrapnel and 'grape shot' at close quarters, was a major factor in the British victory at the Battle of Kambula from which the Zulu army never recovered.

At the conclusion of the Zulu campaign, Sir Garnet Wolseley immediately set out for the Transvaal to conquer Sekhukhune, the Chief of the baPedi. Note the long line of wagons in the distant valley on the left.

Wolseley secured his line of advance with a number of forts. At one time Dennison and the Border Horse were stationed here at Fort Oliphant.

Without the aid of Swazi mercenaries, the traditional enemies of the baPedi, it is unlikely that the British war with Sekhukhune would have been successful.

Chief Sekhukhune of the baPedi. A photograph taken in Pretoria after his capture.

Commandant Pieter Raaff, CMG, proudly wears the Order of St Michael & St George, a decoration that Dennison believed he was denied because he upset Sir Garnet Wolseley.

Above: Cecil Paulett Mountjoy Weatherley, the eldest son of Colonel Weatherley, was conspicuously brave in the attack on Sekhoukhune's stronghold. Soon thereafter he joined the 80th Regiment as a private, but due to Sir Garnet Wolseley's influence, quickly obtained a commission. Later, on leaving the army, he achieved fame as an explorer and hunter in Central and Eastern Africa.

Above right: A group of young burgers, ready to do battle in the First Anglo Boer War of 1880. Note their antiquated firearms.

Today, Dennison's lonely and untended grave in Plumtree Cemetary, Zimbabwe, formerly Southern Rhodesia, where he was buried in 1932 at the age of 88.

Above: The late Thomas Burghers, President of the Transvaal in 1876 and 1877.

Above right: A garrison fort on the Rustenburg Heights.

This old gun was used against the British Fort at Rustenburg in 1881.

Officers and NCOs of Dennison's scouts when first raised. 1. Sergeant W. Staynes (died of wounds, November 1900) 2. Sergeant-Major Staynes 3. Quartermaster-Sergeant H. J. Dennison 4. Captain Dennison 5. Lieutenant J. Streak (killed November 1900) 6. Corporal Harvey Smith.

Dennison's scouts: Officers' quarters on line of march.

A squadron, Dennison's scouts.

Lieutenant Herbert Brown, screen leader of Dennison's scouts.

Pack drill: a trooper of Dennison's Scouts is punished for cruelty to his horse.

Officers of the Kimberley Column.

Lieutenant Kidd, DFA, and his pom-pom.

Mode of travelling in the Transvaal.

War result: remains of a farmer's house near Rustenburg.

Ox-wagon crossing Sterstroom, Rustenburg district.

cruel murder, if possible, but the natives had all, except for a few old men and women fled on the place being attacked by our forces; a half-hearted defence was made, a few natives were shot in the attack and the rest escaped. Galishwe fled on horseback with some of his followers in the direction of Manthe, then crossed in to the Transvaal and later escaped away into the Langberg and, aided by Luka Jantji, chief of Langberg vicinity, he defended himself against the Cape force under the command of Col. Dalgetty, for several months. This was known as the Langberg War of 1897.

I had been offered the command of the Stellaland Burgers but refused, as circumstances connected with the war was not to my fancy. I left Vryburg with my wagons, transport riding, for Bulawayo. After my return, about three months later, I was pruning my orchard, when Inspector Ayliff, 'Daddy' as he was called, rode up to the garden fence and after greeting me said:

'You are wanted by the Government to undertake an expedition, will you do so?'

I asked where to.

'I cannot tell you unless you accept,' replied Ayliff.

'I will let you know in an hour's time. Will that do?' I replied.

He agreed and rode off. I went inside and told my wife, who said:

'I would accept if I were in your place, you will come to no harm, you bear a charmed life.'

And within the hour I rode up to the police camp and accepted the offer.

After hearing where I was expected to go and the various objectives, I was told I had to raise a force of a hundred white men, arrange the transport and go into the Kalahari and capture Galishwe who, it was said, had gone from the Langberg with some of his followers, on horseback, into the desert.

'A case of hunting for a needle in a haystack,' I said, 'but I will go, and mention my conditions which, besides a few minor details, was that I be allowed to raise a force of 120 mounted Europeans and twenty Basutos, the latter for intelligence work.'

Barely an hour later a policeman knocked at my door with a telegram which read: 'Terms accepted. Enrol at once.'

I employed two recruiting agents, one of whom was our then magistrate's son, Lenard Tillard, the other being John Gerringh. Both are still alive and no doubt recollect the details of my story as will others who took part in our memorable march into the Kalahari desert. The former is now a magistrate somewhere in the Transvaal, the latter is in Vryburg.

Within three weeks we were fully equipped and off. Our course was past Geluk and Hassfort down the Mashowing River past Uadebing to the junction of the Mashowing River with the Kuruman at lower Lehotlong. We were going through a country occupied by herds of natives who were not in sympathy with whites and of whom many had taken part in the Langberg Rebellion. I knew the native character well. My force was a small one, about 140 effective as combatants, and about thirty wagon drivers and leaders besides a few servants. We had to be stern and just in our intercourse with the natives; on our way an incident occurred at Hassfort then in the occupation of the owner, the late Carl Hassforther, so well known in the earlier days of Vryburg.

We were camped about half a mile below the house, having breakfast quite near the road, when fifteen young kaffirs passed without greeting us, but made some jeering remarks, which several of us heard. A sergeant was ordered to stop the youths and orders where given to administer two stripes to the bare backs of each with a wagon strap. When this was done, they were brought before me and asked if they knew why they had been punished? Of course, they replied, they did not know. They were told that: 'The next you meet white men you will greet them, now go.'

Readers will say the action was cruel and arbitrary: to any who know the native character it will be quite apparent that such action was, in the long run, one of mercy and not cruelty, for it prevented action on the native part, through fear, that would, or might have, resulted in greater harm on the whole.

Our convoy of wagons was fourteen besides three scotch carts and four water carts. The wagons carried both the men and the horse rations and were used as transport from one base, or depot, to another, having to return for supplies at times to the depots in the rear, when necessary.

Owing to the difficulty of watering our animals we could not take more than two wagons at a time; in some places water had to be got from the beneath the sand, in the dry riverbed of the Kuruman and thrown into the hollow of buck sails on the sand, where it had been hollowed out; in other places, old wells had to be deepened and the water hauled out with buckets and the animals watered in the hollows made by the natives. It was slow and arduous work, the thirsty animals were as a rule difficult to keep back during the water-sifting process.

I omitted to state that I had as Captains Commanding troops, Angus Hannay and Arthur Cullinan (now DSO), the latter only accompanied us as far as Madebing where he got letters from his home which necessitated his immediate return. I appointed another to act in his place. We captured a few rebels at Madebing. After a tedious and trying march we arrived at Khuis on the Malopo, our destination, on the 20th August 1897, having being twenty days on the march from Vryburg, for we left there on the 31st July.

I should have stated that the natives en route did not give us much trouble for our reputation had gone ahead of us, for we were feared. We surrounded Madebing one morning before daybreak, and when it became light a number of natives were seen on horseback galloping away westward. I sent off some men, with Capt. Cullinan, who rounded up a few but the majority got away; they were not fired upon for I had given orders that no firing on the natives was allowed except in defence.

Our doctor, Hancock by name, and about half-a-dozen men remained with me near Madebi's kraal, Madebi was the name of the chief of Madebing. We saw a light among the huts, and heard the low murmur of voices.

'Come, Doctor,' I said, 'let us see who is inside the kraal.'

We went and guided by the light of a fire and the voices, we got to a hut around which was the usual wind screen, made of wild currant branches. Looking in at the entrance we saw about twenty natives sitting and standing around a fire, one of them remarked in their native tongue:

'Here are the white men!'

We were not greeted, but were scowled at by faces that bespoke the venom lurking beneath. Some guns and sticks rested against the screen; one of the natives put his hand back towards a gun standing near him but was felled by one of the native stools I had quickly caught and with which I hit him. I then took out my revolver but on reaching the entrance, and after looking at the crowd for a minute or two, I put it back in its holster. I then heard a noise behind me and on turning found our doctor about to hit another native in a similar manner.

'Stop it, Doctor!' I said, 'or you will have to spend the morning closing up holes in kaffir heads.'

With that a servile 'Dumela Morana' greeted our ears. My prompt action had produced a most placid effect among the gathered natives.

I have diffused from the thread of my story. A certain amount of egotism may appear in the use of 'I' so often, but if I had not been where I was and what I was I could barely give a truthful statement of the facts. So come what may I must appear in the story despite all prospective criticism. I have said we arrived at Khuis on the 20th August 1897, it was before the dawn of day we crossed the Molopo River in the Kalahari. I had about forty men with men, the remainder were at the different depots we had left some miles behind. As quickly, and quietly as possible, we crossed the Molopo Valley and surrounded the native town of Khuis on the dunes of the desert west of Molopo. We dismounted and waited for daylight; then, on reaching the town all we found was one old native who, on being asked where the people were, said they had fled away into the Kalahari for they were afraid of the white men. I knew the headman's name was eTouwnig, and asked where he was. The old man said he ran away first for he was very much afraid. We guessed the reason was that he was one of those who took part in the rebellion and so it was as we later found out.

Our wagons arrived towards evening and the day following I had my camp formed by having camel trees sawn down and dragged around the wagons, forming a circle of about sixty yards in diameter, within which all our animals were secured at night; and the high fence protected us from the August winds to a great extent. No hunting or patrolling was allowed. I did not want to frighten the natives further so would allow no firing of guns either. Mounted vedettes were, as is customary, placed about a mile from camp on either side, who had orders to watch for stray natives and bring them into camp, and to treat them with kindness for through such means I might gain valuable information. A couple of days after our arrival at Khuis, a young native was brought into camp by one of the vedettes. He said he was the headman eTouwnig's son and that his father was away about three days' journey on foot into the desert with a number of his people. I said:

'You must go back to your father and tell him he need not be afraid, he must return to Khuis with his people and no harm will be done to them. Tell him also that I can give them some food.' For I knew they were hungry. 'You can rest here today and eat.' I continued, 'and tomorrow you can go to your father and tell him what I have told you.'

The boy was fed and some mealies were given to him to take back on the day following. Five days later, while I was watching the watering of our cattle at the waterhole in the Molopo Valley, information was brought to me that eTouwnig, the headman, had arrived at his kraal and that his people were also returning. I went back to camp and shortly after, on being sent for, eTouwnig turned up with a couple of his followers. He took off his jackal-skin cap and greeted me in the usual servile manner of a whipped Bechuana; he had an oily tongue and lots of it. According to his account he had ever been a loyal subject of the British Crown, he had been with Sir Charles Warren's force some years previous and had assisted in the taking of Takoon, Bechuanan Batlapin town, on the head waters of the Mashowing north-east of Kuruman and that most of the other Bechuanas were very wicked people, etc., etc.

I said:

'Yes, I know all about what you have done, and now I want you to do more for the Government, and that is why I sent for you, and you being such an old and faithful servant of our Queen can, I am sure, be trusted to do what I want you to do. I have not been sent to punish innocent people, I am seeking for those who have done wrong. I want Galishwe and you have to find him and bring me the information as to where he is.'

I let this sink in and then continued:

'This day is Saturday and before next Saturday you are to be here with the news I want, otherwise beware, for you cannot escape me if you act falsely. Now Go!'

I ordered food to be given to him and he left looking very down in his luck, for it was apparent he did not relish the work I had given him to do, and I felt convinced, also, that he knew where Galishwe and his followers were hiding. Three days later, the headman of my Basutos, Jan Fick, by name (who by the way, told me he had been a servant of Gen. Fick's when a boy in the Orange Free State about the time of the Basuto War of 1865. Fick was the Commandant-General of the then Free State Force who fought against Moshesh, the Basuto Chief of that period. The Bloemfontein Rangers under Capt. Hanger, of which I was a trooper, joined part of the Free State Commando), came to my tent and said eTouwnig was outside with a Makaluka servant (bushman servant); I said:

'All right, bring the servant in.'

He was brought in and was proved to be not a Makaluka but a wily bushman of the fine old sort. (The Makaluka were also called bushmen, but they were more like the low caste Batlapin.) I said, speaking in Dutch:

'What is your name?'

'I'm Charlie, Baas,' he replied.

119

'Well, what have you got to tell me?' I asked.

'No, Baas. Nothing. I only came with eTouwnig because he said I must.'

'Oh, you know nothing. Then you are no good,' and gave him in charge of one of my sergeants, saying: 'Keep him out of sight and send eTouwnig in' – who shortly after was brought before me. I said: 'Your bushman has told me everything, now I want to hear it from you.'

He seemed a bit upset when I said this and replied:

'Sir, you know the bushmen are liars.'

'Yes,' I said, 'but I know a servant of the Great Queen won't lie.'

'No, sir. I cannot lie to you. I will tell you I have been down to Mopoling but there are no kaffirs there. They are all gone.'

'Go,' I said, 'Now I know you are lying. You still have three days to tell me where Galishwe is and on Saturday I must know.'

He left, looking very depressed.

The next evening Jan Fick again came and said eTouwnig had come again and old Charlie was also with him.

'Let eTouwnig come to me,' I said.

He came a few minutes later and after greeting in his usual servile oily way, said:

'Sir, I told you the bushmen are liars. Charlie was down at Mopoling and saw Galishwe and his men. Galishwe is shot on his heel' (the latter I knew to be true) 'Old Charlie told me after we left yesterday.'

''Tis well,' I said, and turning to a sergeant said: 'Take him away and sent old Charlie to me.'

After old Charlie had arrived and greeted me I said:

'Bushmen never tell lies. Is it not so?'

'I don't know, Master,' was his doubtful reply.

'Well, I know,' I said, 'and now you have to speak the truth.'

'Yes, Master, but what did eTouwnig tell the Master?'

I replied:

'eTouwnig told me lots and now I want to hear what you have to say.'

He hesitated a moment or more, then looking me fairly in the face, said:

'Baas, you must take me with you when you go from here or eTouwnig will kill me.'

I said:

'All right, I will keep you here and when we return to Vryburg you will go with us; now tell me what you know.'

'Ja Baas, I will tell you, Baas knows the day we went away from here, I

120

went with eTouwnig down the Molopo, and next day we met two kaffirs coming from Mopoling' (the name of a cattle post between the Kuruman valley and Molopo and not far from the former where water was got from a well in that valley) 'and he told me that Galishwe was hiding with his men in the dunes near their cattle post but that he, eTouwnig, must not speak about it; because the white men at Khuis might hear and it would cause great trouble. eTouwnig said his mouth 'was shot', for Galishwe was their friend. We then turned back and rode with the man, who later left us and went away across the dunes towards Bushman's Huts. We then, the next day, came here and the Baas knows what eTouwnig said.'

'Very well, you can go now,' I said. 'I will call you again later.'

I had eTouwnig brought to me again. He appeared very nervous and seemed to apprehend danger.

'You must not be afraid of me, I will not hurt you,' I told him. (I wanted to allay his suspicions and to think I trusted him.) 'I am going to Mopoling tonight,' I continued, 'and you are to go with me to show my men and myself the path.'

I was watching him keenly while talking, his faced changed, I noticed, the anxious expression was again apparent.

'I cannot go,' he said, 'for I am sick.'

'All right,' I said. 'You stop here in my camp till I come back.'

He was handed over to our sergeant-major with instructions that he be kept a prisoner in the camp for the present. My men had gone down into the Molopo Valley to drill with Capt. Hannay, it was about 3 o'clock in the afternoon. I sent to call them in, and meantime sent for old Charlie who shortly arrived. I said:

'Now, Charlie, I have sent for you to tell you I am going to Mopoling tonight, and you have to go to show us the path.'

'Ja! Baas,' he at once replied. 'Yes, I will go and the Master will see that Old Charlie does not lie.'

I gave orders and preparations were made to start at 5 o'clock that evening. A corporal with four men were ordered to follow with a water cart and wait about twenty-five or thirty miles down the Molopo Valley for our return. I had this arrangement made for I knew we should require water on our return journey. We started about 5 o'clock that evening, fifty horsemen besides old Charlie and six mounted Basutos. Fifty-seven including Dr Hancock, our corps doctor (a regular good sort and qualified doctor).

It was a moonlit night that followed the evening of our departure from camp and we traveled at a walk down the Molopo Valley until about 10 o'clock that night. It was an early evening in September and a keen wind blew all night from the south; we off-saddled under the shelter of a sand dune covered with furze for an hour; no fires were allowed, or smoking either while marching, for the light of a match can be seen a long way off at night in the desert and every care was taken to hide our approach to Mopoling. During our halt I questioned old Charlie again and from his answers I felt assured that we were on the right track to capture Galishwe. After we marched on again, led by our guide for about another hour, we left the valley and entered the sand dunes of the desert. We traveled in a south-easterly direction for about two hours, then decided to halt between two high sand dunes and there fires were made to warm ourselves by, for now it was bitterly cold. Also, old Charlie had missed the path which he, however, found again and we mounted. Then despite the biting cold we rode on and over the sand covered stretches and dunes, with our weary horses till daylight. Finally, our guide halted and coming to me said:

'Baas, we must wait here a while. I go and look for Mopoling. It is not far off now.'

He left and walked to a bush on the top of a dune then beckoned. I went to him, the sun was just rising and away in front against a sand dune, about three miles ahead, I saw some cattle browsing.

'Mopoling is there,' said Charlie, pointing to the right of the cattle.

I had my field glasses and was able by their aid to plan my further advance. I returned to where my men were waiting, they had dismounted and were sheltering themselves as best they could behind the furze bushes that were around. On calling to Capt. Hannay he came to me, and I told him my plan of encircling the place. That is, he and his men to file off to the right in single file, well apart, and to keep out of sight as much as possible from the natives in our front; I would take the left and we were to advance as quickly and as quietly as possible. We started off, Hannay with his men encircling away to the right, while I took my course away leftward. We rode as fast as the heavy sand and mouse burrows would allow, our horses going knee-deep into the sand every now and then, always keeping out of sight as much as possible, and it was only when we showed ourselves on a dune, about 200 yards away from a native encampment, consisting of several wagons and bush fences, that they became aware of our presence. There was a shout and several men ran with their weapons in their hands into what was a trench or hollow below the fence. I had advanced my men in an extended line on to the top of the dune. Our doctor rode near me.

'Doctor,' I said, 'Get back. Those kaffirs may fire and we cannot have you hit.'

But he did not obey.

'My place is here,' he said. 'I cannot go back.'

While we spoke a native appeared with a white flag from behind the fence and came towards us. I galloped forward to meet him. He took off his hat as I rode up to him and said:

'Schleim is there, Baas,' pointing to a dune some distance below us.

I beckoned to my men who quickly came to me. I divided them to cover right and left flanks and we went forward at a gallop. We had not reached the dune when one of the men that went with Capt. Hannay appeared on top of the dune, waved his hat, and shouted. We crossed quickly over and found Capt. Hannay with his men surrounding eight natives, Galishwe and seven others. Caught at last after being tracked from one spot to another and causing war, bloodshed and a costly campaign. They were on the point of fleeing on their horses, which were already saddled, when Hannay and his men captured them. All were armed but one, Galishwe's uncle, who denied having a gun. I had them searched (Hannay had already disarmed them, and found on Galishwe a leather purse in which was a cheque and some cash, the cheque was drawn in favour of Benn, a trooper in the CMR [Cape Mounted Rifles] who fell at Langberg, a bloodstained saddle and bridle, which Galishwe said was the one Trooper Benn had ridden on when he was shot. We camped near the wagons and, after having our morning meal all hands, except the guards and myself, lay down and slept. Most of our party were tired out with the long night march of fifty-five miles and no sleep. Capt. Hannay and myself took turns to rest. I took the opportunity while the others slept to get Galishwe on one side and talk to him. I asked him to tell me the cause of his rebellion: he said the police shot his cattle and certain white men over the border told him that the English wanted his country and were forcing war upon him and that he should fight for his country. He continued to say that the white men would help him with arms, ammunition and men. I asked him had this happened?

'No,' he replied, 'they sold me two cases of ammunition and four rifles for which I had to pay £40 in cash, that was all the help I got.'

'And where were you going from here?' I asked.

'I wanted to get help and fight again and I should have got away from here if you had not caught me. Dennison,' he said, 'you are like a dog on a spoor. I heard there were white men at Khuis but I did not know it was you. But still I am glad you have come. If it had been the police they might have shot me.'

My turn to rest was on, Hannay came towards Galishwe and myself. I left him to talk to the prisoners and laid down for a much needed rest, the strain was mental as well as a bodily one; I was determined to catch Galishwe and while others slept I either walked about at nights or lay awake.

'Catching Galishwe was nothing to make a fuss about,' a certain police officer was reputed to have said and which was later repeated to me.

I said: 'Remind him of Christopher Columbus, the Spanish officials and the egg.'

Well, anyhow, we caught him and some adventurous spirits won money on the capture – we did not! Kudos was our share of the spoil, even the £500 reward offered for the capture of Galishwe did not fall to our lot under the Sprigg Government.

Galishwe was tried in Kimberley and sentenced to a long term of imprisonment, but was released long before the expiration of the sentence and is now living near his former country, at Magagong on the Taungs Native Reserve.

I sent Galishwe and his men out via Kuruman with one of my officers and twenty-five men, and remained to try and affect the arrest of another noted rebel Sampie by name; but a few days after the departure of the prisoners, a dispatch arrived from Vryburg to the effect that having accomplished the purpose for which we were sent, we were to return at once 'to save further expense'.

'How about the Langberg picnic that cost the Government over £200,000?' remarked Capt. Hannay, 'we have finished the job and I am sure it won't cost the Government more than £25,000. Golly, this is a funny world!' he exclaimed.

'Yes, it sometimes is,' I commented, 'but it is the people in it that makes the world a funny place.'

We started on our back trek two days later and arrived in Vryburg fifteen days thereafter. The capture of Galishwe ended the Langberg War, and in all probability saved the Cape Government the spending of many thousands more in a prolonged engagement had Galishwe got away and had been able to carry out his intention of getting other tribes further north to rise, and with him fight the white man. And it wanted but little at that time to call several tribes to unite in a rise against their common foe, in many cases urged on by renegade white men.

Old Charlie came with us to Vryburg and after being in my service for some months disappeared and I believe went back to the old haunts in the Kalahari desert, which has an enchantment to all who travel in it and, no doubt, to a greater extent, to those whose home it is.

Editor's Note

At this point in Dennison's life, circa 1899, the unpublished manuscript and the book, *A Fight To The Finish*, merge (see Introduction) with the first seventeen pages of the published volume merely mentioning, ever so briefly, many of the important events in Dennison's life that he has re-counted so ably in his hitherto unpublished manuscript. For this reason, these seventeen pages of *A Fight To The Finish* have been omitted from the replication that follows.

Having got this far in the narrative, the reader will be aware of Dennison's intimate involvement in many happenings of high drama yet, for instance, the battles of Hlobane, Kambula and the Sekhukhune campaign were each given little more space than a few paragraphs in the seventeen pages mentioned above, while the Kalahari desert expedition of 1896 was not mentioned at all. So the mystery remains: Why were these events of historical importance either omitted or brushed over?

Having worked on the manuscript for several months, the present editors offer the following as a possible explanation: there is evidence of an earlier editorial hand attempting to discipline Dennison's unruly grammar, but the corrections, in a small spidery hand, soon peter out. So, perhaps, editor and raconteur lost patience with the each other causing Dennison's earlier adventures to fall short of the publisher's desk with the attention of both parties concentrating on the Anglo-Boer War of 1899–1902 which was fast losing its topicality. However, now, after more than a hundred years, the two halves of Dennison's life are finally joined and we have been given glimpses of history hitherto unseen; much of which is unsavoury and cruel but bear the merit of straight reporting even if observed through the eyes of a long-since redundant colonial outlook.

The text of *A Fight To The Finish* which follows has been subject to a minimum of interference by the present editors, the grammar and style remaining much the same as originally published; and it must be mentioned that the book was well received in 1904. We have included extracts from one review that appeared in *The Daily Telegraph* of that year:

'. . . the South African War seem rather belated now – so much has happened since the last shot was fired, and memories are so short. But a good word must be said for a very modest and unassuming little book just published and written by Major Dennison, DSO, the leader of a well-known band of scouts which bore their captain's name, and did it and themselves honour . . . The outbreak of war in 1899 found him with his family in Fryburg; two years and a half later, when he counted up his experiences, they included capture twice, a couple of wounds, countless skirmishes and hot corners, and the loss of two gallant sons . . . When he found that the war was not over in the middle of 1900, Dennison became attached to several columns operating in the Western Transvaal . . . He raised a body of scouts about 200 strong who acted as eyes to the Kimberley Column, Dennison did not approve of the policy of farm burning and the ruthless destruction of stock and his little book is valuable because he does not spare criticism. Here for example, is a pungent passage in which he stigmatises the notorious jealousy between certain column commanders: 'From all sources we heard of train-wrecking, capture of convoys and men by the Boers. De Wet, the Will O'the Wisp, the man who might have been caught again and again were it not for that curse of the British Army, jealousy . . . Anyone can thus judge that there must have been something most glaringly wrong – and that something was jealousy, deplorable jealousy. A nation's cause, the honour of the flag, everything, counted as nought, everything endangered for the aggrandisement of self, in so many instances.'

Thus the review approved of Dennison's reminiscences and his frank and fearless criticism of those in high command who otherwise, more often than not, received nothing but obsequious approbation.

Part II
A Fight to the Finish:
Reminiscences of the Great Boer War
of 1899–1902

Chapter 13

'The Boers have crossed the border at Kraaiban' was the news given me hurriedly by a friend as I rode up Vryburg Street on the 13th October, 1899, on my return from a scouting expedition to the border the night before, 'and broken up the line at the bridge. The armoured train goes tonight with guns and ammunition for Mafeking,' he continued.

'And,' I queried, 'who goes in charge and when does the train start?'

He told me, and that evening I went down to the station just in time to see the armoured train steam off to its destiny, its destruction, and its fated cargo of brave men recklessly rushed by folly into the hands of the enemy. Thus, then, did the war for the predominancy of races break out, the war foreseen by so many of us for years past. The war as ascribed to many causes, franchise, etc., but the inevitable struggle between Britain and Boer had commenced in dread reality.

I had for some time being in charge of the Intelligence Department for the District of Vryburg previous to the war. The ill-fated Maj. Scott, CP, was in command of the district, sent up from Kimberley but a few weeks prior to the outbreak to manage, with a handful of Cape police and a volunteer corps, the Vryburg Rifles, in whose ranks rebels were not wanting; a district whose inhabitants counted 95 % of a people in open rebellion. The one and only wise course open was adopted by him, and that was the evacuation of Vryburg. A bare fortification, untenable, un-provisioned, away from the only means of obtaining water, he was at last forced by dint of persuasion to abandon and fall back on Kimberley; no means of communication either with Kimberley or Mafeking, as the wires were cut north and south by the Boers; suffering from mental affliction, a respected, brave, and good soldier, the strain was too much for him. He imagined himself disgraced, and died the day after he left Vryburg. The remainder of the Cape police with their maxims safely reached Kimberley, and nobly aided in the defence of that place. The part the Cape police took during the siege and later during the war is one that will ever bare comparison with the best of corps that served during the war. I cannot refrain here from remarking that the Cape police, as I knew them six months after the war, was, through mismanagement, by no means the good, able old force of warriors that served before and during the long struggle. Youths, fresh from England or elsewhere, formed the principal part of the strength, old hands drifted away. Many tried and good men wished to join, in many instances men I myself had recommended, but they were over thirty years of age, beyond the age laid down by the sage rulers of the corps, experience and service sacrificed to ignorance: how often again is history to repeat itself? As the facts connected with the evacuation of Vryburg by the Cape police are not generally known, I have mentioned the foregoing, and may add that repeated efforts were made by the loyal inhabitants of Vryburg to induce the Cape Government to send us men, provisions, and arms, but without avail. The following is a copy of a statement sent by me to Col. Kekewich from Kuruman, October 13th, 1899:

Col. Kekewich, OC, Kimberley

From the first I pointed out to the late Major Scott that the position he held at Vryburg was by no means a good one, and recommended that the prison be fortified and the point opposite, commanding water be fortified with sandbags thus the prison could be made a very strong position. I told him that a number of English colonials were willing to assist if he did so. On a night of a false alarm I again went to Major Scott at midnight with a Mr W. Crosbie, of Vryburg, and spoke about the position of his camp and its extensive area to be commanded by a limited number of men under his command, etc. He said: 'Do you wish me to lay down my arms?' I replied: 'Certainly not, there are other ways of doing things.' He said: 'My orders are to defend this camp.' Mr Crosbie also made some remark about the place being a difficult one to protect, and afterwards said to me as we walked back to town that he would also take part in the defence if Major Scott would move into a better position.. On Saturday night, the 15th October, The two Hannays – Robert and Angus –, my late eldest son Alec, and myself agreed to go into the camp and assist

Major Scott at any cost. We went to the camp that night to see Major Scott, but were refused admittance. On Sunday morning the magistrate, a Mr R. Tillard came to my house and asked me to attend a meeting at the courthouse at 12 o'clock midday, that he had seen Major Scott again, and that the Major had asked him to get the feeling of the people on the subject of withdrawal of the Cape police. The meeting was held, and a resolution passed that the OC forces be requested to withdraw and the volunteer corps be disbanded. I had previously strongly recommended the disbandment of this corps, as there were many among them who could not be trusted. This can be borne out by the Vryburg loyal people, such as Messrs. Crosbie, Fincham, Hannays, Browns, and many others.

I was placed in a most awkward position, as the people wanted me as their leader, and I could not act without authority. I did not see how I could command a town guard under the adverse circumstances. I wished to act with Major Scott, but was debarred by the position he took up. I again and again offered my personal assistance in any way he might consider most useful, but he never made use of my offer. He seemed very much depressed on several occasions that I met him. On one occasion, on returning from the border, I found him in the compound behind the police barracks. He seemed very much distressed, and said: 'At Kimberley and Mafeking they have the best engineering experts, while this place is left to one police officer.' I said: 'Scott, I have repeatedly offered to help you.' He replied: 'Yes, true; but I cannot move from here.'

I consider that the wisest course Major Scott could have adopted was the one taken, viz, the evacuation of Vryburg; and I fail to see that any dishonour could be attached to such an act under the circumstances. The Vryburg people again and again had pointed out through the RM [Resident Magistrate] Mr Hoole (prior to the arrival of Mr Tillard), and also by direct communication with His Excellency the High Commissioner, the defenceless state of Vryburg, and asked that 400 men with artillery be sent to assist us. The majority of the Vryburg loyal men were willing to fight to the last, had an opportunity been given to them. The conclusion I came to regarding Major Scott was that at last he knew his position, in case of an attack, was a hopeless one, knowing, as he did, that the Boers had artillery and were in strong force, but wanted a resolution of the loyal townspeople to support his action. I wrote to him on Sunday morning, and attach a copy of my letter.

(Sgd) C. G. Dennison.

The following is a copy of my letter to Major Scott referred to:

Vryburg, 15/10/99
To the OC, Vryburg
Dear Sir,
As I feel that my efforts have been misunderstood, I shall not again approach you at your camp on any subject concerning your position at present. I may merely say that whatever I have suggested as being with the best intentions, and I now for the last time take the liberty of pointing out the fact that your camp is one that, under ordinary circumstances, would require 'some protecting'; that I do not and cannot think that the Commissioner realises that the position of your camp is in any way bad. May I suggest as an open course that you evacuate with your men and maxim, and give the volunteers an opportunity of disbanding? Your force is no protection to the town, nor can you prevent the Boers from hoisting their flag in Vryburg. The wire is cut, and you are now left to use your own judgement; by evacuating you can fall back on Kimberley or Mafeking. You will thus retain you arms and ammunition and maxim, which will otherwise fall into the hands of the Boers, as well as those of your men who might survive the attack. Shortly summarised thus: Your position is one you cannot hold against artillery; resistance means loss of life and the endangering of the town – your loss, the enemy's gain. Then how do you best benefit your country? By saving to that country the lives and services of good men, besides the arms, ammunition and maxim. Your communication with Headquarters is cut off. You have now to use your own judgement; and I say and say it earnestly, that when the time comes leave your position and no dishonour attaches itself to you, but will be execution of judgement.
Yours faithfully
(Sgd) C. G. Dennison.

On Sunday afternoon 16th October, my daughter and some her friends walked up to the cemetery, but returned quickly to inform me that they had seen clouds of dust in the direction of Vlakfontein, which was presumed to be the Boer commando advancing. I changed my clothes, bade farewell to my family, mounted my horse and went to Kuruman, ninety-eight miles west, passing on my way whites and blacks fleeing the advancing foe. Native women and men carrying large bundles on their heads, infants on their backs, and dragging their young children along, flying from the dreaded Boer. In many cases whites were in the same state of terror. No advance of a barbarous foe could have caused greater flight. 'Where are the Boers?', 'Are they coming on?', 'Will they shoot us?' etc., etc., were among the many questions put to me. The scene was pitiful but ludicrous.

On account of my horse getting sick, I was delayed, and did not reach Kuruman until the 18th. At Kuruman I met Capt. Bates, who was in charge of a detachment of the Cape police in the district, and whom I had known in the earlier native war of 1879. A good plucky sort was Bates, and a man of considerable experience.

Immediately on my arrival I wired to Col. Kekewich, OC, Kimberley, for instructions and was ordered by him to assist in the defence of Kuruman if necessary, and by all means keep open communication between Kimberley and Mafeking. This I did by means of native runners who usually succeeded in getting into Mafeking by circuitous routes, and later, when, during the siege of Mafeking, the place was being closely invested, the dispatches were handed by the natives to Lady Sarah Wilson, who was staying at Mosita at J. Keely's farm and by whose kind aid the letters were sent on by her trusted boys to their destination. Several of the native runners were shot in cold blood by the Boers, many of whom take a delight in putting natives up in a road and coolly shooting them down. The shedding of native blood is not counted as murder by many of them; on the contrary, they talk and laugh over the deed, describing the fear and agony of the poor sufferer with jeers and laughter. But all are not thus; too many, nevertheless, can be charged.

I had many difficulties to contend against, and some caused by men who should have given every assistance.

By the aid of my late son Alec, who remained in Vryburg, I was able to get information to and from that place. This was just after the occupation by De la Rey, who had hoisted the Transvaal flag, and stated in his speech: 'that the flag he had that day hoisted would never be struck otherwise than over the dead bodies of his burgers.' Vain boast! One is apt to recall the words of General Sir Garnet Wolseley: 'As long as the sun shines', etc. No dead bodies were there to get over for the purpose; no defence was made by them; they deemed the alternative course the best, and acted on it. Acting on information I had got from Vryburg, that we were to be attacked, we built small fortifications around the base camp on the most prominent positions, dividing our small force of fighting men, sixty-three in all, among the different redoubts. We had rarely about 120 men of all sorts, black and white, the majority refugees, but only the number I have given were available for bearing arms. About this time I had occasion to warn Van Zyl, who, I knew, was inciting the Boers to rebel. Capt. Bates and myself were walking down from his camp to the courthouse when, on passing Van Zyl's house, I noticed several saddles outside and some horses grazing about. I immediately went to his house and called him outside, telling him that I knew perfectly that he was inciting the people to arms against the Imperial Government. He laughed aloud and said:

'Do you think I should be such a fool?'

I replied:

'I say what I know, not what I think, and I warn you that severe punishment awaits you after the war, if you live.'

I then left him, but had him watched, and this man was never punished, but lives now in the Transvaal on his ill-gotten gains. On a Sunday in the early part of November, 1899, came the Boer Ultimatum from the commander, one Visser by name, demanding our surrender, to which after consultation with the magistrate, Capt. Bates, and myself, a reply was sent suitable to the occasion. We refused to surrender and defied the rebel gang. I was in command of twenty men on the south-east ridge, about a mile and a half from the base camp.

On the Monday morning following, having made all the arrangements necessary at the camp, I rode up to my forts, for I had two on the ridge, one with ten men in charge of Herbert Brown – a Queenstown lad, full of pluck, of whom I shall have more to say later on – about one hundred and thirty paces distance from my fort, commanding from this position the approach from the south side; nine commanding the north-end, also east and west, as was the case with Brown's position. Capt. Bates, with Mr Hilliard, the RM [RSM] Roger, were in charge of the main camp with about twenty-five men of all sorts.

On my arrival at the forts, I sent my horse back with a man who accompanied me for that purpose. And hardly had the man gone with the two horses ere the head of the Boer commando came in sight on the Pokani road. When about 2,500 yards distant, fire was opened on them, unfortunately, from one of our forts, about 2,500 yards on my north in charge of Corp. Gass. This scattered the Boers who might otherwise have come on to closer quarters and given us a better opportunity of damaging them. On getting with about 1,000 yards of my position they opened fire from the low ridges in our front, which we returned with a cheer from both our small forts. The war with us had begun, the war only to last about six months, as so many of us thought!

'Only a gallop over from Mafeking to Johannesburg' as one of Baden-Powell's officers said to me at Mafeking.

'No Jameson affair this time, old chap.'

True, as a whole, a legitimate war, but in many cases how much worse the blunders, the disasters, the Great War history can bear record.

The Boers, after making several attempts to get the best of us, moved round on to a fort held by a few men under Sgt. Child of the Cape police, where they made a most determined attempt but were repulsed, losing several of their number. Again and again did they make such attempts (as their well-known want of solid pluck allowed them) to take one or another of our little forts, but without success, outnumbering us as they did by twelve to one.

Thus for a week things went on, when, on a Saturday night, they suddenly withdrew. On the Sunday morning not a sign of Boers was seen. They had gone – but only to return the following week with reinforcements. A force now over 1,300 men to take sixty three! Again, the same as before, attack after attack was made on our little fortifications, but with as little success. One large gap, affording the Boers an opportunity of getting within our lines, we could not defend. This was a rugged ridge behind the magistrate's dwelling and public offices – a rugged ridge out of which the Kuruman River takes its rise. But just before the Boers sent us their ultimatum I sent for the native headmen and warned them to keep their people and stock away from the ridge, as we had placed dynamite mines there, knowing that this information would soon reach the ears of the enemy. And so it proved, for the Boers carefully kept aloof from this point. And only after their reinforcements had arrived from Griqualand West, under one Field-Cornet Wessels (who had more grit in him than the other leaders), did they venture down this ridge, and take possession of M. Colley's store, thus cutting me off from the water, as we got our supply at night from near his house out of the river.

It was on the same night that the Boers got possession of Coley's store that they made, for the fifth time, a most determined attack on Brown's fort. Actually getting up to the walls, they pushed some of the sandbags down on the men inside with their guns. I plainly heard Wessels call out in Dutch:

'Will you give in now?'

But the reply he got was:

'No! I have never given in to a Boer in my life, and less so tonight.'

This was from W. Dunbar of the Cape police, as brave a boy as ever carried a rifle; his dash cost him his life at a later period of the war.

'Then,' said Wessels, 'I will have you all dragged out and your throats cut.'

'Come in and try it if you are men,' was the reply of Herbert Brown, who sat on the ground wounded in the head.

The men inside managed, by standing on the sandbags and some stores, to reach over with their revolvers and rifles and fired on to the Boers below, with the result that one Van Aswegen was killed and others wounded. This cleared them off, and the same night I had to evacuate both forts and get over to that in charge of Gass, narrowly escaping some Boers whose front we just had time to cross as they were coming along the road to Colley's store.

I left the men at Gass's fort, after enlarging it, and went down to the main camp at the request of Bates, to assist him. Some of the men left at Gass's were afterwards also sent for to strengthen our meagre force at the camp, as the Boers were now only 300 yards from us, at Colley's store.

I must mention that every assistance in his power was rendered us by Michael Colley as long as he could do so. He was an old and true friend of mine, and one I shall ever respect. Among the trials we had to endure were the locusts (*Voetvangers*), 'infantry', i.e. young locusts that hop along in myriads. The sun was scorching hot, and as we lay in our small forts under partial cover these insects crawled over us, into our trouser legs, into our shirts – in fact, where ever there was an opening, they got in. Our clothes and anything lying about were destroyed. We suffered torture, and the Boers were in even worse plight, lying flat in the open behind a few stores, barely sufficient to cover their heads, our constant fire in front, the blazing sun above, and the locusts crawling, hopping, eating, torturing (as they themselves later described it) as they at times cursed or prayed or, in sheer desperation, sprung up and rushed away, daring exposure to our fire rather than endure the unbearable torture they were submitted to. Yes, ye fat-quartered civil servants, some of ye at the head of departments now under imperial rule, holding your positions in so many cases by the only qualification you can claim, viz. that of favour, who had never seen a day's active service during the last, or maybe any war, what I have mentioned are some of the minor discomforts you have missed, and which perhaps had you endured might have broadened your narrow minds, or at least embellished them with some truth and Christian charity towards at least the South Africans who had fought so hard, endured and sacrificed so much, despite what one calling himself an officer has said in public print, which perhaps is only worth paying attention to from the fact of the malicious ignorance displayed by the writer when he describes the Irregular Forces of South Africa as 'little better than a rabble, disobedient to their officers', who in their turn 'had no knowledge of their duties'. This base mis-statement, in as far as the mass of colonials and their officers are concerned, is more than contradicted by the good work done by them, and with which they are credited by Lord Kitchener and many of our best British generals. But enough! Perhaps I should not have wasted material on such insignificant nonentity.

Chapter 14

Pretty well during the whole of the Kuruman siege I was able to get dispatches away to Mafeking and Kimberley, many of which never reached their destination. In some cases the natives, acting on my instructions, destroyed the dispatches when escape seemed hopeless, but too frequently they were caught and shot in cold blood. As I have before stated, I was greatly assisted by Lady Sarah Wilson, who deserves great credit for the service she rendered our corps while outside Mafeking. Many deeds of daring were done by individuals during the war, many not known, too many unrewarded.

Day after day, from daylight to dark, were the Boer bullets rained on our defences; our cattle and horses, kept alive by the aid of green reeds cut in the river near the main camp at night, and watered there also, fell daily, killed by Boer fire. But, although we had about a third of our force hit, we lost but one white man (Poor Ward of the Cape Police) killed by a random shot at dusk on a Sunday evening. He was a good man, and in charge of one of five forts surrounding the base.

Christmas Day at last came round. About 10 a.m. we saw a Boer with a white flag between Colley's store and Gass's fort above us, then one of the men from the fort met him, firing ceased, and presently we were informed that Field-Cornet Wessels had offered an armistice. We accepted, and agreed to suspend hostilities during the day, but were warned by him not to venture too much until he had conferred with the Commandant, who was camped near the mission station. Shortly after we got word that it was all right. Our men scattered about revelling in the outside freedom, many went into the fruit gardens below and gathered the half-ripe fruits, meeting in many cases our enemies, only to engage in friendly banter. Some met their friends fighting on opposite sides.

I had just returned from having a bath in the Kuruman River – a luxury not to be despised after weeks without it. Messrs. Hilliard and Bates went down shortly after my return to indulge as well, and on returning when near the camp were suddenly fired on by Van der Merwe's men. Wessels did not fire, but sent word to us to let our men come down on his side; this could be done by running a short distance down the ridge below which they were not exposed to Van der Merwe's fire. Wessels faithfully kept his word, and the following day withdrew from the attack with his Free State men, as we heard, on account of Van der Merwe's treachery.

During our siege I heard on several occasions from Vryburg. My family were at first not interfered with, but later on my sons, Alec, Harry and Fred, with all loyal families, except my wife and daughter, were sent away first to Christiana, then back to Vryburg, then down South. Fred, my youngest son, managed, in company with a son of our congregational minister, Rev. Olver, to escape from their guards, and got into Kimberley, narrowly escaping falling into the hands of the Boers by falling flat as the Kimberley searchlight turned towards them in its circuit just as a patrol passed about a hundred yards from them. They were arrested by our guards, but, as my son was known, was soon released. They remained and took part in the defence of the place, Fred assisting his brother-in-law, J. E. Symons, as one of the six millers on the Conning Tower. Far above all shelter, exposed daily to the fire of the Boer guns, including the 9-pounder, they stuck to their post without a mishap, although under constant fire. It was during the siege, the bursting of shells and constant firing of other guns and small arms, that my daughter, Mrs Symons, gave birth to her first child; both mother and child survived. Close to Symons' house, a Mrs Soloman was killed by a shell. About this time also Labram, the maker of 'Long Cecil', was killed by another shell. At the attack on Carter's Ridge, near Kimberley, my second boy, Cliff, was killed, with Major Scott, Turner and many more. I cannot dwell on Kimberley Siege, others more able and in a better position than myself have given the details; suffice that I write what I personally know, with a glance at time at other scenes during the war.

My wife and daughter were treated with kindness by the last Boer magistrate, P. Bodenstein, whom we had known as a boy in Rustenburg in days gone by – in fact, Bodenstein acted most nobly to those of the loyal families who remained in Vryburg.

Self-sacrifice was not wanting at Kuruman, as was shown in the case of

141

Mrs Harmsworth, the wife of Sgt. Harmsworth, of the Cape police, who was also with us. She nobly remained with her husband, though a cripple, and did all she could to aid and add to the comfort of those in defence. And it was only by dint of persuasion that she moved on to the mission station, and there assisted Miss E. Chapman in nursing some of our sick and wounded. It was the intention to give both these ladies some token of recognition, but circumstances prevented this being done. I will now take the opportunity of saying that what they both did was well and nobly done, and merited the sincere appreciation which was felt by one and all of us. Many noble women from the old country, as well as the colonies, assisted the sick and wounded during the war, and no thanks of ours can adequately compensate them for the gentle, careful nursing many a lad experienced at their hands.

The grey dawn of morning was just tingeing the east as I lighted my pipe on my morning watch (for Capt. Bates and myself took half-nights about duty) on the 1st January 1900. And barely was it light enough to distinguish the fort on the ridge opposite, when we heard a distant boom. It sounded like a cannon. Relief at last, I thought, and was on the point of calling the others in the shanty we slept in, but waited for another shot to be sure. A few minutes, and again a distant cannon boom from the north-west, and as I looked out of the porthole a cannonball struck up the earth on the other side of the river. No doubt about it being a cannon this time, but not of friends. I called Capt. Bates and others, who seemed to doubt at first; but scarcely had they joined me outside when we heard another shot, and saw a shell burst near Ward's fort. We all felt that the end had come, but determined to hold out as long as possible. Perhaps relief might come at last, Vain hope!

After pounding away for some time at Ward, the Boers moved their old 9-pounder round south, and then opened upon us and the stable fort; the latter they could not hit, but after many attempts at us from a ridge about 3,000 yards distant, they succeeded at last in striking our embankment twice, and put one shell in an old parapet on which a goat was standing, which threw the animal up some distance, to alight on its feet straight down unhurt. The ordinary black powder was used by the Boers, so that a look-out could give fair warning, as he saw the smoke from the gun, to take cover. No one, excepting some women and children (native), seemed much put out by the Boer's shelling – in fact, joking and banter was kept up all the time. After throwing shot and shell at us from daylight to 3 p.m., they moved their gun round east and commenced giving Gass's fort their attention, their first shells nearer hitting us than the object of their fire – in fact, about as close as the majority of shots aimed at us. At last we saw a shell burst on the fort wall, then another shortly after inside, besides which the men were exposed to heavy Mauser fire, caused by the breach the shells had made in the wall of their fort.

'There goes the white flag,' said one of our party, and sure enough something white – I believe a shirt that once was white – was hoisted by the party on the ridge. Shortly after 1, Henry Thompson, a Vryburg rebel, rode up to our camp with a message from Commandant Visser demanding our surrender. After conferring together, we decided it was our only course. We had done our best, and had held out for several weeks against overwhelming odds, and longer resistance meant more loss of life. Capt. Bates, Mr Hilliard, and myself went down and met Visser at Chapman's store. The only terms we could get were that our private property would be respected; and thus, after fighting hard against fearful odds for so long we had to submit to the inevitable. Conan Doyle says in his work on the war that Kuruman was garrisoned by 130 Cape police. He is wrong. I have given the correct number, sixty three in all, fighting men, Cape police, civilians, half-castes and blacks. My statement can be borne out by the Rev. J. T. Brown of Kuruman, as well as by many others not of our Defence Force.

What was done at Kuruman was never recognised by the authorities. We kept a considerable force engaged that might otherwise have swelled the number of the enemy elsewhere, and had the cannon not been brought to bear on us we should, in all probability, have held out another month. We had nothing but small arms.

Previous to our surrender, the Boers had used a gun, probably a Hotchkiss, that fired a small shell. On one occasion one burst in one of the portholes of Brown's fort, and again on another occasion one struck a stone outside my fort and, bursting, wounded five of us, including myself; two of the wounded went to hospital and recovered, the remaining three including myself, more slightly wounded, were able to continue our work of defence. Our wounded were ably attended to by the local district surgeon Dr Beare.

Among the commando to whom we surrendered were many men we knew of the Vryburg rebels. One, John Myburg, was very prominent; he came galloping up to the others, waving his rifle over his head, and

143

shouting, 'Yes, I told you so; 'tis because I came to assist you.'

We were kept in one of the rooms of Colley's house that night, the next day, and following night, and then moved by ox-wagons to Vryburg. We were, however, treated with every kindness and consideration by our captives. Tobacco, a luxury we had been out of for some time, was freely supplied, and as they had no sugar, they sent for some on the farm on our way out and got some. I cannot commend too highly the treatment of our guards, numbering, if I rightly remember, 150 men.

On our arrival at Vryburg we were all put into the jail. My wife and daughter came to see me there. Before we were cut of from Colley's store, and prior to the Boers' taking it, I got a draft from him for £16; this I sewed in the waistband-lining of my trousers, and, on giving some things to be washed to my wife, I mentioned quietly the fact about the draft, and requesting her to change it for notes, placing two of five pounds in the same place. This was done, besides which I had a few pounds in my purse, as the Boers had not robbed us of everything. We remained at Vryburg two days, and then were taken on to Klerksdorp. On our way we passed a farm called Rietfontein, and as we passed two carts with women drove up to our wagons from the farm. The wagons were halted, and the commandant in charge of our guard came up, and speaking to me in Dutch, said, 'This is Mrs Coetzee and her daughters. I want the officers to dismount that they may see you all.'

I said:

'I shall not get off the wagon; if Mrs Coetzee wants to see me, here I am; the others may do as they please.'

None of us got off. On this the young women commenced jeering at us, one of them saying:

'Wait until you get to Pretoria into Kruger's hands; he will treat you all as you deserve. You dirt! You dogs!' and such epitaphs were freely cast at us.

I stood on the front of the wagon for some time, looking at them; and said:

'And so this is the language of a people who call themselves Christians?'

'Ha!' said one of the girls pointing at me, 'he talks of Christianity; what can such a heathen know about it?'

At which they all burst out laughing. Our men on an open wagon in front gave a cheer, and some of them jumped off the wagon and started plaguing the girls, who at first seemed to resent, but soon appreciated the attention paid them. They shortly drove back to their farm amid cheers from the men.

The action of Willie Dunbar and others in chafing the girls had sent them away in good humour and completely changed the current feeling.

I noticed that they were all dressed in black, and, on enquiring, found that the father, two sons and son-in-law had all been killed at Mud River. The Boers did not lose by any means as many men as we did, but they lost heavily nevertheless, as was proved by the fact that few families in the Transvaal had not lost one or more relatives.

'One killed and two wounded', became the set rule of number of their casualties, whereas the number of killed on our sides were multiplied by any number. They are not a particularly truthful people, and truth is only used when it might be beneficial to the party using it. The South African Boer has many good traits in his character, but he is, as a rule, untruthful to a degree; it is, I am sorry to say, a national failing. '*Jy lieg*' ('You lie') is no insult to a Boer, and the expression is commonly used by them one towards the other.

We arrived at Klerksdorp and were again placed in the common jail for the night, and the morning entrained for Pretoria, where we arrived in the afternoon of the same day.

Immediately on our arrival we were ordered to get off, and were kept standing for fully two hours, then marched off (all excepting the magistrate, Mr Hilliard, who was taken to the model school prison) to 'Die Transvaal Hotel', as the Hollander officer who gave the order called it. He meant the common jail, and to the jail we were taken, there arranged in a row, searched, everything of any value taken from us, including our pocket knives, then all marched to the reformers quarters – an iron building in the prison yard. This was the room occupied by the Johannesburg men after the capture of Jameson's party. Shortly after, on walking across the yard, I met face-to-face a stout man whose face I recognised but whose name I could not find in my unfaithful memory for names. We shook hands.

'Who are you?' I asked.

'I will not tell you,' he replied, 'you must find out. You know me well.'

'In what capacity are you here?' I enquired.

'I am jailor of this prison,' he replied.

'Oh, are you?' I said, 'and is it your custom to crowd men and officers into one room?'

145

'No, how many officers are you?' he enquired.

'Two,' I answered, 'Capt. Bates and myself.'

'Well,' he said, 'you see those two men standing in the doorway of those rooms there?' (pointing to the opposite sides), 'they are two officers. There are two rooms, Jameson's rooms. Go there and I will cause your blankets to be taken to the rooms at once.'

I called Bates, and we went together. The two officers were Capt. Kirkwood and Lt. Tarbut of the South African Light Horse, who were taken prisoners at Colenso and Nicholson's Nek. After chatting a while, I asked who the jailer was. 'Du Plessis is his name,' replied Capt. Kirkwood. And so it was. A man, Jacobus du Plessis, whom I had known in Burgersdorp as a youth in 1860, and later in Rustenburg. The same man served with me in 1879 with Sir Garnet Wolseley's column against Sekhukhune.

We were pleased, as can be imagined, to get into comfortable quarters and to find such genial companions. Poor Tarbut took ill later, was removed to the hospital, and died there of enteric fever.

The first few days passed pleasantly away as we killed the time by recounting to one another our experiences of the war, but as time dragged on, prison life became monotonous, even reading became tiring to my restless spirit. The monotony was often broken, as batches of fresh prisoners were brought in, in seeing them searched and watching their faces and actions when their first ration of mealy meal porridge was given to them. The hungry would generally eat it, or at any rate a portion of it, but, as a rule, smell it, turn it over in the round tin bowls, then put it down in disgust.

Kirkwood suggested marbles, and sent for some, but after an hour at the game we had to give it up, concluding that the game was no good, and this we realised more the next day, as we both were almost too stiff in our joints to walk.

The game of Patience with cards was the most popular past-time in jail, and certainly suited our environment better than marbles.

During the day we were only allowed to make use of a space within chalked lines enclosing an area of about thirty feet square, but after the cells were locked at night greater freedom was given us. We could walk all about the yard, which was a great boon, more especially as this gave us an opportunity, from the corner of the prison yard, of seeing the hills outside; and on one occasion I was allowed, by special permission of the President, whom I had known in former years, two hours on parole to enable me to visit my sister, who lived in Pretoria, and who was ill. No one but those who have suffered prison life can realise this great boon, to be able to wander about free, even for a limited time, and breathe purer air.

After all, there were many worse off than we were, for the treatment was by no means unkind. We were allowed to make use of the money that had been taken from us, by giving orders, through the warders, for necessities, which were booked against the amounts held in trust for us by the prison clerk. Then, besides, friends supplied us with food and reading matter – in fact, the kindness experienced by us from the Pretorian friends deserved our sincerest appreciation and gratitude. And in these lines I would convey to them the fact that we valued their kindness greatly. How can I forget the kind consideration of the American consul, Mr Hayes? He proved himself (excuse the phrase) 'a white man'.

We were not without news from the outer world either, for the local papers, which were not allowed to any prisoners by the prison rules, were frequently brought us secretly by one or other of the native (Zulu) constables at their own costs. One of the warders, Jarvis by name, had been an NCO in the Border Horse under me; in 1879 he rendered me great assistance in getting dispatches out. Frequently men were arrested on suspicion in the town, placed in prison, and later sent down to Delagoa Bay as undesirables. Jarvis would give me this information, as well as more useful intelligence. Then at our Sunday service I would manage to pass a letter to one or other of those being sent away, to be posted at a British port to the Chief Intelligence Officer, Cape Town. Letters from home came frequently to hand, via Delagoa, of course after having passed the censor. Thus I had news of the welfare of my family from time to time, as did my fellow prisoners from theirs.

The newspapers, teeming with news of the disasters of our troops – fairly truthful accounts at times, as we found out later – were read aloud by one or other of us, while one stood near the window on guard against intrusion. On the approach of anyone the paper was hastily hidden beneath the mattress. Copies of State wires not infrequently came into our possession by the aid of two war prisoners in the cell adjoining us, who got them through a trusty native constable. How they were obtained I do not know, but can fairly guess. These wires were tied to a stone and thrown through the window bars at night to our friends by the constable, and eagerly were these wires awaited and the contents devoured by us.

The story of the 'Man with the dog' at the Model School Prison, where the officers were first kept, has appeared in print before, but I will recount it again.

A man with a dog was frequently seen by the officers in the prison at the Model School, whose actions seemed peculiar. He would walk slowly past the prison windows, suddenly halt and talk to the dog, who would wag its tail knowingly. He was thought by the prisoners to be mad, but by degrees it dawned upon them that the man was trying to attract their attention. This was conclusively proved to be the case at last. He would, for instance, say to the dog, 'Lady relieved, ey! Old dog?' and so on. The dog of course, always wagged its tail as if in a scent. By this means much information was conveyed to the eager prisoners-of-war inside the, again, by means of signalling from a friendly dwelling opposite, in which some young ladies lent their aid. As I have not the permission of those, who aided our officers so much, to give their names, I shall refrain from doing so in these pages. Suffice it to say they were rewarded for their self-sacrificing work.

Chapter 15

About two months after our arrival in the Pretoria prison, Captains Kirkwood and Bates were removed to the officers' prison. I was left alone.

'Why is this?' I asked the jailer.

'Because,' he replied, 'you were formerly a burger of this State.'

True I had, in the days when I lived in the Transvaal, been a burger until the annexation by the British. Then, during the armistice of 1881, I left the country, and although a burger, I never was other than loyal to the flag of England.

After remaining in the rooms alone for a few days, I asked the jailer to give me a companion. He asked me whom I would like. I said Cray Nourse. He sent for Mr Nourse and asked him if he would like to join me; he assented and became my companion the same day. Nourse had been taken prisoner near Colenso, had served on one of the Intelligence Staffs of our troops, and was in a room on the opposite side of the yard to us.

One day, while we were sitting at table together, I said:

'Nourse, I am going to try what I can do to get out of this to the officers' quarters, by writing to the Attorney-General that, as I am now so comfortable here, I hope they will not remove me, but allow us to remain here together.'

'And what good will that do you?' he asked.

'It can do me no harm,' I replied, 'but as these people seem to have a happy way of doing the opposite of what is asked of them sometimes, they may decide not to grant my request.'

I wrote the letter and the next day the jailer sent for me and gave it to me back, with the reply from the Attorney-General on the corner, containing briefly the words: 'The request cannot be complied with.' I had got what I wanted, had beaten the wily limb of the law at his own game. I was satisfied.

I have forgotten to mention that two prisoners-of-war in the same cell adjoining our rooms, later occupied by the men who got the copies of the State wires I have mentioned, made up their minds to try and effect their escape by cutting a hole in the iron of their roof. We assisted them with a can opener and night after night could hear the grating sound of their cutting. After many nights of arduous work they at last got on to the roof, only to be seen by the guard at the back gate who gave the alarm. They were caught, locked up in the murderers' cell, next day tried and condemned to six months' hard labour. Daily afterwards did we see them in ordinary convict's garb paraded and marched about with criminals to work. Hard justice, we thought, for trying to do their duty.

A day or two after receiving the communication from the Attorney re – my request, the acting jailer Van der Walt, came to our rooms and said that a policeman was waiting to take me over to the officers' prison. 'But,' he said, 'if you will pay for a cab I will drive you over', to which I willingly agreed. We drove over about 11 a.m. and the gate of the compound of the triple-barbed wire fence a crowd of officers were standing, among whom I recognised Kirkwood and Hilliard. An eager crowd at once surrounded me for news, but only to be disappointed when they heard I was only a jailbird, a prisoner like themselves. Here I cannot do better than give an extract from my diary, which may prove of some interest to readers of this scanty history of my personal experiences of the war, to which could be added many more details. Much I could write, and too much perhaps that would not reflect credit on some of our imperial officers or of the management, or want of it, of some of the campaigns I served in. May England's experience of the last few years be the means of adding lustre to her fame, by weeding out incapacity and supplanting it with ability and experience. She has an unlimited supply of it obtainable by the burial of false pride, and by the aid of ordinary common sense, making use of experienced practical men as officers, and doing away with favouritism, that is so much the curse of the civil as well as the military department.

I give the following extract from the altered biography of William Amslie, one of the earlier settlers of the Cape colony, showing that in the past things were mismanaged in the same way as of late years. England's rulers in this country sacrificed those who fought hardest and suffered most to benefit the stranger, men wanting an experience required of the subjects they have to deal with. He says, referring to the granting of land after the kaffir war of 1851–2:

'We, who had acted as buffers to the hordes in Waterkloof, thought we were sure of getting in first, but we were woefully disappointed. Men who had never smelt gunpowder were appointed to considerable claims. Men who were strangers to the position and all that had taken place, etc.'

And this was after much valuable service rendered, much loss, sacrifice and wounds endured by brave borderers. And this was but one of the many acts of injustice suffered by our forefathers at the hands of the autocratic and incapable rulers of the earlier days of the Cape Colony.

Chapter 16

The following extracts from my diary while in prison, dating previous to my arrival in officers' quarters:

1900, April 23rd, Monday – Kirkwood and Bates, besides about twenty-six others, were removed today; the former to the officers' quarters. Three men, by names of Turner, York, and E. Ferreira, were put outside the prison gate and simply told to go; the other men were sent to Waterfall. Informed today that a number of Irish-Americans, who came out ostensibly for ambulance work, were relieved by the Red Cross and armed in front of the President's house, after having been addressed by him. Received parcel of books and a set of chessmen with board from Transvaal Masonic Lodge; a welcome boon.

24th, Tuesday – My first whole day alone, but I did not mind the solitude of my prison room; it seemed to suit me. Got information re explosion of Begbie of Begbie Iron Foundry at Johannesburg; loss of life reported, 133 killed, 58 in hospital wounded.

25th, Wednesday – Went to see jailer; asked for permission to have a companion at times for a game of chess. 'Would you like to have Nourse to live with you?' he asked. 'I shall be very glad indeed if you will allow it,' I replied. Calling to Sgt. van Tonder (one of his assistants), he said: 'Tell Nourse to come here.' Mr Nourse shortly arrived and agreed to the proposal.

26th, Thursday – My sister, Mrs W. A. Tennant, with her three boys came to see me today.

27th, Friday – Peach, one of my old Border Horse troopers, arrived in jail today, was taken near Berkeley-West in the Cape colony. Was glad to meet him.

28th, Saturday – Reported all English to be sent over the border. Too good to be true.

29th – This is Sunday, and I have now been in prison one hundred and four days. What those days have been can only be realised by those who like myself, have had to pass away the weary, monotonous time, each day like the other, varied a little by the stolen news from the outside world, rumours of success and failures of our arms (too often the latter). Rev. Batts, Baptist minister of Pretoria, preached again today. This gentleman is much respected by us all. Owing to his exertions, the prisoners-of-war have been for the last month getting meals from an outside source, and are looking much better in consequence. Rumour today that Boers have been driven from Wepener and other positions; that foreign corps have been cut up. Boers also driven from Fourteen Streams, on the Vaal River.

30th, Monday – Piet Grobler (one of the warders) informs me that he has to get one of the native youths from Kuruman promised him by the jailer. These boys, about thirteen in number, brought up by us from Kuruman, and who were some of our water carriers to the outpost that night at Kuruman during the siege, have nearly all been given out to work as servants in the town. My niece, Mrs Cooper, came to see me, brought some magazines and a cake. Rumoured the British had occupied Winburg. Dr Newman, about thirty natives, and one white man arrived in prison today. Both Nourse and myself were struck with the fact that things were very quiet at the railway station this evening. Here all British subjects are to leave Transvaal towns within thirty-six hours, excepting those as get special permission to remain.

May 1st, Tuesday – Hear Boer forces retire from Wepener, and that severe engagements had taken place east of Bloemfontein. P. Grobler (warder) informed me this morning that no more milk will be supplied in future. Presume jailer's daughter does not care to supply one bottle per diem, which is all we now require. This woman has done well out of the prisoners-of-war by selling milk at sixpence per bottle. Received a letter from Alec (my late eldest son), dated 30/2/00, giving account of Paul Cliff's death (my second son, who fell at Carters Ridge, siege of Kimberley).

2nd, Wednesday – Rumours earlier this morning that British have taken Winburg. Boers have taken 400 prisoners, and that De Wet has been surrounded for several days. The day commences well. – Letter from home (Vryburg). State fever very bad in Vryburg and district. Numbers, both black and white, stated to be dying; that provisions are becoming very

153

scarce. Am feeling anxious about my family at Vryburg. More men, all warders, left for the front last night, together with the jailer's two sons, Snyman and Abraham. Rumoured that Boers are tired of war, and that we may have peace within a month – had a shower bath today at Reformers-room, an improvement on the bucket bath, and a luxury indeed.

3rd, Thursday – The day commenced with the usual jail rumours, but, on the principle that 'There cannot be smoke without fire.' Heard of Lord Robert's notice to Republican Government re treatment of prisoners-of-war. Volkstem leader denies that any prisoners-of-war are kept in jail there. As a direct contradiction, we are at present in jail; Nourse, Natal Scouts; Ferreira, Cape Police; Hildane, Cape Police; Hanson, Cape Police; and myself.

4th, Friday – Morning rumours: that President Steyn is moving; that Boers are making preparations to fall back here. Considerable commotion during last night at railway station, wagons and carts going to and fro, evidently the removal of valuables. The jailer, most friendly, had a long chat with him during the afternoon today; quite a new departure, as he has been most distant and surly lately. He said, 'I am going to the Front today, and if I am made a prisoner you must put in a word for me.'

I said: 'Yes, I will give you a card.' He came again in the evening and had a long chat with us. I gave him a few lines recommending him to the mercy of our troops, in case he became a prisoner; for, on the whole, we had been well-treated by him. Sgt. van Tonder also came in and sat down to chat with us for the first time. What does this mean? We guess, but do not know. Perhaps some of the rumours are true. Perhaps De Wet has been captured and Liebenburg cut up. Had a message on the quiet from an old friend, Dr Flynn, of early Rustenburg days, but he is not allowed to see me.

5th, Saturday – Usual rumours. Troops at Brandfort, general advance started.

6th, Sunday – Authentic rumours this morning as follows: Brandfort in hands of English, Boers retreating in all directions. Our troops crossed Fourteen Streams. Troops, via Berea, near Mafeking, Irish Brigade at Brandfort all killed or taken prisoners.

Sunday afternoon – All very quiet, the air balmy and refreshing; everything in prison seems peaceful and serene, and one can hardly realise that not far from us strife, bloody strife, is raging.

7th, Monday – Jailer informs me that he has got me permission to visit

154

my sister, who is ill. Good news! I go for two hours tomorrow. An old bushman died in prison today, one of the Kuruman prisoners, believed to be the man who shot a Cape Police sergeant near Langberg about the outbreak of the war.

8th, Tuesday – This is being a red-letter day for me, for I have been granted two hours parole, to visit my sister. Never were two hours more happily spent, never more valued. I shall ever feel grateful to President Kruger, for it is to him I owe this favour. Poor old Paul, there are many worse than you, and with all your faults it is perhaps just doubtful that imperial rule will be better than yours. Various and contradictory rumours as usual regarding the war.

9th, Wednesday – Rumoured that the Boers are retiring on Vereeniging. As they retire so our hopes are raised for release. May it be on the 24th! This evening the jailer leaves for the Front with his son Jan du Plessis, and also Warders Harn, Hennings, and Hatting. Du Plessis, the jailer, again came to bid us goodbye; he has so often being going that we doubt him; his son came, as also a younger brother, about eleven or twelve years, whom I ask if he too were going to fight. He said: 'No, but I wish I was.'

10th, Thursday – This morning private note from outside states: 'All going well. Fourteen Streams in our hands. Boers have taken up position about six miles from Christiana. Boers are now finding pressing duties at their homes calling them back. No stand will be made at Pretoria by Boer armies. Roberts wired to Cape Town on the 3rd to provide accommodation for about 4,000 prisoners. Suppose that General de Wet and his commando are the prisoners referred to. Preparations are being made to move seat of government from Pretoria to some place north-east, probably Lydenburg.'

Since getting the foregoing, a number of prisoners have been removed from the jail here to Barberton.

One of the sergeants of the jail (Van der Walt) has refused to go to the Front with the jailer. He like many others, knows the game is up, and will be satisfied to live under the British flag.

I often spoke to the sergeant and pointed out the folly of the struggle, and that they (the people) were being misled by the rulers, guided by a fanatical president, whose constant Biblical quotations greatly influenced the simple Boer. I feel sorry for the people, brave but misled men. Patriotism, or fanaticism, has reached the zenith, for women are now offering their services to do battle for the States, vide Volkstem of the 8th instant.

11th, Friday – This morning I was told that I was to be moved to the officers' quarters. I had written asking to be allowed to remain here, and this is the result. I packed my few articles, and, in company with Sgt. van Tonder, left my prison abode of nearly four months. Van Tonder was most kind. He got a cab and saved me a walk to my new quarters. After a few minutes' drive we arrived at the 'Bird Cage' (name given to officers' prison quarters). I was met by a crowd at the gate to hear the news. Among others, I met Kirkwood and Bates (my former fellow prisoners) and Hilliard of Kuruman, the only ones I knew at the time. Later on I met others, among whom was Pat Hockley, one of our best colonial boys, who had been captured at Magersfontein; was one of our corps of scouts. Col. Hunt was senior officer of about 140 all told in this prison abode. The prison building stands in the centre of an enclosure of about 200 yards square, fenced by three lines of barbed wire interlaced, and is of iron and wood and about 315 feet long, in which are the sleeping apartments, one long dormitory, and a large mess room; good bathrooms outside and other accommodation; all lighted outside and in by electric light. The guards here are all Hollanders, are polite and obliging. I met also the Rev. A. Hoffman, whom I knew at Mafeking. He was taken at Lobatsi, while on his way to Lake N'Gami with his family. His all was confiscated and himself imprisoned. Met the United Stated Consul, Mr Hayes, today; he was most kind to me, and very popular with all.

12th, Saturday – I found my new quarters much colder than the old but slept well.

Extract from Volkstem of 12th May shows to what length the leaders will go to mislead the ignorant Boer. Consequences: 'From Landdrost Schweizer Reneke to State President, 11/5/1900. It has been reported to me today by burgers in Bechuanaland that the behaviour of the British troops is terrible, and that the destruction of property is wholesale. Sick persons are being driven out into the veld, and their homes and furniture burnt; cattle, everything is destroyed, nothing is left. To such lengths has these barbarities been carried that a newly buried body has been exhumed and thrown upon the veld.'

13th, Sunday – Reported that that Mafeking had been taken by the Boers. We do not believe this. Volkstem of 12th states Mafeking was being again attacked and that the native town was burnt.

14th, Monday – This morning we hear that heavy fighting had taken place at Mafeking, that Boers had lost 140 killed; later that all were captured but three.

Here I may mention that, besides the daily papers (local) which in these officers' quarters are allowed us, we get a deal of information from the baker's boy, who brings in everything with the bread cart. Two of us, as a rule, meet the cart at the kitchen door, and one – usually myself speaking Dutch – keeps the guard engaged in conversation while the others pumps the baker's boy, who, being an English colonial lad, gives us all he can and gleans all he can for us.

Our meals would be most amusing to a spectator for everyone is free to make as much noise in talking as he likes. All – like a group of ladies at a tea party – talk at once. Not being adept at doing three things at once – viz. eating, talking, and listening – I am rather out of the game; but all seem happy, so what does it matter?

15th, Tuesday – I am getting to like the life here more and more. So much freedom, so many to talk to and interchange ideas with, so many accounts of the different battles fought, so much criticism, so much to criticise, time passes pleasantly and quickly by; so different to the cruel monotony of jail life. Nothing particular today.

16th, Wednesday – Rumoured that we have had a big reverse; I was told this by the Assistant-Commandant of our prison guard but do not believe it, as the man is very bitter against the English, and the only one of our guards we do not care for.

17th and 18th, Thursday and Friday – Nothing of any importance re the war, but received some home letters, which were a boon.

19th, Saturday – Articles in the Volkstem referring to Lord Roberts, evidently untrue, mentioning atrocities committed by his order, etc., etc., in the Orange Free State.

20th, Sunday – Rumoured that the public of Pretoria expect peace in five days' time. We hope so. We knew now that relief was not far off. Lt. Everton, PAG, gave me the story of his capture today. He says:

'I was out buying porridge, etc. from Kroonstad, with six men, including my servant. We had gone to several farmhouses, when on nearing one about ten miles out, on which a white flag was hoisted, we rode boldly up to it. Suddenly a number of guns were pointed at us from round the gable end of the house, and a voice called out: 'Hands up!' followed by a volley. Three of my men fell, one killed and two wounded. One man escaped. Myself with the other two were captured. The

Volkstem does not publish such acts as these. D. Theron was the man in charge of the enemy's party.'

21st, Monday – Heard today again that we are to be removed. I doubt it.

22nd, Tuesday – Volkstem of yesterday is changing its tone as the government mouthpiece; now states facts re British treatment; prints a statement from Lichtenburg, dated May 19th, which states that 'The account of British brutality in Stellaland have been much exaggerated, and that families in want have been fed.' This, to my mind, is another little bit of our usual Boer leader sliminess. They find it best, at the present juncture, to contradict themselves, to colour the minds of their followers by publishing ostensibly the contradiction of a lie. It meets their ends to tell the truth now. 'Do not fear the English; the English are not monsters, your families are cared for.' We hear Buller is advancing, that he is in possession of Laing's Nek, and that our forces from the west are near Rustenburg. We murmur as we hear of delay of Roberts at Kroonstad, and, from our point of view, it seems suicidal not to push on after a flying foe, to whom delay gives the opportunity of reorganising. But we must not judge, for we do not know the circumstances of such delay. Pleased are we all to see by the paper this evening that the train is now running to Mafeking and Bulawayo. Our people deserve credit for pushing on at last on the western border; there seem to have been some thoroughness in the carrying out of matters on the western side. Same paper gives account of defeat of a small body of our men on the eastern side, and the capture of thirteen of our men and forty killed. The usual 'one killed and two wounded' on the Boers' side.

23rd, Wednesday – Nothing particular today. Wild talk about distant gun firing south-east, which I think our keen-eared boys, had they carefully investigated, would have found to be from the knocking on our iron building by a mischievous somebody. I believe it was one or other of our soldier servants, who had also at different times been the cause of the captive monkey's release from its pole, and escapades on the iron roof in the morning, dragging its chain across the iron, much to the annoyance of the lazy members of our prison house. 'Tommy' found it an excellent way to make an early clearance, so as to enable them to commence the daily making up of our dormitory.

24th, Thursday – No signs of the relieving column yet, and this is our Queen's birthday, the day we looked forward to. But the day is only commencing.

The dinner bell sounded for an unusually early gathering, when it was decided to send a congratulatory message to Her Majesty from all the prisoners in this cage. Some opposition had been made regarding the civilians in our midst, who should not be included, but this was overruled. I felt rather sorry for the 'little' men who ventured to give vent to their 'little' ideas. I had begun to think that the education of the British in England had raised them above the once proverbial, and to us colonials, disgusting littleness of those who claim to belong to the greatest nation on earth.

25th, Friday – Usual routine of rumours: Potchefstroom in our hands, etc., etc. Another prisoner came in this evening, an officer of Lumsdens Horse, from Hospital. He was taken at Brandfort wounded. Drawing today for our prison newspaper, called The Gram, inaugurated by Lord Rosslyn and others, a most cleverly got-up. I was among the unsuccessful drawers. Hilliard, Bates, and Kirkwood were among the lucky men.

26th, Saturday – Two more officers arrived today, taken at Lindley, OFS. They state the Lord Roberts has 120,000 men with him, and is sweeping all before him.

27th, Sunday – A Wesleyan minister preached to us today. I asked how it was that no Episcopalian minister performed, and was told that the local parson, who used to officiate at the Model School Prison, prior to the removal to the 'Bird Cage', refused to conduct services after the escape from prison of Winston Churchill and others. Wasn't he a caution? I reckoned he would take Cape Owls' cake, that parson. Couldn't have been a big man, eh? 'Chucked a chest', they say, 'once but got the hump' later. Guns distinctly heard this afternoon in the direction of Krugersdorp. All looking forward to speedy release. All hands excited.

28th, Monday – Another officer today, Webber by name, of the RE, taken at Heilbron. Rumoured today that our troops have crossed the Vaal. Boers are holding a place called 'Eagles Nest', seven miles south of Johannesburg. That we are to be moved to Pietersburg. Cannonading heard in direction of Johannesburg and Krugersdorp.

29th, Tuesday – Heard this morning that Mafeking column is two miles from Johannesburg. Another that the column is in possession. Guns distinctly heard again in direction of Johannesburg. No further news re our removal as yet. Our guards have been strengthened. Twelve o'clock, rumoured that our forces are at Krugersdorp. 1 p.m., that we are in possession of Johannesburg. Heavy guns firing all the afternoon in direction Krugersdorp. All very jovial tonight. Hear tonight that men at Waterfall refused to be moved to Middelburg. Col. Hunt was approached during the evening and told that the men's refusal might result in bloodshed. His reply was:

'If such does occur your government will have themselves to blame for what the other soldiers may do in avenging their comrades. The officers here will not do anything to aid in the removal of the troops, and, if I am allowed to suggest I will say that if you will allow some of the officers going to speak to the men, and that no removal of prisoners is attempted, the officers would guarantee their conduct.'

While at dinner Col. Hunt was called out and shortly returned with Mr Leigh Wood, manager of the Standard Bank, Pretoria, who took his place with us. Shortly after the United States Consul, Mr Hayes, also joined us. This unusual event was most cheering; all said that something important had happened. The commandant of our prison came in and told us it was believed that our troops would be here tomorrow, and hoped that, as we had got on so well together hitherto we as soldiers would remember that he still had his duty to perform. 'He's a jolly good fellow' followed the commandant's remarks. Col. Hunt said there were two gentlemen present who had much for us quietly, namely, Mr Leigh Wood and Mr Hayes, the United States Consul. The proverbial song was repeated, followed by 'God Save the Queen', sung as I have seldom before or since heard it sung; it was truly meant. We hear that Generals French and Hamilton have forced through with a large cavalry force and were this afternoon twenty-four miles from here, and in possession of the railway line to Johannesburg. That we are in possession of the Krugersdorp line also.

Several officers (at the request of the President, with a promise that no prisoners should be moved), including Kirkwood, Major Murray, Burrowes, Spencer, Gray, Lord Rossling, and others went to Waterfall to aid in quietening the troops and prisoners there. All excitement this evening, and little sleep there will be tonight.

30th, Wednesday – All dressed in their best this morning. All who could raise any uniform at all were dressed in it to meet the long expected relief. Heavy cannon firing commenced in the early morning, and our gaze was towards the south from whence the advancing forces were expected to enter the capital. The morning and noon passed, but still no signs of the expected columns. About 3 p.m. another prisoner, an Australian officer, was brought in. He had been captured riding in to Johannesburg on Monday last. States he witnessed a fight in rear of the train which brought him in, and that the Boers were flying in all directions. Hundreds tried to mount the train, but could not; many were pulled off by their comrades by the legs. That they intend making a last stand about six miles south of this. That the Burger Master of Pretoria told him he was prepared to hand over the town at once. That Lord Roberts' program was to enter Johannesburg on Tuesday, and Pretoria on Thursday, so that we have another night at least in our prison quarters. Another long night! How long these last nights and days seem to us! Volkstem says that Bloemfontein is retaken, that De Wet is busy reorganising in the Free State; the usual routine of lying inventions. And as a fact we hear that the President has fled and has taken £2,500,000 with him in bullion.

31st, Thursday – Everyone rose this morning early in anxious expectation, but no signs of the relief column yet. Much excitement apparent in town. Natives and Boers flying. Two miserable objects (Boers) turned up on foot out of some bush near our prison, with their guns and blankets. They were taken to the commandant of our guard, fed, and, accompanied by one of the guards, went into the town to hand in their rifles, it was said. Rumoured that train communication with Johannesburg was resumed. Several trains going north on the Pietersburg line. About 150 Boers passed our compound; one said in English, 'Your friends are close by.' Later, about 400 mounted Boers came from the west, halted for a time near the town, then went off through Dasport to the north. The first lot were recalled and sent back to Irene Station, where the leaders intend making a stand. Two officers and men brought in today, captured at Elandsfontein. Looting of government stores today in the town, populants [*sic*] enraged at the action of Kruger and his satellites in taking away all the bullion and leaving useless notes to pay their hirelings and officials with. Great excitement, we hear, prevails in consequence. The Boers are burning the veld all around the town; object, to make the place as useless for stock as possible. Hear that four Polish Jews were shot today by the police while looting stores. Several shots were heard by us in town.

June 1st, Friday – Lord Rossling, who had been let out of prison, returned today, and states that it is rumoured that several hundred of Gen. French's men were captured and let go on parole, and that another Jew had been shot while looting; he tried to defend himself with a revolver. We hear that the Boers are gathering in strong force at Irene

Station. A number of mounted Boers passed through today, about 300 or 400, with several mule-wagons loaded with footmen, all trekking north. We all received a bonus today of £25 each from some good Samaritan or Samaritans. God bless them, for many of us want the means of buying necessities.

2nd, Saturday – Rumoured that our forces are at Modderfontein, fifteen miles from here, south. That Baden-Powell is at the Crocodile, fifteen miles north-west. That our forces have had a knock-out at Senekal in the Orange Free State.

A Boer commando of several hundred is reported to be off-saddled about three miles west of town. Numbers are passing through to Six Miles Spruit, south of the town. Botha is said to have about 1,500 men there. The final battles may be fought there. I am, and we are all, eager to get out and join in the finale.

3rd, Sunday – Boers on south of town have moved a wagon, and a few horsemen only seen moving.

4th, Monday – This morning all was quiet until about midday, when the booming of cannon was distinctly heard in the south, and continues as I am writing now, about 3 p.m. Shells and shrapnel can be plainly seen bursting on the ridge and forts south, south-west and south-east of the town. Some have burst on the outskirts of the town, with what result we cannot tell. Heavy firing in the distance can be heard extending over miles south of the town. A balloon was twice visible to our eager gaze beyond the ridge south and, as I write, it is again descending. The intense excitement existing can more easily be imagined than I can describe it. Boers with carts, wagons, and on horseback, are leaving the town, going north.

We have from our quarters a fine view of the shells which continue bursting on the ridge and forts above the town, which are not defended by the Boers. Some in the know say our forces are feeling the country, and that it is only a reconnaissance in force. It seems to me a waste of ammunition and certainly a dangerous feeler for the town inhabitants, as many of the shells appear to be bursting within the outskirts.

5th, Tuesday – About one o'clock this morning the commandant of our guard came in and, after waking us, said that Gen. Botha had sent him orders to move us; that we should walk about four miles to a railway station and then go by train east, whereto he did not know. Col. Hunt, as senior officer, refused to go; we all backed him. I went out with the intention of escaping if possible, but found it not possible. Our guards had been doubled and a party of mounted men were at the gate. I returned to the house, when I was met by Capt. McInerney, of an Australian contingent, who said:

'What do you think? Will the Boers fire on us if we make prisoner of the commandant?'

I said:

'No, I do not think so.'

We entered together and went to where the commandant was standing, surrounded by some of my fellow prisoners. Placing his hand on that officer's shoulder he said:

'You are my prisoner, sir!'

'What?' said that individual in surprise. 'Do you mean it?'

'Yes,' replied McInerney, 'I do. Your General is trying to play us false; President Kruger gave us his word we should not be moved if we assisted to keep the Waterfall prisoners quiet. We have fulfilled our part of the contract and now you want to move us.'

'Well, gentlemen,' said the Commandant, I cannot help it; it is Gen. Botha's order. However, release me, and I will tell the Boer guard that you refuse to go, and will explain to them what I know were the conditions made by the President, and give you my word that I will return to you.'

We were all satisfied that the man was in earnest and let him go. I followed him to the gate and heard him fairly fulfil his promise to us. The Boer party then mounted their horses and galloped off, glad apparently of the opportunity to get away. One shouted, as he rode off:

'Now I'm going home and shall fight no more.'

Shortly after the commandant left us his assistant and his secretary came in and remained till he himself returned. The guards' things had all been loaded on a wagon and ready to start when the commandant went out, but were at once offloaded. Thus a little determination saved us from being removed and the possibility of a further long time of imprisonment. I believe that the action of Capt. McInerney saved us. About 8 a.m. troops were seen in the west formed up in long columns. Our hearts beat high, and many a grateful tear crawled down some cheeks, I know. No firing, all was quiet. What does it mean? Suddenly a shout rose from the rear of our prison building: 'Hoorah – Here they come! We are all free!'

Two horsemen rode up to our gate, the Duke of Marlborough and

Winston Churchill. The gate was rushed, opened, and we went out. The position was reversed, for our prisoners' servants became the guards of our late guards, but now our prisoners. We walked over to the town, free once more after many months in prison. Everywhere was khaki; many were the greetings of friends.

Already the advance guard of the column were arriving, and at 2 p.m. began the grand entry from the south. Lord Roberts with his staff arrived amidst the cheering of thousands (not all); many looked scowlingly on without raising a hat or waving a kerchief; but who could blame them? They were not all visitors.

From the east, south, and west, division after division marched past the General and his staff, who had taken up their stand near the Dutch church on the Square. Alternatively cavalry and infantry, travel-stained and worn (many of them) marched past, headed by small bands – truly a never-to-be forgotten sight. A small silk Union Jack, made by Lady Roberts to hoist at Pretoria, was run up, then, after all the troops had passed, a large 'Jack' and was hoisted to wave over the Transvaal, this time as long 'as the sun shall shine'. The British Empire has placed the flag now, and not all the hypocrisy of Kruger or his associates can ever cause its removal again. Kruger – Where is he? Gone, with all the gold, and left worthless paper to pay his servants and others with. Those who blessed him before now showered curses on his name. And are they to be blamed? God grant that we may never have cause to regret the change of flags.

I slept at my sister's house. About one o'clock something shook my bed. I woke, and lo! The door I had securely locked stood wide open! I felt for my candle and matches; and they were gone. I felt for my clothes; gone too, money and all. I woke my brother-in-law; we searched and found my shirt and hat lying at the corner of the house, and, later on, my trousers near the well behind the house. My purse was gone, but a small bag in one of the pockets, containing gold, was still there. The thief had got a fright; for immediately on waking, and seeing the door open, I jumped up and shouted out: 'Stand, you devil, or I will put a bullet into you!' This was bluff; an empty revolver hung on the bedstead, which I grasped, holster and all; but it had the desired effect evidently.

6th, Wednesday – We were today inspected by Lord Roberts, having formed up in a semi-circle before his quarters at Sunnyside. He came round to each in turn, from the right, and shook hands, enquiring the circumstances of our capture. His face struck me as one indicating a kindly spirit, but one of great willpower. A little man in stature, but not in mind. Boers coming in all day to lay down their arms. Soldiers about, disarming the townspeople quietly; no noise or violence displayed.

7th, Thursday – Our late jailer's wife, Mrs Du Plessis, sent for me. I went to see her. She complained that some soldiers had taken her cows' milk (She kept a few cows and had been in the habit of selling milk), but said an officer had interfered and she was satisfied. Said she wanted to go out to the scene of the last fight near the town, for her husband, sons, and some friends had fought there and some were missing. I gave the acting jailer, Jarvis by name, a note to the Provost Marshal, to get her a pass if possible. I asked her why her husband and sons did not stay in the town. She replied that her husband was afraid that the English would make soldiers of the sons, and that was the reason they left. He himself left because he intended fighting to the last. She said she was 'surprised' that the soldiers caused so little trouble to the people. They acted just like '*Christi menschen*' (Christian people). 'We were told they were worse than kaffirs. There is no noise, no burning or robbing of the houses; it is not as we were told as we were told it would be.' And by such lies have the ignorant been misled and goaded on to a continuance of the hopeless struggle. Her husband, Jacobus du Plessis, knew better; he had been, as I have before stated, a British subject. I knew him first in Burgersdorp, in 1861; he trekked into the Transvaal, and in 1879 served under me at Secocoeni's.

Prisoners at Waterfall were fired on yesterday by Boer artillery, and although the shells fell in the camp and one or more struck the hospital, fortunately no one was hurt. 900 were persuaded to go by train east, under the promise that they were to be released on the border.

8th, Friday – Reported that Botha's commando is surrounded at Donker Hoek, farm of Hans Botha of 1881 renown.

9th, Saturday – Reported that Botha was to meet Lord Roberts today. Paul Kruger said to have sent word to fight to the last.

Nurse Alma, of SAR German Ambulance, says of the last attack on Mafeking, that the German corps led the way through the native town to the wire fence; that, owing to the many tins in the way, their advance was discovered; that the Boers ran when the first cannon shot was fired; also, that on the day of the relief of Mafeking the Boers, including Commandant Snyman, all ran and left the nurses with the wounded in the ambulance to the mercy of the kaffirs; that Col. Baden-Powell sent them protection. This account corroborates more I have heard of the same nature, and that the foreigners are cursing the Boers now for cowardice.

10th, Sunday – Fighting reported at Zwaartkopjes. Lord Kitchener gone to Heidelberg.

11th, Monday – Saw Col. Hume, DAAG. I asked what I had to do. After some conversation he gave me a note to Capt. Hughes, Intelligence Officer at the Government offices, by whom I was engaged.

12th, Tuesday – Commenced work today in Naturalisation Office of the late Transvaal Government translating, after having made a list of some of the numerous documents I found there.

Rumoured that British have had severe losses today at Donkerpoort, several officers killed, among whom is Lord Cavendish. That Free State Boers have blown up Renoster River Bridge, also that the railway line beyond Kroonstad is destroyed, and that a convoy of fifty wagons of ours has been captured. That the mail train between this and Bloemfontein has been captured and the mail burnt.

13th, Wednesday – Several ambulance wagons in with wounded yesterday and today.

14th, Thursday – The morning is bright and clear and looks peaceful here, while a few miles away men are striving to destroy one another. Why will Botha not give in? It seems criminal the manner in which the ignorant Boer is misled. What is he fighting for now? For they are practically conquered. 'Fighting for freedom,' they say, poor ignorant mortals! Will they not be really free under the flag of old England, if England is but just to herself and to her people this time, and retains to the Empire what it has cost so much blood and so many millions to attain?

Error on error has marked the track of British rule in South Africa in the past. We can only hope that the errors of the past, so dearly paid for, be severe and lasting lessons to benefit England's future generations in South Africa and the Empire. Why, why are the people of the country ignored? Why not a proper standing Court or Board of Investigation, comprised jointly of men of practical experience, sons of the soil, combined with imperial men, appointed? Even now one sees the beginning of errors, and I fear the future.

15th, Friday – Official news today that Gen. Buller had crossed Laings Nek; that Gen. Baden-Powel and Gen. Hunter are at Potchefstroom; that Methuen has smashed up De Wet's commando; that Botha's rearguard had been severely punished at Donkerpoort; that our losses since Monday the 4th are about a hundred all told.

16th, Saturday – Usual routine of news today. Among the list is that Baden-Powel had occupied Rustenburg; that a thousand rifles had been laid down there; that a notice will shortly be issued by Lord Roberts, 'that as the cutting of telegraph wires is of such frequent occurrence all houses in the vicinity of said cuttings will in future be burnt.' Andreas Cronje's commando laid down their arms.

17th, Sunday – Went visiting today after church. Heard that Herbert Brown, who assisted me at Kuruman, was in hospital.

18th, Monday – Went to artillery barracks, passed Court of Enquiry on Prisoners-of-War. Saw Herbert Brown at artillery barracks hospital. Baden-Powel and staff arrived today from Rustenburg, where his forces are stationed.

19th, Tuesday – Met Baden-Powel and McKenzie this morning. The latter I had known previous to the war, a smart and intelligent fellow. Baden-Powel asked me whether I would like to be exchanged to his command, which I gladly agreed to and am looking forward to the transfer and the chances of leave to return home to see my family.

20th, Wednesday – Finished 1,178 documents today, inspected some and translated others, chiefly applications for full franchise and letters of naturalisation. Commenced Waterfall papers. Had lunch with Coute Green; met him first in 1864 at Tchabn'Chu, prior to the war of 1865, in which he took part as one of the Bloemfontein Rangers, of which I was also a member.

21st, Thursday – Rumours of a speedy close of the war. I don't think so.

22nd, Friday – At usual work today, inspecting and translating Dutch documents.

23rd, Saturday – Went to artillery barracks again at 11 a.m., to see Lt. Col. Briggs in regard to Court of Enquiry into treatment of Prisoners-of-War. Met Davey of the Glosters.

24th, Sunday – Went to Johannesburg to meet Maj. Reade of the Intelligence, had great difficulty in finding quarters; succeeded at last, by the aid of an old Border Horse man, to find a place where I could get a bed and meals.

25th, Monday – Went to the Military Governor's office to ascertain where Maj. Reade could be found. After sending in my name to the DAAG, one Capt. —, I was ushered in and was met with a curt 'Well, what do you want?' in that Little Englander tone that we Afrikaners don't like.

I looked at the individual and replied calmly that I had come to find out the whereabouts of Maj. Reade of the Intelligence, and that I had been told that the only one who could give me the information was the Military Governor. I gave him my pass, which he took away and brought back with the words: 'Maj. Reade has left for Heidelberg yesterday afternoon,' written on the face of it. I did not meet Maj. Reade, and so had my trip for nought. Met some blunt but courteous colonial friends later, which made some amends for the other man's manner; but then he wore scars, and they don't fit everybody.

26th, Tuesday – Returned to Pretoria. Browning, of the Canadians, and myself, travelled together. Reported at the office and got instructions to proceed to Rustenburg by post cart next morning.

27th, Wednesday – Started by post cart at 8.30 a.m., arrived Wolhuter's Kop about 2.30 p.m.; found Capt. Glynn, with a party of men of Plumer's Force, there collecting Boer arms. He had a prisoner by the name of Ras, a field-cornet, who had been sent to commandeer men in the district of Pretoria by his commandant. Was asked by Glynn to take Ras with me to Rustenburg, which I did. We arrived here at about 8.35 p.m. I handed Ras over to Col. Plumer; he was placed in jail. Met the General, Baden-Powel, who informed me that I should now take my orders from Lord Cecil, who was in charge of the Western District as Special Commissioner.

28th, Thursday – Met many old friends, and many memories of the past came to mind as I walked that well-known paths of years ago. Arranged to board and lodge in the house that was once mine and that I lost for loyalty in 1881. Saw the General again at 11 a.m. Maj. Godley, Staff Officer, wired to Lord Cecil re myself.

29th, Friday – Met Major Godley again, and was by him informed that Lord Cecil wished me to report to the assistant commissioner, Capt. Marsh, which I did. He offered me the billet as Magistrate's Clerk, which I declined, and was appointed as Assistant Native Commissioner of the Western District, which included Rustenburg, Zeerust and West Lichtenburg districts. Capt. March informed me that my salary would be the same as that paid by the South African Republic, 'and perhaps more, certainly not less'. Capt. Smitherman of the Rhodesian Force, under Plumer, was Acting Commissioner of Natives for the Western District. I took over the work, and thus commenced my work in old Rustenburg once more. Is it to be my home again? Am promised leave to go home to Vryburg to settle my affairs there as soon as Smitherman returns; he is away on Intelligence work. Had supper with old friends, Mr and Mrs Dawes and family.

30th, Saturday – Sent native cyclists with dispatches to Smitherman, who is at a native kraal beyond the Crocodile. Met old friends from Blaauwbank today, Messrs. John Jennings and Tom Hinds, also Mrs W. Jennings from Nooitgedacht.

July 1st, Sunday – The morning is cloudy and the air damp. A steady rain poured down during last night. What will the superstitious Boers say? Will they call this a blessing? Will they say that the sky weeps for the downfall of their oligarchic government? Or will they say that it is a forerunner of blessing on the land?

2nd, Monday – Sent two native cyclists to Bethanie with dispatches for Smitherman. Constant reports of cattle stealing by Linchwe's natives from the north of the Crocodile. It is said that Linchwe himself was with the party of natives looting the Boer farms.

Chapter 17

This far from my diary, which ends on the 2nd July. The following are the translations I made from the Volkstem while in prison at Pretoria, which show how every means were used to incite the Boers to continue the strife.

An exhortation from the Volkstem, Wednesday, 16th May, 1900:

'How long halt ye between two opinions? Fellow burgers, what is the reason that ye are so doubtful? Why do you turn your backs on the enemy? Why do you withdraw from the strife? Where is now your faith? Where are the people of heroic courage? Where is the spirit of the pioneers? Why do you allow the enemy to say in derision, 'Where is now their God?' Can it be that the children of the able Voortrekkers, who for years struggled undaunted against endless troubles, and countless numbers of the enemy, will, after months' fighting, give up the struggle? Have ye no faith more? Do you mean that you are acting as God would have you act, when you cease the struggle, which is not of your seeking, but which was forced on you? Do you give to the arch enemies of our race the inheritance bought with blood and drenched with tears of your forefathers, without first using all your efforts to retain it? Is this the gratitude you show towards your forefathers, who suffered so long to secure you one inheritance, one free state? And do you not fear the curses of your children and the children's children, when they become acquainted with the fact that they, through your faults, through your cowardice, your carelessness, your selfishness, have lost the glorious and dearly bought inheritance of your fathers and become, instead of masters and free, slaves and hirelings in our Fatherland? Is this a war of Kruger or Joubert? Is it not a general national struggle for the people's existence? Which of you did not when our old President, fearing this war (which some of you dare charge him with bringing about), tried by every means in his power to avoid; who of you, I say, did not call out with indignation, 'No! Not an inch more give, rather fight'?

Fellow Burgers, has not God showed in an undoubted manner that He is with us? Did He not in the first months enable us with a handful of ours to overcome a mighty multitude of the enemy? Has He not spared the lives of our braves in a most wonderful manner against thousands and tens of thousands of bullets which the hellish machines of the enemy cast on them? Have not friends and enemies been astonished at the small numbers of our killed and wounded, as against the hundreds and thousands of killed and wounded on the side of the enemy? And is the same God not mighty enough to preserve us still, though small in numbers? Not alone your leaders, but also the foreign officers, who up to the present have fought or sympathised with us, assured you that nothing is lost if our people will only stand firmly. What is the reason that so many are withdrawing from the strife, deserting or remaining at home, thus causing their brother burgers – fellows in the strife – who up to the present are full of faith and hope on your account, and through your neglect of duty, to be killed, wounded or taken prisoners, or in time lose heart also?

Fellow Burgers, there must come a change, and that at once, otherwise our country is lost and your freedom forever gone.

'Do not imagine in your souls' as Mordecai said to Esther, 'that you will escape'. The sentence is fixed, resolved against us. Milner let it slippen [*sic*]. Did he not say: 'Afrikanerdom must be broken'? The English government is already making plans to give your lands to the soldiers and volunteers who fought against us, whose hands are still dripping with blood of your fellow burgers – relatives probably – and who will after our fall be called upon to assist in conveying us away. Do you not know what has occurred in the south and south-western districts of the Free State and in Bechuanaland? Do you not know that, according to official reports from Gen. de Wet and Froneman, the subjected parts of the Free State are totally ruined, not withstanding the petty proclamation of Roberts? Do you not know what brutalities have been committed during the past week in Bechuanaland? How women and children in sickness have been driven from their homes, their houses burnt, dead bodies exhumed and cast on the veld? Is it not known to you that, according to official reports, the soldiers ran about the streets of Boshoff naked, and their shameful conduct with kaffir women? Is it not known to you that in Bloemfontein disgusting diseases, from which, according to English statistics of 1896/97/98, the pet of the English Army suffered, have broken out among the poor whites and kaffirs? And when all this occurs in the Free State, which was so friendly towards the English, and out of which a portion are now so willing to lay down their arms, what can we expect in the hated Transvaal, which has always been a thorn in England's side? What will happen, if God does not preserve us from it and you do not do your duty, is this:

The English troops will, out of revenge, plunder and rob you of everything.

All burgers will be disarmed; no one will be allowed a gun or a cartridge in their homes, and they who dare disobey and are discovered will be treated like the poor Du Plooys at Bloemfontein (Father and son sentenced to one year's hard labour on the breakwater), and see all their property confiscated.

Through the disarming, the Boer – the independent man of former days – becomes defenceless even against the kaffir, who, under English rule, becomes the equal of the white man, and surely more than formerly protected and indulged. Think of Bezuidenhout and the Hottentot!

Through the Discriminating Act, which naturally during the first years will strictly be carried out, hunting will be stopped and the Boer will see his lands destroyed by wild animals. Besides this, he will have to put up with the shooting and hunting over his lands by British officers or Lords, and taking away the game killed, which he (the Boer) has the first right to.

Through the unlawful equality of kaffirs and all coloured peoples with the white man, the Boer, who has been accustomed to treat and look upon them as children and minors – in the street, train, church and school, in the courts of justice, and everywhere – will have to treat them as equals; and where he may venture to uproot this, a strong hand will quickly remind him of his subjection.

Through the existence of equality and through the instreaming of so much of the English element of all sorts, mixed marriages will become the rule instead of the exception; thus a class of bastards will increase, who so readily inherit the bad, but little of the good qualities of the white man. Bad disorders and sin will spread.

In the interest of the new arrivals, who by all possible ways will be encouraged to settle here as agricultural and stock farmers, a strict fencing law will be enacted, and those who do not fulfil the requirements of the law will be heavily fined, or see before his eyes that the government has the work done, and then the account will be sent to him for payment, and in

172

case he is not in a position to pay same his property will be sold to cover the amount of cost.

The tremendous war costs that England has incurred to destroy us will have to be paid by the Boer. His already too much taxed farm will not bear the additional heavy tax, and the result will be that the farm, the heritage of his fathers, will be sold for debt and fall into the hands of strangers.

Milner has spoken of it, and others with him: the Afrikaner must be broken, and a second war like the present must forever be made impossible. The Boer must go down, must be totally destroyed. Disarming, equality with the natives, and taxed are not the only means whereby to obtain that object. By low railway tariff on articles from other English colonies, competition will be so keen that the Boer will not be able to stand against it; he will not make his expenses, not be able to pay his taxes, lose his land, and from master become servant!

The new administration will take care that the Boer, the feared antagonist, will not be able to earn anything, and thus not be able to rise again.

The Dutch Church will be superseded by the English State Church, and, owing to the poverty of the congregation, the Dutch ministers will lose their influence with the people.

The national language will be superseded by English, and whoever does not understand English will have but little to break into his milk.

The sons of the soil will be kept out of all official positions, and, as farming will not pay, they will have to endeavour to earn their food by hard labour, and to compete with the English and other uitlanders, who in trade and ability in labour far exceed them.

The capitalists have already said that they intend to reduce the number of white labourers after the war and make the kaffirs work for less. For the sons of the soil there will be little or no chance at the mines to succeed, or even get work, and so they will by poverty and want be driven to join the English army, and side-by-side with the longsuffering and low standing Tommy Atkins, fight in strange lands for England's flag. But already enough!

Fellow Burgers, think over these points, and if you do not yet feel that it is in your own interests at once to take your weapon, and stand alongside your brothers at the front, well, then you have earned the lot that I have endeavoured to sketch, which will be that of the conquered Transvaaler; then you are jointly with others responsible for the death of

173

your fathers and fellow burgers who have fallen in struggle for right and freedom. Then you are ungrateful to God, who will make you hear His words, 'I wanted to make of you a great nation, but ye would not.'

Signed: A fellow Burger.'

I have given the foregoing as literally as possible. Many such effusions grace the columns of the Volkstem during the war, written, no doubt, by men who knew that the statements contained in them were utterly false, but done to urge on the credulous and ignorant Boer. Much may have been meant by some writers in a purely patriotic spirit, but the majority of those who filled the local organ of the day with their trash were of the class who urge others on to do the hard and dangerous duties of war while they remain in safety at home, being in a position to pay for substitutes. Oh such, alas! There were too many, but the quality or numbers were not confined to the Transvaal; the Cape Colony had its share, among whose number could be counted men from whom better things might well have been expected. Some may not have had their substitutes to fight for them, but urged others on to do the dirty work while they sat in safety under the shadow of Table Mountain, or elsewhere.

I give another letter translated from the Volkstem by myself while in prison, an amusing though ridiculous concoction of untruths under the guise of religious exhortation, the best suited to reach the ignorant Boers. The extract is from the Volkstem, of 17 May, 1900 and dated Carolina, 12th May, 1900 and is as follows:

'To the Editor of the Volkstem

Sir, as matters in our country are becoming so serious, and the sun of our Afrikanerdom threatens to go down, I will also write a little bit to encourage our striving burgers and to show those staying-at-home burgers their duty.

It is a thorn in my heart to hear that the burgers have so little courage to fight. Oh! Dear burgers, have you then no trust or faith? Do you place no trust in your Lord Jesus Christ? 'Whosoever trusts in the Lord hath not built their house upon sand'. We have read that Jonathan and his armour bearer beat the enemy. Why could he do it? Because he put his trust in the Lord. Saul had much success in his reign until he failed to do the commands of the Lord; he neglected the Lord and God deserted him. What was the result of his disobedience? He fell in his strife against the enemy.

Oh! Burgers, neglect not the Lord, forget not to pray; in the fight pray; a single sigh the Lord will hear. Let us people of the Transvaal and Free State raise our voices to Zion, from whence shall come our help. Let us humble ourselves before God and leave all that is sinful. Let those who have unrighteously taken loot or stolen give back the booty or stolen goods. Some will say, 'I am ashamed to be a thief before the eye of the world,' but I say to you that if you in truth repent it is no shame.

You burgers that are remaining at home, does not your manly heart call you to the front? Truly a shame that still so many healthy men remain at home, the one for one reason, the other for another; others trek away. Why does the government not stop the trekking? They may get stock again, but never again our country. When will such men regret their acts? When it is too late. Those who remain at home have no national (or patriotic) feelings in them. Some say: 'I have not caused any war'; then I can thus stand by and see how my fellow householders strive to save our burning homes and say: 'Strive away, all of you; I did not light the house'. Deborah says in her song of praise: 'Curse Meros' etc. but I say 'Curse those who stay at home and take no part in the strife'.

Dear burgers, have you thought over the case? Is it not terrible to think that, if the enemy gain the victory, they will exhibit the head of our beloved president in a dish in the London streets? If your little children should ask you 'Pa, why did the Boers lose?' – will you say to them: 'It was because I, and more such cowards, stayed at home and took no part in the strife?' Will you not blush before your children? Is it not terrible to think that the farms you have so long occupied have fallen into the hands of others? Almost on every farm are graves of loved ones. How will you feel to have to leave those graves and trek away into the wilderness? You will then regret it, but, alas, too late. Some may say: 'It will not be as hard as all that'. To such I say: Read the history of Ireland, or ask the Irish; they will tell you what it is to be ruled by England. We women are too weak to go into the strife; we can help the men by praying for them. Dear burgeresses, pray for your husbands, encourage them to go to the front, do not needlessly call them home.

Awake burgers! See what danger our country is in. I pray you read my writing, and think earnestly of what will become of you and yours. I have much more to write, but am afraid of requiring too much space. Sir, Editor, I thank you in anticipation for placing theses lines and name myself

A young Burgeress.'

Many more like the foregoing appeared in the columns of the Volkstem, too plainly showing that the Boers were tired of the war, hence the necessity of such exhortations; but, as I said before, they emanated from those who had taken no part in the actual strife. The poor worn-out burger had, in most instances, enough of war, but was urged on to contend further in the futile struggle by his ministers. Leaders, and in many cases the women and letters such as I have quoted, had much to do with it; but later on the burning of the houses by our troops, in pursuance of Lord Roberts' notice, did more to combine the scattered and shaky Boer forces than all the prevailing and women influence could do. It was a fatal error and tended to make them fight more bitterly, though perhaps more warily than before. The burning of houses had brought about unity among the burgers again, and they fought and destroyed in sheer desperation. Again a little want of judgement brought about what Lord Roberts' saying would have undone, had it been possible.

Chapter 18

On the evening of 3rd July I had just gone to my lodging when Thornton, my clerk, came in and said Col. Hoare wanted me at the telegraph office at once, that some important news had come in from the General. (I must here mention that Gen. Baden-Powell had left east-ward with the whole of his force, excepting about sixty mounted men, a few dismounted details and a considerable number of ox-wagons of his transport; Col. Hoare was left in charge of Rustenburg.) I went over at once and found Col. Hoare outside the telegraph office in a nervous state of excitement. He handed me a note from the General and one from Col. Godley. The latter was requesting me to get horses and take Mrs Godley (who was in Rustenburg) on to Zeerust. The other note contained a repetition of that to Col. Hoare. The orders to Hoare were to evacuate at once and fall back on Zeerust, taking all transport with us, and to turn back all convoys on the road hither, and to wire Lord Cecil to entrench at once, that Rustenburg was to be attacked that night by 2,000 Boers with cannon. After sending the wire to Zeerust we hurried up to the camp near the prison, and orders were at once given to break up and go, which was done in all speed. No time was lost, for 2,000 Boers with cannon was too tall an order for us. I asked one of the conductors to get my kit at Mrs de Lange's boarding house as the wagons passed. He promised, but then the Boers were coming, and so he forgot. After seeing all off and having arranged with a Major of the New Zealand contingent, who had a cart, to take Mrs Godley on to Zeerust, I went the rounds of the village to commandeer horses and equipment. Thornton had a horse. I had neither horse, saddle, or bridle. I first got two horses and a saddle complete from Mr Schoch, an inhabitant of the town; but later, having got a really good horse, in the possession of an old friend, Duncan McKenzie, belonging to

S. le Roux, I left the other two to be brought on by another young man who was to accompany us but did not start, as I later found out, but returned the horses to Mr Schoch. I was ably assisted by some of the inhabitants, among whom was Piet Kruger, son of the late President, in getting information as to the advance of the Boers, for I remained behind for the purpose some three hours after the column had left. Up to the time we left about 10 o'clock, no Boer commando was anywhere near. We caught up to the column about 12 o'clock, south of Magoto's Nek; they were still trekking along the heavy muddy roads, for it had been raining. After some difficulty in the dark, I found Col. Hoare, and suggested outspanning, which he would not hear of. I pointed out that he would be the gainer by doing so, as it was over the cattle's time to sleep, that if he gave them an hour they would travel on again all night, but if not, when the sun rose, they would be fairly done-up. After some persuasion he agreed, and asked me to arrange about the camping ground. I knew of a bare piece of rising ground on ahead, and immediately rode on. On reaching the spot I heard a wagon on ahead travelling. I was some distance in advance of the other wagons. The conductors were not attending to their duty, or this one wagon could not be so far ahead. I rode on and caught up to the wagon near Selons River Drift; so there was no help for it, all would have to cross. I told the driver of the wagon to span out on the other side. The other wagons came up by degrees some time after, and, as the last outspanned, those that had first arrived were again inspanning. 'No time, for fear the dreaded 2,000 and guns would be on us.'

I had meanwhile gone to a store near the drift, and, after knocking for some time, managed to get someone to answer, but no door was opened. I offered payment for some coffee or tea. The reply was: 'I have nothing.' So with nothing I had to content myself, and after offsaddling I managed to find some forage for my horse. I was content, and lay down for some time, sleeping for about half an hour. Thornton I had not seen since we caught up to the wagons near the nek.

Just as the day was dawning I saddled up and found that the last of the convoy was leaving, the others were miles ahead. I rode on and found wagons scattered along the road, covering several miles. About 7 o'clock I found Thornton, or rather he found me, as he had missed me in the dark or the night before. We rode to a farmhouse nearby to try and get a cup of coffee. There we found two men and two women, with their children, and got a cup of coffee, or, rather, a beverage made from the roots of a well known tree, called '*Witte bast*' (White bark). However it was something warm, for we were cold and damp. We stayed talking to the people for some time, about the war principally. They seemed to be glad there were prospects of a speedy end to hostilities; but said: 'You people are now going back. The commandos of De la Rey, Lemmer, or others, will come round here and force us to take up arms again. We have all surrendered our arms and bound ourselves to remain neutral. We do not wish to fight anymore, we have had enough of it and are satisfied we have done our best and cannot do more. Now, what protection do you give us? Your generals' plans are wrong.'

I tried to satisfy them and said: 'We are not leaving you. Gen. Baden-Powell is still in the district with his forces, and we are shortly returning to Rustenburg.' They were not satisfied, but said: 'Yes, the English in 1879 caused us great trouble, for you know that many of us in this part would not fight, but went into laager at Coster's River, as we did not fight against them. Many of us wanted the British Government here, but what did you do? You went away and left us to the mercy of the Transvaal Government. Sir Garnet Wolseley said 'that the British flag would wave over this country as long as the sun shone.'

I could only say: 'It will not be so this time,' but too well I saw the mistake. All who lay down their arms should have been removed to some place out of reach of the Boer leaders, ostensibly as prisoners, but really only out of harm's way for their own sakes and ours.

By the time we left the wagons had all passed, and we found a rear guard, consisting of some Australians, riding in a straggling manner along the road. A sergeant was in charge, whom I asked what his orders were. He said: 'To ride behind the wagons and act as rear guard.'

I said: 'But you are absolutely useless as you are now riding, for who is to warn you of any approach of an enemy from the rear? Have you no rear scouts out?' He said: 'No, sir.' I then sent Thornton to find Col. Hoare, with a note pointing out what I thought necessary, and told him to explain besides, that as we were crossing a rugged country, full of ridges, how necessary it was to have proper precautions taken, for, if attacked at all, it would be from the rear. He returned, after being absent about an hour and a half, with a note from Hoare asking me to take charge of the rear. I then showed the sergeant what to do. The men all seemed pleased when it was explained to them that eight men should remain behind the rear guard

179

on the highest points until the convoy crossed the next ridge in front, then four were to proceed on to that ridge, and as the next was reached they were relieved by those left, and so on from ridge to ridge, thus always being able to give notice of the approach of the enemy. I, with Thornton, also remained with them, as per Col. Hoare's wish.

We camped for breakfast at Woodstock, the farm of Willie McDonald, who had a store on the place. I was most hospitably treated by him. We arrived at Elands River about 10 o'clock that night, without any misadventure, and, as neither Thornton nor myself had blankets, I told Col. Hoare that I would push on to Zeerust, and in company with Lazarus, a young man of Wiel's Transport Service, who by the way, was staying for a few days at the same boarding house in Rustenburg as I was, but whom we had forgotten. He woke, the morning after we had departed, and finding how matters stood, hurriedly followed on horseback, and caught us up during the day, I think at Woodstock. We went down to the drift, where a mill was situated, and having been informed that the owner was at his house behind the mill, we called, and saw a white woman working in the kitchen. I asked her if we might get a cup of coffee or something to eat, for which I offered payment. She said she had none. We had to be satisfied, and, cold and hungry, we rode on. Lazarus said he knew a man named Leon a few miles further on, whom he was sure would do all he could for us. We arrived at Leon's place about 11 p.m., and, after waking him, got all we wanted and civility into the bargain. Of course we paid for what we got, including a bed each, for we decided to remain till daylight.

The next morning he was up before the day broke and had coffee ready for us. We hastily drank one cup each, and continued our journey, arriving at Zeerust that evening. The next morning I reported to Lord Cecil, and at the same time got leave to go home the following week, as there were some matters requiring attention there, and also regarding the working of the Intelligence of the District.

The natives employed for Intelligence work were local men, and, knowing the influence of the Boers had over them, I suggested to the Commissioner, Lord Cecil, that I should bring up some Basutos from Vryburg when I went down; this he agreed to. The men I intended bringing up were some of the Basutos I had employed before in campaigns in Bechuanaland, and were most useful and trustworthy.

After settling a dispute about the chiefdomship at Dinokani, Kalafins

Stadt, and some other matters, I left for home by post cart to Mafeking, and from there by train to Vryburg, where I was again united with my family after ten months absence, five of which I spent in prison life in Pretoria.

Before I left Zeerust, and knowing that an acting magistrate's clerk was required at Rustenburg, I suggested to Lord Cecil that my son Harry should come up, knowing that he was qualified to fill the billet; he consented.

After twelve days spent at home, I returned having a few days previously sent the Basutos, sixteen in number, on to Zeerust; my son accompanied me. On arrival at Zeerust I heard that Rustenburg had been occupied by detachment of our troops under Maj. Tracey a couple of days after we left; that the Boers had attacked them, but had been beaten off, but that the road was closed to Rustenburg. Col. Hoare was still at Elands River, where he had been ordered to remain. That the Boers had been forced, such as had surrendered and were left on their farms, to take up arms again in the Zeerust, as in most other districts. The event, by some of us expected, had come true.

I again settled down to my work at Zeerust. My son was engaged pro-tem in the office of the District Commissioner, Lord Cecil; his salary, like mine, had not been paid. We boarded for the time being at a hotel, intending to get quarters of our own later.

The Basutos I had engaged for my Intelligence work proved both good and faithful. The news they brought me could always be relied on. A report brought in by them that Col. Hoare had been attacked proved true, and that the Boers were taking up positions around his camp.

A short time after my return to Zeerust, Sir F. Carrington arrived with his column, consisting of about 1,700 men of a thorough good stamp, chiefly Australians, Rhodesians, and Cape Colonials. I stool alongside of Carrington as his force marched through to the relief of Hoare, and certainly I never saw a force I liked better. Horses and men were fully fit, besides which the artillery was all that one could wish. I remarked to Gen. Carrington with such a force he could go anywhere; but he didn't. He came back without relieving Hoare at Elands River, who was besieged by a force consisting of about 400 Boers under Lemmer.

The evening after Carrington's return I was in the hotel, and was informed that there was talk of evacuating Zeerust. I asked Lord Cecil, who said he was not aware of any such intention. We all went to bed late that night. The next morning Capt. Blum, who had been acting as magistrate of Lichtenburg, came into my room about 7 o'clock and said:

'What! In bed yet? Why, the column is moving, and they have already set alight to the stores.'

'What?' I said, 'Clearing out and evacuating? Why? What for?'

'I do no know,' he replied; 'they are the general's orders.'

Both my son and myself hurriedly dressed and went out. Sure enough, there were the stores burning on the hill, while the village was all bustle and confusion. Men galloping madly hither and thither. Anxious loyalists on foot seeking means of conveyance for their families. Everybody seemed in a hurry, and no one seemed to know why. I found Lord Cecil at last, at our offices, and saluting, said:

'Why are we evacuating this place, sir? Do not go; let us remain here. I am sure with a force of 300 men we can hold it.'

'Dennison,' he replied, 'I have to obey orders, and so must you.'

'Very good, sir' I replied, and walked away disgusted and mad.

I sent my son by the coach. Our kit was left behind as the wagon had gone, and there was no room on the coach for it. I remained behind until my horse was jumped by a Boer and late that evening, about 9 o'clock, I rode out, having being helped by a friend in Zeerust with another horse and equipment, which I got late. It was moonlight, and, as I rode at a gentle trot near Jacobsdal, I was suddenly fired on from both sides, but not hit. I at once galloped forward, and could hear horses' hooves behind me and a shout. I kept on until I saw an open place towards the ridge on my right. I turned short at right angles and made for the ridge, on reaching which I hurriedly dismounted, gave the horse a cut with a small switch I had in my hand, and away he went towards Zeerust. The reason why I drove the animal off was that I could not ride him in the ridge, and, had I left him, the Boers following would have got him. Barely had I crept into the stony ridge when I heard my pursuers coming on towards me. They had passed the open glade, and finding later that I was not in front of them, they retraced their way and found my spoor by moonlight, which they followed on to the hill above the glade. As they dismounted one of them said: 'He is hiding in the ridge; he is an old *skelm* [scoundrel].'

I knew that voice, but could never call to mind the owner of it, and was satisfied, however, that I had been waylaid by men of Zeerust – there were two. Had I been armed I should have been alright, but I had only a switch in my hand. I crept gently up the ridge, being careful to make no noise.

The Boers did n*f*ot ascend, but walked about the foot of the ridge for a short time, then mounted and rode away. I then walked on for about an hour or more, and then, feeling sleepy, crept into a bush, broke down some of the bushes, and went to sleep. Just as the day was dawning I awoke, and walked along the ridge towards Malmani. I could look down on the farmhouses below, and when it became unwise to go any further, I hid among the rocks and bush on the ridge. About midday, feeling very hungry and thirsty, and noticing some kaffir huts below me some distance from a farmhouse, I resolved to descend and seek food and water. As I approached one of the huts a woman came from a stream nearby carrying water in a can. She gave me some to drink, and having some small coins with me, I purchased a few raw eggs and some boiled corn, which I hastily ate. The woman was friendly, and said that she would not tell her masters that she had seen an Englishman. She said she had heard that morning that a commando of Boers were beyond Jacobsdal, and advised me to wait in the hills until it was dark and then push on to Mafeking. The woman was very intelligent for her class, and asked why the English were running away again. She said, 'The Boers are afraid of the English, but the English are worse than the Boers, for they run away and are the stronger.'

Alas! Yes, one of the most disgraceful things enacted during the war that ever came to my knowledge was the evacuation of Zeerust and the burning of 90,000 worth of stores, or thereabouts. Not only the hurry, but the contemptible haste to get away from a foe distant at least twenty-five miles at the time.

The woman seemed inclined to talk more, but I dare not delay, at any moment a stray Boer might turn up, and I was not anxious to be a prisoner again. So bidding her goodbye, I hurried back into the hills again, taking care to keep as much under cover of the trees as possible. I again hid until the sun was about down, then walked quickly on along the ridge until I got at the extreme end of the valley above Lemmer's Farm, where I found some water, and, after a drink, went on again. On reaching the high country I suddenly came face-to-face with a friendly Boer, in search of cattle which, he said, he now had reason to think had been taken by our forces on their way out. Very probable, I thought.

'Now,' he said, 'do not delay for Lemmer's commando is not far off – in fact, his advance is already on that hill', pointing to a bushy hill about a mile off, 'and,' he continued, 'they may have seen you already, but go quickly until you get among the rocks yonder; it will soon be dark and you will be safe, but be careful in passing Malmani.'

I did not delay longer, but shaking hands with him, I went and did so with all the energy I possessed until I got among the rocks, about six miles from Malmani. Rested up for a few minutes, and again walked, arriving at Malmani about 9 p.m. Walking warily along the road, I got opposite a house with a verandah covered by creepers, I heard women's voices speaking English, and went to the gate; there was sufficient light from the moon to distinguish three ladies sitting on the stoep. One of them, an old lady, got up and came towards me as I greeted her. She hesitated, and then it struck me I was without a hat, with a handkerchief tied round my head, so that my appearance was not conducive to the confidence that one would like to inspire, more so when you are hungry and thirsty. However, matters were soon explained, and a kindly welcome, with a cup of tea and some bread and butter, was given me besides which the old lady gave me a cap to replace the hat I had lost and the coloured handkerchief which had been my headgear for the last twenty-four hours. I found out that one Henrik Gey still lived at Malmani, and, after bidding my kind hostesses farewell and thanking them, I made my way to Gey's house. (I may here state that most people, farmers and others, had commenced their peaceful avocations since shortly after 5th June – the date of Lord Roberts' entry into Pretoria – thinking that the war was practically over.) On my arrival at Gey's house I was welcomed both by him and his wife; the latter hastily got me some food, while I rested on the sofa in the dining room talking to my host. He said he had two horses in his stable, and both were at my service; 'and now,' he said, 'try to sleep for a short time until my wife has something to eat ready for you, and then I will wake you.'

I turned over and was asleep in a few minutes, but awoke shortly after by people talking, and found that some neighbours – two women and two men, Boers all – were in the room. As I rose and greeted them, one of the men left, apparently in a hurry. I had something to eat, and then reclined on the sofa again, waiting for Gey, who had gone out. He came hurriedly in after a short time and said:

'There is danger, and I am in a fix; the man you saw go out has gone to the commando camp at Malmani to inform De la Rey that you are here. Now, if I assist you to get away I shall get quite into trouble, and as you are my friend I cannot let you become a prisoner.'

'All right,' I said, rising, 'Where are your horses?'

'In the stable close by,' he replied.

'Well,' I said, 'Let your son mount one and I will mount the other and we shall ride hard for about four miles; your son can then return with the horses and I will proceed on foot.'

'For your sake,' he replied, 'I will risk it but I know I shall have trouble.'

The horses were saddled and we went off at a stiff gallop for about four or five miles. I then sent the horses back and walked on. For assisting me Gey had everything taken from him by the Boers, and was later on sent to St. Helena by our forces. I, however, did what I could for him later by writing to the magistrate at Zeerust after peace in reference to compensation for his losses.

About midnight I caught up to a wagon outspanned, and from a native, who sat shivering over the remains of a fire, I ascertained that his master was an Englishman, who, with his family, was fleeing from Jacobsdal. The owner of the wagon hearing my voice, got up and came down from the wagon. I told him my tale. He inspanned at once, and I rode on his wagon for some miles until, when near Mafeking, we came on the rear of Gen. Carrington's column. I then walked on into Mafeking and reported to Maj. Pilson, Lord Cecil's chief staff officer, who advised me to go home and have a rest, which I did after paying off my Basutos and disbanding them. Sick, weary, and disgusted, I went home by train and arrived in Vryburg the evening of the day I left Mafeking.

As Commandant at Vryburg I found Col. Galway of the Somersets, whom I had known in Pretoria prior to 1881, as Adjutant of the old 13th. After having being home for about a week, I felt that I ought to be doing something, so decided to raise a corps of scouts, after getting permission from Lord Cecil, who was then in Cape Town, and whom I wired for permission. His reply was:

'I have no objection to your going into military service providing military pay you.'

What he meant was that I could not expect to get paid by his office while doing military service. This, of course I knew and did not object to, but I felt that I should be doing something for the pay I considered I was receiving, although up to that time I had only received an advance of pay enough to pay current expenses. No rate of pay had up to that time being decided on for either my son or myself. My son had preceded me to Vryburg and was there a day or so before me.

I had several conversations with Col. Galway about raising the corps.

He was highly in favour of my doing so, and on the arrival of Sir Charles Parsons, shortly before that of Gen. Settle, the necessary order was given and I started raising the corps of fifty men, purely to act as scouts, which was a duty I knew well and in which I had considerable practice in earlier wars.

Chapter 19

Having got the necessary order, as I have stated in the previous chapter I set to work at once enrolling men, and in a short time had about the number I wanted. James Streak, an old Grahamstown Boy and a man on whom I could rely, was appointed as my Lieutenant, my son Harry as Quartermaster, and young Willy Staynes, son of our former congregational minister here, as Sergeant-Major. The photo given is one taken, by the resident photographer, of the officers and non-commissioned officers of the first batch of scouts I raised in Vryburg.

I had barely got into working order when we received orders to accompany Gen. Settle's column to Schweizer Reneke and onward on a circuitous campaign, spying out the land. We saw a lot of country, of the Transvaal and also of the Orange Free State; Boers, some also, but we had not lost any, someone said. I wondered what we had lost, as we were not finding much. At any rate the Boers found us on two or three occasions. Once when a portion of our convoy was left behind near the *weg draai* (i.e., turnaway) on the Vaal River, when they crept up close during the night and fired continuously into the camp, killing a number of the animals and wounding several men; creating a deal of disturbance but not doing any particular harm. And again, on our return to Hoopstad by the same road, the Boers found us but too well. Of this, however, I will give an account anon.

After the night attack we marched on up the river towards Commando Drift on the Vaal. On a Sunday morning several Boers were noticed riding about on the opposite side of the river, and shortly after it was reported to me by Lt. Streak from the left flank of my screen that a laager was located on the river in the thorns, and that the Boers could plainly be heard singing. I at once reported back to Sir Charles Parsons, who was in command of the mounted brigade, and rode down to the left myself, when sure enough the Boers could be plainly heard singing, singing lustily – a Sunday service evidently. On returning to my centre I met Sir Charles Parsons, who had ridden up on getting my report. We were then where the roads divided, one going parallel with the river, and the other turning off to the right. I was ordered to take the right-hand road. No effort was made to attack the Boers. 'Magnanimous reasons, perhaps!' I thought. But of course one should not think sometimes. We camped near a farm shortly after, and while away about two miles ahead with my men off-saddled, an orderly rode up with a note from Sir Charles, requesting me to come to camp. I immediately had my horse caught and saddled, then rode back to camp, where I met Sir Charles, who gave me orders to go on to Commando Drift and hold it until the column advanced saying that I should be supported by the Cape Mounted Rifles, a good corps. I immediately returned to my men, and quickly saddled up and marched forward across the flats in my usual extended order; my front covered by my screen, which usually extended about three or four miles; the distance between two men of a half-section was always about fifty yards, and between each half-section about three hundred yards. Thus four men covered a front of four hundred yards, but in wooded or rugged country the men were much closer together. The screen was supported on either flank by the remainder of the corps riding in open skirmishing order, myself in the centre with a section of gallopers; besides which, individual scouts in advance were often used, and always connecting links in my front to the officers in charge of the screen.

Commando Drift was about eight or nine miles ahead. When we got to within about three miles of the drift, and near a farm house and some large rocks, I saw a column advancing towards the drift from the east, and shortly after saw a helio[graph] at work on us. I at once sent a man back with a note to Col. Parsons, and placed my men and horses, whom I had concentrated on seeing the column, behind the rocks, which afforded safe cover against any description of fire, besides which I placed a picket on a rise and a single lookout on another point of vantage, sending two of my most reliable men on to reconnoitre. Shortly afterwards I rode out towards the picket I had placed on the rise, when I saw my lookout galloping towards me gesticulating frantically. As he neared me I shouted:

'What is the matter?'

'The Boers are coming round on our right rear, sir,' he shouted, 'about

200 horsemen galloping hard.'

And while he was still talking a drove of blesboks came over the rise from the direction indicated by the man.

'There are your Boers,' I said, 'and the next time you come to report be sure you tell me what kind of horns the enemy carry! Get back to your post.'

But, suddenly, looking around I saw no supports, which had been advancing some distance behind us a short time before, nor yet the dust of the artillery that should have followed an hour or so after us with Sir Charles Parsons, and which I had also noticed far behind us on the long bare flat before we took cover.

'What has become of the supports and guns?' I asked the man.

'Gone back, sir,' he said, 'some time ago.'

'Well, here's a mess,' I thought, but said nothing. I returned to my men and on looking through my glasses at the column in our front I could plainly see the guns being unlimbered, evidently to open fire on us, but immediately limbered up again. Knowing that De Wet was not far off, I thought perhaps it was his commando; but, to my relief, my two men returned and reported having come in touch with Australian scouts, and that the column was that of Col. Porter and a portion of Gen. Hunter's column, which we were to meet at Bothasville. I rode forward at once with my party and met Col. Porter, to whom I explained matters, on which a hearty laugh followed. I asked him what I should do. He said:

'Oh, camp where you think fit, but I should suggest beyond me on the river as the best place for you.'

I saluted and we rode on and camped about where Col. Porter had shown me. I forgot to state that he said:

'You know, I was just about putting my guns on you when I heard who you were.'

I said:

'Yes, I saw it; but we were quite safe.'

'You scouts are cool customers,' one of the staff remarked as he rode a short way with me. 'Supposing this column had been De Wet's instead of ours, what would you have done?'

'Stayed where I was,' I replied, 'and done my best. I had no order to retire.'

But I did not feel at peace with everyone that evening. Col. Porter kindly sent me word to draw provisions, which I did, for we had none.

About 8 p.m. I heard that Col. Parsons had arrived, but I did not see him until next morning. I got orders to start work with him at six the next morning. Nothing of any importance occurred beyond some straggling shots at the outposts, and next morning, just at dawn, we saddled up and rode to Col. Porter's camp, and after waiting for some time for Col. Parsons, we started back to rejoin the column.

We returned the way we had come, towards Hoopstad, and on arriving at Wegdraai again, camped there, after passing the site of the camp that had been attacked and where the remains of many cattle and horses lay stinking in the open veld. Boers were seen galloping about on the opposite side of the river, and firing from the bush lining the northern bank was frequent. Col. Porter had told me that De Wet was in the vicinity, and the actions of the Boers gave one the idea that someone was in command whom they trusted; their actions were bold, and not as usual. Col. Parsons' two horses had been sent to water, and, becoming frightened at our maxim fire, got away from the native who had them in charge, and stampeded past one of my pickets, who turned them towards the river. A Boer was seen to drive them away and they were not recovered again. Another who was coming through the river, ostensibly to surrender, was shot by our maxim fire and died at the farmhouse at Wegdraai the next day.

I repeatedly approached Sir Charles Parsons, asking that we (the mounted forces) might be allowed to cross and attack the Boers, but was informed that the General would not allow it. The following day, while dozing under my screen (we had no tents), I heard mounting orders given, and looking out from under the screen I saw Maj. Berrange of the Cape Police mounting some of his men. I went to him at once and asked where he was going. He said:

'Down the river.'

'What?' I replied, 'With eighteen men only?'

He said:

''Yes, and two maxims.'

'Well then, I will try and go with you,' I said.

I immediately went to Sir Charles Parsons' tent and asked him if I might accompany Berrange with my scouts. He said:

'No, I cannot spare the scouts for we are marching shortly for Hoopstad.'

I was persistent, and at last he said:

'You may send half of your men.'

I said:

'Thank you, sir,' and immediately had eleven horses saddled and my own, taking some of my best men. I only had about twenty-five horses fit for service.

We had barely gone four miles from camp when I was fired on from the river bank opposite; one of the CP [Cape Police] maxims opened on them and stopped their fire. We proceeded down the river for about another three or four miles, and crossed a peninsula running into an abrupt bend of the river; in the distance we could see a number of Boers coming up the river on the off side at full speed. Berrange had just driven up, and I pointed out the Boers to him. A few horsemen had galloped away from a farmhouse on our left front.

'We turn here,' said Berrange; 'This my guide tells me, is the place indicated as our turning point.'

'Very good,' I replied, 'and in that case I shall scout through that brushwood.'

I pointed out to where the few Boers had ridden from, and taking the right flank of the screen (leaving the left in charge of Sgt.-Maj. Staynes to scout for Maj. Berrange), consisting of five men, including a non-commissioned officer, I galloped towards the farmhouse in the brushwood, and found that a party of Boers had been camped there. I then turned to the left to join my centre, and when within about 500 or 600 yards from Berrange and his men, heard firing and saw confusion among the Cape Police. We galloped up, and dismounting behind a bush I went back with my handful of men on foot (our horses were meanwhile with my servant – a Hottentot). Riderless horses passed us again and again as well as animals. I saw Maj. Berrange doing his best to stop the panic, but at last he gave up the vain attempt. Some of the best men had taken what cover the country afforded, a few scattered camel tree thorns and ant heaps, that were in the vicinity, being the only cover. The game was up. One of the maxims was already in the hands of the enemy; the other, with a wounded horse and one wounded man had gone forward. I sent my men back to get their horses and to send me mine, which my boy brought, and, as the men mounted, I ordered them to clear, for the Boers were advancing rapidly on us, firing from their horses. As my servant handed me the reins of my horse, I shouted to him to go and I would follow. I threw the reins over the animal's neck and tried to mount, but the horse was panic-stricken and would not allow me to mount. The bullets were cutting up the sand thick and fast around me. I felt that my time had come, when suddenly Sgt.-Maj. Sheppard of the Cape Police rode up and, hastily catching hold of my horse's reins said:

'Mount Captain; I will hold him.'

This saved me, and barely had I swung myself into the saddle when the horse put down his head and bolted for all he was worth. Sheppard had saved me! And this was the second gallant act of his that day, for I later on met Maj. Maloney, CSO [Chief Staff Officer] to Gen. Settle, whom I informed of Sheppard's brave act. He said that early in the day Sheppard had acted in a way worthy of mention, and asked me to write reporting the matter, and request mention for him, and that he (Maj. Maloney) would endorse it. I did so but up the time I am writing, now two years after the event, this gallant non-commissioned officer has never been recognised.

After some considerable difficulty I succeeded in quietening my horse a bit as I reached the remaining maxim, in charge of Lt. Davidson of the Cape Police, who could get no further with the wounded horse. We were, later on, met by reliefs from the column, and got to camp at Hoopstad about 10 p.m. Our losses were considerable in deaths, wounded, and prisoners. Among the former was young Grant, of the Cape Mounted Rifles, who, with some more of that force, had joined shortly before the firing began, but of which I was not aware at the time; and among the latter was Sgt.-Maj. Ball of the Cape Police, one of the best and a general favourite. Ball earned the VC at Carters Ridge during the siege of Kimberly by carrying out a wounded man, but the act was not recognised. (All the prisoners were released later and returned to Kimberley.) Several wounded were left on the field and brought in later by our ambulance.

It appears that Maj. Berrange had sent Capt. Harvey, round the promontory I mentioned in the bend of the river and, later, noticing the men advancing in his rear, had taken them for Harvey's men, and was not aware of any enemy close until fired on from the rear. Harvey and his men had ridden into a trap and had all been captured.

I give the details as they occurred. My readers can judge for themselves, but I cannot refrain from saying that, having a large force available at his command, Gen. Settle might have sent a stronger number down the river, knowing that the Boers were about in considerable strength. But this is only another minor error of judgement.

The following day we marched on towards Boshoff, which we reached a few days later. (I cannot give exact time or dates as a large portion of my diary got lost during the war, and I have to trust to my memory. The details of my story are correct, but I must omit dates.)

On leaving Boshoff, Gen. Settle rode up to the head of the column to me, and after conversing for a short time, he said:

'Now Dennison, you are going with Sir Charles Parsons and the rest of the mounted brigade, and I trust you will have fighting enough to suit you. I shall follow later. Goodbye, I wish you lots of luck.'

And, shaking hands with me, he returned to Boshoff while we proceeded on to Modder River and conveyed supplies to Koffiefontein Diamond Mine, which was garrisoned by some troops and held throughout the war. On our return Sir Charles rode ahead to Honey Nest Kloof railway station, and proceeded to Kimberley by train. We met him a few days later at Honey Nest Kloof Station from which place all the mounted proceeded to Kimberley, excepting my corps, who proceeded to Vryburg. On our arrival there I reported to the commandant in charge, who said he had no orders about us. I wrote to Headquarters, Kimberley, and also to Capt. White, of the Cape Police, who had been acting SO to Sir Charles Parsons, enquiring what we had to do, and after waiting some time, I got orders to remain where I was for the present. Col. Milne – commonly called Lyddite, on account of his violent temper – was in command of Vryburg. I was informed by him that we were shortly to proceed to Schweizer Reneke to convey provision wagons and that he himself was going in command. We left Vryburg in November, 1900, for Schweizer Reneke with a convoy of 140 ox- and donkey-wagons, escorted by 300 of the Welsh Regiment, and a half squadron of imperial yeomanry; also less than half a squadron of Australian Bushmen under Lt. McPherson, a gallant lad, and of my own scouts about twenty seven men. Col. Milne was in command, with Capt. Taylor, of the Welsh Regiment, as SO; Capt. Anthill, of the Australians, with one 15-pounder and the gun guard; Capt. Robert Hannay (an elder brother of Angus Hannay, who was with me in the capture of Chief Galishwe, of Langberg fame, and who was mainly instrumental in the capture of the chief; both were friends of mine, as our fathers had been friends of yore in lower Albany, in the Cape Colony, near Grahamstown) was guide and transport officer; Geoff McBeth, a brave and able young man, who afterwards did good service as second-in-command of Cullinan's Horse, was in charge of captured stock – or stock to be captured.

On our arrival at O'Reilly's Pan (so named after an old hunter, Jack O'Reilly), about thirteen miles from Vryburg, we made our first halt, had breakfast and camped for the night.

Early the next morning we started on, the scouts well in advance, and on nearing O'Reilly's kop, a few miles beyond the pan, firing commenced on my left. The Boers, about sixty in number, cleared as I brought my right screen flank round, and retired down the flat, hastened by the shells of our 15-pounder. With the scouts I advanced at a gallop and drove the Boers on. We camped at New Grennan, Hannay's farm, then moved on again to Peto's (a Frenchman) farm, where some outhouses were burnt by order of Sir C. Parsons on our former trip. We remained at Peto's that night, and moved on early the next morning to William Pretorius' farm, where we camped until about 2 p.m., and then resumed our march. Barely had we got a few miles from our camping ground when my right flank was fired on, but as the supports came up the enemy retired. Constant sniping continued without any casualties on our side, until we got on top of the rise, where I called a halt for the convoy to get nearer. I then suggested to Col. Milne that we should push on as fast as possible, as I feared the Boers would try to stop us at the Koppies Dam, and it was getting late. This was done, getting the wagons two and three abreast, where it could be done. I sent on two of my most reliable men to reconnoitre and report on Koppies Dam if possible. We halted for a short time until McFarlane and Seaward – the two men I had sent on – returned. They reported that Koppies Dam, now three miles ahead, was held by a large number of Boers, as also the ridges on either side. Besides Robert Hannay and myself, who both knew the country well, we had one Terblanche, a loyal Boer, with us, and who had temporarily joined my scouts. This man suggested taking a road leading past the left of Koppies Dam. I recommended taking this road, to which Col. Milne at first objected, but finally agreed to take. On nearing the hill on the left of Koppies Dam, Lt. Streak reported that about 200 Boers had just gone into it from the north; more reinforcements! I saw that we should have to avoid this hill by leaving the road we were on and striking across the veld, the fire by this time becoming hot.

I rode on and found that there was nothing to prevent our crossing the veld; the ground was hard and but few stones, and no sluits. The Colonel objected most strongly, but I pointed out to him that we had the convoy to consider, and that the road we were on went within a hundred yards of the hill I have mentioned. At last he agreed, saying:

'Very well, do as you think best.'

I had sent word by my galloper, (a few minutes before speaking to the Colonel), to Sgt.-Maj. Staynes, who was in charge of the right screen flank, to close on the centre, leaving a few flankers out, but not to advance until they got orders. By some mistake or other poor Staynes did not get the order, and continued to advance towards the hill, with the result that he fell mortally wounded, and was got out later under a heavy fire by our surgeon, Dr Ellis, who acted most pluckily, as the Boers fired on him and the party conveying the wounded man out the whole way to where we were camped, under the ridges at a farm house away to the left. One wheel of the wagon came off, but the wagon was galloped into camp. As it was, the fire was too hot to delay. Col. Milne left me practically to do as I thought best, so I had the wagons turned to the left, while Streak with nine men, whom I had sent, took possession of one of the ridges as some of the Boers, about fifty or sixty, got possession of the one immediately behind the farm house. I asked Anthill to put some shells on the koppie the Boers had got into, while I charge the spot with about a dozen men. We thus got possession of both positions, and camped the wagons in very close order in front of the house. The action of Dr Ellis deserved recognition, and I trust he has got the well merited distinction of the Victoria Cross.

We had foiled the Boers in their own game, and the convoy was saved. Great assistance was rendered by Hannay, McBeth, and Capt. Taylor WR [Welsh Regiment], in fact, all hands did their best. Especially I must mention the Australian Bushmen and Lt. McPherson, their leader. Of my own handful of scouts I cannot speak too highly; both officers and men did their duty, including my son Harry, who always showed cool pluck in danger, and who was Quartermaster-Sergeant at the time.

Every precaution was taken against a night attack. On one ridge to the east of the camp some infantry were placed as night pickets; but as it was too long for them to defend, I left Streak with his men there with orders to remain until dark and then fall back to camp. By this means the Boers were led to think we held the whole ridge. Streak and his men were wanted elsewhere.

The next morning before sunrise we marched onward, and struck the main road via Koppies Dam about one and a half miles off; we had, by crossing the veld the evening before, really saved in distance, as the road described the half-side of a square and we had cut off the angle. From ridge to ridge the Boers opposed us, but always gave way as we advanced on them. The long front of screen was too much for the Boers, there was always the danger of being outflanked, and individual men were poor targets, for my screen rode in very widely extended order.

After camping that night on M. Pretorius's farm, we arrived the next day at our destination without any further mishap, although the Boers showed up in fairly strong numbers. Poor Staynes died the day after our arrival at Schweizer Reneke. By his death I lost one of my bravest and best lads. He was buried with full military honours. The day following, we started on our return march to Vryburg, taking the upper, or northern road, not the one by which we had come, and the next day captured a considerable number of stock, cattle, sheep, and goats.

As we had to bring out some families from near New Grennan – R. Hannay's farm – one of which was that of Terblanche, whom I have already mentioned, we diverged to the left, and went towards New Grennan on to the road we had come by. As we neared Losasa, the stream on which the New Grennan is situated, Boers were seen riding about in the distance, usually a sign that a force is not far off. We camped for the night on the Losasa, and the next morning continued our march and reached Terblanche's farm about sunrise, where the families were that we had to bring out. They were hastily placed in our wagons, and in the meantime, during the halt, I had ordered Streak to advance, supported by the yeomanry, and secure the positions on the ridge facing New Grennan Farm. Shortly after he left I heard heavy and continued firing, and on immediately galloping forward was met by one of Streak's men, who said that his officer and several others had fallen in the advance on the ridge. The gun was quickly brought forward and opened fire on the Boers, and under cover of fire I took the position. We found poor Streak lying riddled with bullets and picked up three other men wounded besides. Streak died as the doctor, who had accompanied me, turned him over; he was lying on his face. Another of my best and bravest gone! It seems the Boers saw him advancing and waited until he got within thirty paces of the schanses – they had hastily built rough stone walls about one and a half feet high as they saw us advancing – and then fired on our men, who were not supported as they should have been. I felt bitter, hard, and wished for a stronger force.

After placing my pickets in the best positions, I went back to the wagons which had camped at the farm house. We buried poor Streak in the little graveyard on the farm, where lay the remains of Robert Hannay's father and uncle. The other men were seriously, but not mortally, wounded. After a short halt, only allowing time for the burial and for breakfast, we moved on – or rather the convoy did – after the advance guard of the yeomanry, while I got the men out from their positions on the ridge under cover of the gun. On rejoining the convoy I found it halted on the top of the rise, and the ridges held on our front and left by a strong force of Boers. I found Col. Milne near the gun, and got orders from him to try and dislodge the Boers on the ridge on the left; and barely had I got my men – a detachment of yeomanry, Australian Bushmen, and scouts – ready for the advance on the rear of the ridge, when I noticed that we had no protection on our right, and at once sent a sergeant and twelve men – six scouts and six yeomanry – to take up a position on the right flank, which a slight rise afforded. I waited a few minutes and saw the men swerve and go to cover at some old kaffir huts, or rather the walls of them, as they had all been burnt by the Boers – near the wagons, where several others from the wagons had also taken cover. Then putting spurs into the flanks of my always-willing and swift pony, I galloped across under a heavy fire all the way from the left ridge and turned the men out to the position I wanted them in. As I turned to go back to my men my horse shied, and as I drew him tight by the reins, felt that I was hit in the elbow. The ambulance was close by, so I rode over and dismounted. The doctor and assistants were dressing some wounded. My coat sleeve was quickly ripped opened and the wound bandaged by the able and willing doctor, of whom I shall ever think of kindly, for he was a good man. When the bandaging was finished I turned towards my horse to mount, but was stopped by the doctor and made to sit down. A faintness came over me, and I felt that I was no good anymore that day. Col. Milne and Robert Hannay shortly after came up. I suggested to the Colonel to strike away across the flat eastwards well out of fire from the ridges, for our force was too small to attack them and defend the convoy as well; in fact, I often think that it was as well that I was hit and thus the attack on the left prevented. Otherwise it might have gone badly with us, for, as it proved later, we might have been cut off, and that would have given our enemy the opportunity they wanted. My suggestion was acted on, and the direction of our course was changed. Again a disaster averted, for the Boers would not venture on the open flats. As I have said, the course was changed east across the open flats, and then we inclined slightly to the west and camped in a large dry dam at a farm house near O'Reilly's Pan, from whence that night I sent two of my scouts to Vryburg – acting on the orders of Col. Milne – for reinforcements. We knew the Boer force to be strong – as they themselves stated about 800 men – whereas we had only about 200 mounted men all told, and about 250 infantry, while our big gun ammunition was expended, on which so much depended, for Capt. Anthill worked his gun well, and without him and his gun we should have faired badly. Our total was five killed and fifteen wounded; no prisoners.

The next morning just at daylight we moved on again away into the flats around the pan, and barely had we moved a mile from our camping ground when we saw in the distance our relief force advancing from Vryburg, among whom was my late eldest son Alec. Later on, as we neared the town, my wife and daughter met me in a trap, into which I got and drove with them into Vryburg. My wound proved not so serious as was anticipated, but very painful. However, in the course of about three weeks I was fit again.

I cannot here refrain from saying that whatever may have been the faults of Col. Milne, he was at least a brave man, and one who had the sense – so much wanting in the war among so many commanding officers I knew – to take advice from others who knew the country and Boer modes of fighting better than he did. I always like Col. Milne and could get on with him. He was, at any rate, a soldier.

Chapter 20

After remaining in Vryburg for about a month I was ordered to proceed to Kimberley, and there we formed the nucleus of the Kimberley Column. Again, under Col. Milne, we started for Boshoff with a large convoy, but with a considerably stronger force than our former one. Our mounted force consisted of 50th Company Hampshire Imperial Yeomanry, under Capt. Nicholson, a squadron of the Diamond Fields Horse, and my own corps, now 175 men, as I had got authority to raise the force of scouts to 200 men, and had some excellent officers in H. P. Browne (my son-in-law, seconded from the Cape Police and now my adjutant and 2nd-in-command with the rank of Captain, an efficient and good officer), Watty Brunton, and Herbert Brown, both colonial boys and excellent officers. Herbert Brown I made screen leader and he became one of the smartest officers I had. The whole force was good and I was justly proud of my scouts. Brunton was a most plucky and good officer and did a lot of really good work.

Besides the mounted men, we had 300 infantry. Our artillery consisted of two 15-pounders, under Maj. Paris of the Royal Marine Artillery Force. One of the officers who served with him was Lt. Nesham, who had also being with us on Gen. Settle's column. Nesham was a fine and brave young English officer of the right stamp. We also had two pom-poms, in charge of Lt. Kennaway, RFA, C Squadron, 5th, NZ.

Besides a number of ox- and mule-wagons, numbering, if I recollect rightly, all told about 130, we had traction engines with their loaded trucks. After leaving Kimberley we camped at a farm on the Frankfort road, which about six miles ahead wound through a narrow and most dangerous pass in the hills, and which could be defended by a small force against large numbers. We were waiting for the traction engines and their trains.

The next morning, after our arrival at the farm I have mentioned, a white man (Englishman) turned up on foot – having come from Boshoff – and stated that the Boers, about 200, under Jacobs, were waiting for us at Frankfort Pass, and that he had escaped during the night, and the Boers had taken his cart, horses, and money. Later in the day we had positive information through our Intelligence that the pass was held by the Boers in strong force. I had had breakfast with Col. Milne and Capt. Gorton, his staff officer, and the advisability of going via Frankfort was discussed. I gave it as my opinion that we should have great difficulty in getting through the pass, if we got through at all, providing Jacobs with his commando were there. Col. Milne would not hear of taking the other and more northerly road over Slabberts Nek, and which we knew was easier to attack if held than Frankfort Pass. I shortly after went to my camp, and later in the day, after hearing that the Boers held Frankfort, I again went to the Colonel's tent, being determined that we should avoid the pass, if I could do anything towards it. I knew that I had the sympathy of all the other officers, besides which I had a plan to suggest. I met Col. Milne at this tent and found him in good humour and most cordial, as he was to me as a rule.

After talking for a time I said:

'Colonel, I have a plan to suggest to you.'

'All right,' he replied, 'What is it?'

'It is this,' I replied, 'We know that Frankfort Pass is held by the Boers in strong force; we know also that the traction engines cannot go via Slabberts Nek on account of the heavy sand, but the wagons can. Now, if you will allow me, I will start within an hour and hold Slabberts Nek; I shall ride hard, and you allow our wagon transport, in fact, our whole column, excepting the traction engines to follow half an hour later. The Boers, seeing the column changing course, will make for the Nek, but I shall be there before them. We can thus get our convoy of wagons through to Slabberts Farm, and I can go and hold Frankfort while the traction trains get through, by starting tonight at 2 o'clock.'

'I agree with your plan,' he replied, 'Start away as soon as you like.'

I did so, and it was completely successful. Maj. Paris with his guns accompanied me to the Pass. We got everything safely through without firing a shot. The Boers were foiled again. They made for Slabberts Nek, leaving the Frankfort position on seeing the column taking that road, but we had forestalled them, and a few long-range shots sent them back. The traction engines were cursed by us all, as they were constantly requiring water, which was by no means plentiful, and it took us until 3 o'clock the next morning to reach camp with them.

The morning following we started about 5 o'clock, and, as we neared the hills in our front, Boers were reported in strength holding the hills on either side of the road, which passed through between them at an easy rifle range from both sides. I at once pushed on, and when within 800 yards from the entrance, fire was opened on us from the hills. On the left was Lt. Brunton, and on the right Lt. H. Brown. Both left and right flanks dismounted and sent their horses back, then advanced in our usual style, each man acting independently, running forward a short distance then falling flat. I had trained my men to do this mode of advance, as a man lying flat offers but a poor mark to an enemy, even if lying on the bare ground, and is barely visible at 700 or 800 yards, more especially so being in very open order. Our artillery opened fire on the ridges, and the scouts steadily advanced. On the right they were supported by Sir R. Rycroft with a body of Imperial Yeomanry, and who acted well. Rycroft was a good man, and most eager to learn. The left, under a young subaltern – I forget his name – did not seem to grasp what they had to do, and it was only when Brunton and his men got to the hill to their front that any advance was made by the left yeomanry supports, who then madly charged forward past Brunton's right until checked by a heavy fire from the Boers, who had taken up a position further on, and who shot – if I remember rightly – seven of the yeomanry horses; the balance with their riders came as madly back. And this was often the case with some of the yeomanry detachments we had at times with us. They would wildly charge forward, and, of course, when fire was suddenly and unexpectedly opened upon them, it was difficult to prevent the fear-stricken animals they rode from turning and galloping frantically away from danger.

Both positions were soon in our hands, and our convoys got safely through. Near the nek, not far from Boshoff, we were met by the Commandant and some mounted men. among the latter was one of my old Border Horse troopers of 1879, Archer by name, one of the seven who escaped with me on the fatal Zlobanne [Hlobane] day in Zululand, and a man who that day under my own personal observation earned the VC. I was informed that near Boshoff he had saved the life of an officer under very heavy fire. He was not rewarded. This same man later served with me to the end of the last war, always a willing, active, and good soldier.

The day after the stores were all safely delivered at Boshoff, I was informed that we should start on our return on the morning following, but about 5 p.m. I was hurriedly sent for by Col. Milne, and went down at once to see him. I met him coming round the corner on horseback.

'Glad to see you Dennison,' he said as I saluted him. 'I was just riding up to see you. You got my note?'

'Yes, sir,' I replied, 'and came at once.'

'Oh its all right,' he replied, 'but as my man has brought my horse I thought I would ride up and save you the trouble of coming to see me. It seems,' he continued, 'that the Commandant here cannot send a party of infantry to hold the nek tonight – in fact, the Boers are now in possession – and I want you to go at once and drive them out, and hold till we pass in the morning with the convoy. The Boshoff guns have just gone out to shell the ridges, and the Boshoff infantry are to act as your supports, and all take orders from you.'

'Very good, sir,' I replied and turning to my orderly gave him a message to the officer in charge of the camp.

After talking to the colonel a minute or two longer, I rode up to my camp and found all hands busy saddling up; my order had been at once obeyed, and within ten minutes we started; our wagons and camp equipment were to follow on with the convoy in the morning. I found the guns and infantry awaiting me outside, and met the commandant, who, on shaking hands, said he thought we had a risky job to perform.

'And now,' he said, 'You can direct the officers in charge of the guns as to the shelling. I wish you every success, goodbye.'

We again shook hands and rode over to the guns and directed the officers in charge as to the shelling, which, as soon as my men had got clear in front, was commenced.

We advanced rapidly in our usual very extended order, screen and supports, the infantry following on either flank in open skirmishing order. I rode in the centre in line with my supports (the usual position of the officer commanding scouts). The shells from the two guns kept bursting along the ridge until I sent word back to cease firing as I neared the ridge. The Boers opened fire on the left from the ridge, but, being now quite dark, the fire was at random. My men, who had dismounted, crept cautiously but quickly on, then, at the foot of the ridge, with a cheer, rushed in, and the Boers fled; on the right, as the men were able to outflank the position thoroughly, the Boers left it without firing a shot.

The position was gained without a casualty. The infantry came up shortly after, and we held the ridge until the convoy passed next morning, ere the sun rose, and we reached Kimberley a few days later.

Chapter 21

From all sources we heard of train-wrecking and the capture of convoys and men by the Boers. De Wet, the Will 'o the Wisp, the man who might have been caught again and again, were it not for that curse of the British Army, jealousy. Why was he allowed to escape from Oliphants Nek, when the patient, untiring Lord Methuen drove him on to the nek? Where was the much-feted General? Certainly not at the nek, where he should have been. Why did De Wet escape so often? Because of jealousy and incapacity. Why were the colonials never given a chance of attempting the capture independently? Because the military authorities knew too well that the colonials might catch De Wet, and the imperial regular troops would get no kudos. Had a few columns of combined colonial forces, Australians, New Zealanders, Canadians, and South Africans, under their own officers, been given the work to do, De Wet would have been caught, I am confident, without much trouble. Why was he not caught at Orange River below Hopetown? Because the commanding officer of one column wanted the credit of doing it with his column alone, while one of the best columns, one which consisted of good tried colonials principally (the Kimberley column) was left to keep communication open with Plumer, and took no part in the surrounding. De Wet was in a trap in the bend of the Orange River, swollen, impassable, and yet he got out and did not go through the river, and that with all his force, though our troops were all around him! Anyone can thus judge that there must have been something most glaringly wrong – and that something was jealousy, deplorable jealousy. A nation's cause, the honour of the flag, everything counted as nought, everything endangered for the aggrandisement of self, in so many instances.

The Boers, now driven to desperation through the reckless burning of houses and the wholesale destruction of their property took every opportunity they could to do likewise, and one can only be surprised that, under the circumstances, kindness was, as a rule, shown to prisoners they captured, excepting such of their own countrymen who had taken up arms against them.

Referring to wholesale destruction, I have been an eyewitness on more than one occasion to ruthless slaughter of thousands of sheep and goats, and on one occasion, near Boshoff, a number of young horses and foals were shot by orders from our Headquarters. All this stock could have been sent away into safe places, and would have greatly assisted in restocking the country. Many men, hangers-on to columns, and in some cases the Loot Masters (or OC Captured Stock) made pots of money out of captured stock. Many a man I have heard say since, 'Why did I not know what I know now?' Many men who should have been, were not above suspicion. Thousands that had been pressed out of the British taxpayers might have been spared then if all the captured stock had gone to its legitimate account. Those who had fought hardest and lost so much, as a rule, fared the worst.

Some of the corps were allowed a portion of the loot they captured, but not all. Kitchener's Fighting Scouts were allowed this privilege among others. I tried to get the same for my men, but this was not allowed; why the distinction, no one could tell me. Kitchener's Fighting Scouts may have been allowed the extra because they bore the name of the General Officer Commanding. Why they were called Fighting Scouts I cannot tell; the inference is that the others were not. Whereas my experience of scouting corps, or corps of scouts, was that they always came in for the rough knocks, and in many cases had all the fighting to themselves before the columns came up.

Our stay at Kimberley was a short one. We started on convoying again to Koffiefontein under Maj. Chamier of the RA, who took Col. Milne's place. The usual scrimmages took place with the enemy. We got as far back as Jacobsdal, from whence we went to Pietersburg, in the Orange Free State, to bring out all the Dutch families. The Boers held the ridges near Pietersburg which the scouts, supported by the Cape Police, routed them out of. After placing strong pickets on different points where I considered necessary, I rode into the village, and in passing a store noticed a wagon drawn up in front of it. An officer I knew called to me, and as I turned towards him, he said:

'Dennison old chap, do come and help us here; we have a woman to load up and cannot understand her; she speaks nothing but Dutch, and is in a perfect fury.'

I dismounted and entered the dwelling with the officer, where I found in the front room two other officers and a fine big woman who, with her hands on her hips, looked daggers at me went I went in. I spoke to her in Dutch and said:

'My good woman, our orders are to load all families up and take them to Kimberley, and it is of no use for you to try and obstruct us; the orders are such, and all must go. If you required any assistance, we will give it to you.'

She replied:

'I don't want your assistance. I am able to help myself; but have your dirty Tommies driven out of my shop, they are robbing me.'

I spoke to an officer and all men were ordered out of the shop, then said:

'Now, do not delay, but pack what things you require to take with you.'

She replied:

'I shall take my own time. Who are you that you order me in my own house? Get out, you dirt.'

On which I turned to the officer who had asked me to help and said:

'I shall leave you the further honour of dealing here, I'm off!'

After some trouble and some forcible loading of irate Boer women, some of whom were gently but firmly lifted into the wagons amidst curses, screams, and prayers, and the sarcastic but gentle admonitions of Tommy who, with all his faults, was ever kind to the weak, and generally especially so where women and children were concerned.

The British private soldier and NCOs, have gained the respect of friend and foe in South Africa as a rule; would that as much could be said for all others.

On starting, after about three hours' delay from Pietersburg, the women all began to sing the Free State national anthem. One was inclined to lose one's temper sometimes, but oftener to admire the patriotism shown in the State.

Again and again did we go to Boshoff, Koffiefontein, Daniels Kuil, Campbell, and Griquatown, nearly always in charge of convoys – Maj. Paris now in command, as Maj. Chamier was away on sick leave – at times in search of Boer commandos.

On one occasion, after having safely delivered our convoys at Boshoff, we marched at midnight to attack some Boers said to be near a large pan. We surrounded the place quietly and quickly before daylight, but the Boers had fled, and we returned, intending to come again, which we did after leaving our wagons at Winsorton Station. Then, with only our mule luggage and ordinance wagons, we started again in the early morning from Winsorton – about 300 mounted men, including Cape Police, Diamond Fields Horse, Kimberley Light Horse, and a squadron of New Zealanders, besides some yeomanry. We camped that night near a large pan. (A pan is a small inland lake supplied by rainfall, usually dry.)

That evening I was with Maj. Paris and Capt. Gorton, RA, still Staff Officer (Good old Gorton! We all liked him). The Major told me it was his wish to cover a big front the next morning, and was going to put the Cape Police on my screen right and the yeomanry left. I said:

'Well Major, the Cape Police are all right anywhere, but it will never do to place the yeomanry in the front line.'

'Where would you have them?' he asked.

'As supports,' I replied, 'We shall then have the Cape Police cover six miles front.'

He agreed; and next morning we started at three o'clock, and had to pass through about three miles of 'vaalbush' through which the screen rode in fairly close order, but as it became light extended to the limit, viz, 300 yards between half-sections and 50 yards between single files. Capt. Gorton had just ridden up to us (Capt. Browne was riding with me) with an order from Maj. Paris to halt, and he said:

'Do you know you have the yeomanry on the left of your left screen flank this morning?'

'No,' I replied, 'I did not know it for Maj. Paris agreed with me last night not to place them there. However, we may expect trouble ere long, and the firing, I expect, will commence from that ridge on the left' pointing as I said so to a stony ridge about two miles on our left; 'and I should not be at all surprised that the yeomanry will catch it as usual.'

Barely had we ridden a hundred yards when heavy firing was reported on our left, and we shortly also heard it. Presently a galloper came up from Maj. Paris with an order for me to go to the assistance of the yeomanry, who had got into a mess. I quickly got my left flank and supports round, and away we went towards the firing. The Boers gave way as we advanced, and were chased by us for about four miles to a farmhouse, where they

207

took cover behind the buildings and kraals, from which they opened fire on us, when I sent back to Maj. Paris, asking for a gun and that a squadron of our mounted men be sent across behind the Boers; but my request was refused, and an order with it that I was to return at once, which I did, disgusted, for we had Jacobs and Erasmus's men at our mercy. On returning to the column I asked Maj. Paris if he could place some other unit in the advance to scout, as my horses were tired. He replied that the Cape Police would do so. We rode along the road in a column of fours, when on reaching a dam at a farmhouse I ordered the men to water their horses. All rode in to the edge of the dam, as did Maj. Paris and Capt. Gorton, when suddenly a shower of bullets came over us from the ridge about 300 yards in advance. One of the New Zealand contingent was killed a little beyond us. We immediately galloped over the ridge on the right, but the Boers had cleared after firing at us.

We then marched on and camped at a farmhouse in the flat. A strong picket of imperial yeomanry had been left on a plateau about 1 500 yard to the west of the camp; the horses were securely picketed, when I heard shots in the direction of the plateau, and on rising (for I had been resting alongside of the wagon) I saw men galloping from the plateau towards us, and guessing what it was, I shouted to my men to saddle up and mount at once. The men, trained to act promptly, were quickly in their saddles and followed me in straggling order, but soon were in extending line. We galloped swiftly forward, the New Zealanders following us close, through two wire fences, which my wire-cutters on the order raced forward and cut, so that we were not delayed. We gained the plateau just in time to stop the Boers from getting on to the top, and drove them pell-mell back with the loss, as we heard later, of five men wounded, three of whom died of their wounds. Had the Boers got possession of the ridge we should have had a hot time of it in camp. As the Boers retired beyond the range of our rifles, we noticed a solitary horseman riding slowly towards us, and to our surprise, when he came up found it was one of the men belonging to the column, and who had been a scout, one of my men, Page by name, but then a corporal in the DFH. He stated that he had been sent back to see about some oxen that had been left behind, when, on rounding some koppies beyond the plateau, he found himself surrounded by Boers, who relieved him of his horse, arms, ammunition, and other equipment, and took him with them; that the Boers saw the picket on the hill, and crept up to within about 500 yards and opened fire, with the result I have stated.

I left a strong picket of my own men, dismounted, leading their horses back to camp. I knew I could rely on them, and the horses could be fed in camp, as they had done their share of hard work since daylight, and it was then about midday. Maj. Paris informed me that we were to go on the next morning to meet a portion of Lord Methuen's division under Lord Erroll. We started at 3 o'clock the next morning, and just as it was light enough to see I noticed fresh wagon and cattle tracks in and along the road; it had been raining the night before, and had ceased just before we started from the camp, and the tracks were after the rain thus the trek was not far ahead. Men from the screen in front also reported the tracks of a few mounted men, and a little later, as we galloped on the track, a large body of mounted men under a ridge in our front was sighted. I called a halt, and reported back to Maj. Paris, then advanced at a walk until orders arrived. As we neared the mounted horse, and when within about 2,000 yards, firing commenced on us. I guessed they were a portion of Lord Erroll's column, and sent a man on to see; but they fired so hotly on the man that he turned and came back. Owing to Lt. Brunton, who was in charge of the left screen flank, we at last got them to understand that we were not 'Baws'. Brunton had managed to get a man well round on the left showing a white rag.

Firing into one another by our columns was not infrequent, and, in fact, I sometimes thought Tommy was not always particular what he shot at as long as there was an opportunity at something. My men had on several occasions been fired on by one or another of our columns, and on one occasion had rather a hot time for a little while under fire of Col. Plumer's guns and pompoms near Hopetown.

After meeting Lord Erroll, we returned to our camp. I omitted to state that the Boer trek, which had fled from us, were captured by Erroll's men, excepting the mounted men, who had escaped. On our arrival at camp – for we had left all our wagons, well protected, behind when we went to meet the other column – after a restful night, we trekked on to Boshoff, and then back to Kimberley. Then, after a few days, we started to join hands in a big drive on to Pietersburg. Nine columns were on this drive. We started from about twelve miles beyond Jacobsdal, the Kimberley column of the extreme left wing joining us (or rather should have been joining us); on our right was Col. Henry's column. I say should have been, but for some reason or another was not quite in touch with us. The greater part of his men consisted of the MMR, i.e., Metropolitan Mounted Rifles.

Now we had seen some, and in fact too many of this untrained kind, but nothing to equal the MMR. I wonder that Col. Henry had any hair left on his head or any sound brain cells within. What object was there in sending out such men from England? But the war revealed so much – too much!

To give my readers an idea, a number of the MMR was acting as portion of the rear guard to Col. Henry's convoy. A halt was called. The men behind dismounted and let their horses go, as they lay listlessly about on the grass. It was late in the afternoon, and the sun was about going down. The convoy had moved on; our MMR rear guard was not aware of the fact. The horses had turned about and were grazing with their heads down in the direction they had come, for the breeze was from behind, and animals invariably graze towards the wind. When suddenly the young officer in charge got up, looked round, the column was gone – was out of sight. They quickly mounted (or quickly as they could), and noticed some horsemen riding away from them. They followed backwards on their course, oblivious of wagon tracks or any other tracks. There were some men in front of them; it was all right; they followed. When suddenly the men in front of them disappeared over a rise, our young officer with his MMR appeared on the rise and dismounted to the order 'Hands up!' The Boer leader, who spoke English, said:

'Now, Gentlemen, I am sorry to have misled you, but I will not do so any further. Kindly hand over your horses and equipment. I do not want anything belonging to you privately; that you may retain.'

They were quickly relieved of all Government property.

'Now, Gentlemen,' said the polite Boer leader, 'you have been going in the wrong direction. Go back on these wagon tracks, they are big, you cannot miss them, and you will find your friends, no doubt, tonight. Goodbye, Better luck to you.'

And off they rode, leaving our officer and party of MMR to wander back and wander around in the dark.

The day was just dawning when I rose on the morning following the incident I have stated. I was sitting by the fire, for our cook was an early bird, when I heard a picket challenge on the opposite side of a little stream we had the night before camped on. Then the inner guard challenged, and then my horse guard. Immediately after a voice behind me said:

'Good morning, sir.'

I looked round and noted several men – thirteen, if I recollect rightly.

'Hello,' I said. 'Where do you spring from? MMR are you not?'

'Yes,' replied a voice, 'and we have been prisoners, and I am the officer in charge of the party.'

I said:

'Come to the fire and we shall presently have some coffee; and let your men close in too, for they must be cold; a cup of coffee each will warm them.'

The young officer sat down and gave me the story as I have told it.

Needless to say, our drive was not a success; we captured a few youths, one blind, and one maimed man. These we found at their homes; they did not know they would be wanted, they said, or they would have gone into the hills. They were captured by Col. Henry's column, who dashed forward in a most gallant manner as we neared what was supposed to be the enemy's position (without the enemy). We were very slow on the left, not at all gallant, for we knew the enemy had cleared across our front the night before. We saw the tracks of at least 300 horsemen that morning. After returning from the drive, we went to Smidt's Drift with a large convoy, part for Daniel's Kuil and for Griquatown. At Smidt's Drift Maj. Paris divided his convoy, sending on that for Griquatown in charge of Capt. Humbey, of the 74th IY [Imperial Yeomanry], with his men, about a squadron, some details of the DEOVR [probably the Duke of Edinburgh's Own Volunteer Rifles], a pompom in charge of Lt. Kidd of the Kimberley Artillery, and some other details, making a force of about 850 men; while we, with the convoy for Daniel's Kuil, went on to that place. We got safely through, but that going to Griquatown was attacked at the Rooikoppies, and had it not been for the gallantry of the 74th the convoy would certainly have been captured by the enemy. They bravely charged the ridge from which the Boers were firing about 300 yards off, and drove them off, thus gaining the position commanding the road. Their losses were about twenty-three killed and wounded, if I recollect rightly. Lt. Despard, of the 74th, did remarkably well on this occasion, as, in fact, did all the officers and men. Lt. Kidd did good work as well, not only with his pompom, but individually. Maj. Paris made a grave mistake: he had a strong body of scouts, and should have sent a troop at least with Humbey, who had no scouts with him, more especially as he knew that the enemy were in reported strong force in the neighbourhood of Griquatown.

We heard the news at Daniel's Kuil. It was first reported that the convoy had been captured; then, later, we got the correct details. We went from Daniel's Kuil to Campbell, where our wagons were left with the infantry of our column, and then went to meet Capt. Humbey returning from Griquatown, which we did at Rooikoppies, the scene of their battle and victory. Good old Irish Yeomanry! We were all sorry when you left us.

On one occasion, while away to Vryburg on leave, information was sent to me that our column was marching the day following for Pietersburg again, and that my servant, with a section of men, would be left to await my return to Kimberley camp. I returned the next day to Victoria Stables, where, by the kindness of De Beer's Company, I had my lines during the whole of the stay with the Kimberley column, in charge of my son Harry, who held the rank of Lieutenant and was my Quartermaster and Paymaster. Nothing went wrong in Harry's case – in fact, he was my mainstay in camp.

I caught up to the column that night about 9 o'clock, having got in by train about 5 p.m. We camped that night about nine miles south of Kimberley on the Paardeberg Road, and the next morning at daybreak we moved on again. I accompanied the screen myself on the left, as it was reported that the Boers were about in fair numbers. Beyond a few in the distance, we saw none to oppose us, but on nearing the river some shots came from the ridge opposite. After posting a couple of pickets on points commanding the drift on the east, I galloped with the balance of the left flank to the drift and crossed, taking possession of all the ridges near the drift; then sent a troop at full gallop to get a position at the foot of the main ridge in our front; but the fire was too much for them, and they fell back to where I was. We however succeeded, by aid of the guns which had come up, in shifting them; in fact, as we got round on their flank they cleared. The convoy got safely across, and we camped at a pan of water in the flats. About an hour after camping, some of the officers, among whom was the captain of the New Zealand Squadron, said they were anxious to see Cronje's last stand, and whether, if permission was granted by Maj. Paris, I would go with them. I agreed, and shortly after saw Maj. Paris, who said he would allow them to go, providing I went in command. I agreed, and we started about 2 p.m. One captain of the 4th Scottish Rifles, staff officer to Maj. Paris, also accompanied us. We reached the memorable camp of Gen. Cronje about an hour later, and after placing a couple of lookouts on points of vantage, I allowed the party to scatter and look for curios. We were about sixty-five all told, chiefly New Zealanders, scouts, and some Royal Welsh Fusiliers, who were attached to me under Lt. Holroyd. After spending about half an hour, I gave orders to return. The column had meanwhile gone on – and after some little difficulty I got the party collected, and we all started back through the river, when I at once extended the men and sent out the necessary scouts. When almost opposite Kitchener's Kop (so called, being the position held by Lord Kitchener during the shelling of Cronje's camp and trenches along the river banks), firing was reported on our left, and shortly after I noticed two of the four New Zealanders I had sent forward on our left point coming on at a gallop. I rode from my position in front of the men to meet them, and, as they rode up, said:

'What is the matter?'

One of them, Andrews by name, replied:

'My mate's horse is shot, sir, and I think he is wounded under the hill there,' indicating Kitchener's Kop.

'Go,' I said to the other man, whose name was Williams, 'and tell the captain, I say he must change direction to the left, so as to get round the Boer position on the Kop.'

I then said to Andrews: 'Come along,' and rode at a fast gallop for the ridge with only my servant and Andrews with me, never doubting that my order would have been obeyed. I was barely 300 yards from the captain and the men when my servant suddenly said:

'They are running away, sir!'

I looked around and sure enough the whole of the men were galloping in the opposite direction.

'You go,' I said to him, 'and tell the captain, they must come to my assistance with the men.'

A few bullets were passing over our heads in the direction of the retreating party.

The captain was near me when I galloped to the left to meet the two men. Had my orders been carried out, the left flank of the men would have been immediately behind me, and the whole position would have been different, as the result proved – for they rode right into a trap and lost several men wounded and taken prisoners in the wild and disgraceful flight.

On getting about 100 yards from the Kop we saw the wounded man Atkinson walking slowly down the foot of the hill, but he suddenly dropped. I saw nothing could be done, and galloped along the foot of the hill in the direction the column had gone. The fire was directed on us by the Boers, and the bullets came thick and fast from the summit of the hill.

Andrews' horse was shot dead under him. I drew in, and he walked alongside my horse; we were neither of us hit, though the fire continued for several minutes on us after the horse fell, then suddenly stopped, which I thought strange, as we were still within easy range. We had barely gone 500 yards from where Andrews' horse was killed when three Boers dressed in khaki suddenly rose from behind some boulders. I said: 'There are three of the scouts,' taking them to be three of our men I had sent on in our immediate front. Being some 300 or 400 yards, I could not distinguish clearly. A shout of 'Hands up!' and the sight of several rifles pointing at us over the rocks proved I was wrong. It was 'Hands up!' and boiling with rage and disgust, we became prisoners, and were immediately rushed. They were a party of nine – all youngsters but one, a grey-haired and bearded man. While two were taking my leggings and spurs off, and quarrelling over them, one snatched off my glasses, which hung round my body; another my Kodak, while another brute dragged me around by my cross-belt, which he proceeded to take off in a manner that roused my temper, which I showed in a manner most plain.

'What is your name, you old . . . ?' the fellow asked in broken English, for I pretended not to understand Dutch.

'Oh! Smith will do for you,' I replied; and so I remained Capt. Smith to them.

Had they known who I was, I might have had worse treatment, for I was known to the Boers as the Scout leader of the Kimberley Column and we had given them some rough times and were never beaten.

In my demonstrating rather too plainly to the fellow my opinion of him, he raised his rifle from the ground where he had placed it, and said in Dutch to the others, 'Give way while I shoot him.' But the elderly man interfered and saved me. We were shortly after taken to the back of the hill where some others of their party were with their horses. I ascertained from one of the lot – a Cape lad – that they were sixteen all told, and had been placed on the hill by the commandant, Jacobs, who had gone down to the drift we had crossed in the morning, and that our party had ridden right into an ambush for Jacobs had seen them coming.

'Why did your men run away from sixteen rifles?' he asked.

'I do not know,' I replied. I presume they got the orders to do so.

'They were a lot of cowards to leave you,' he said.

'No, the men are not cowards; there is a mistake made by someone. My men never run away unless there is a great need of it,' I replied.

While we were waiting for orders from their leader, Jacobs, the fellow who had treated me so roughly a short time before came up, and several others with him, bringing five more of our men prisoners, and as he dismounted near us, said:

'Where is that . . . officer who cursed me?'

'Here I am,' I replied and walked up to him.

I knew the class of man he was – a cowardly bounce – and stood before him with my arms folded across my breast.

'I will blow your brains out,' he said.

'You dare not, you cowardly cur! All such as you can do is to insult prisoners, and lay behind rocks and fire while your carcasses are in safety. You would shoot me if you dared for I am unarmed and cannot defend myself; but you know that your own people do not allow cold-blooded murders. And how would your men fare that are captured if you shot prisoners?' I said.

The old man stood close to me again and interfered, saying to me at the same time:

'I will protect you and inform the Commandant about this man's conduct towards you.'

Shortly after this man rode up and said that we were to march; that the Commandant had gone on with the other men to the drift. We all walked a short distance down through the rocks. A horse was then given to me; the other prisoners were marched on foot. On crossing the drift three men rode past us from the rear. I heard one of them say:

'What are you going to do with the Khaki's Commandant?'

'They will all be shot tomorrow. It is Gen. de Wet's orders that any of the enemy caught of a column that must have burnt houses are to be shot; and if I am satisfied that it is a house that they burnt at the drift, I shall shoot them all.'

They passed on and I could hear no more, but had heard quite enough. I did not tell the other prisoners, among whom was Sgt. Pearse of the Royal Welsh Fusiliers. We rode on for about a mile, and then halted and camped for the night; the horses were hobbled and guards put on. We were all placed together near an ant heap, guarded by four men. One of our guards was most friendly, and spoke English fairly well. He informed me that Jacobs had not gone as far as the drift, that he saw our party had halted on the ridges east, and that when our men bolted he laid low until they got close, and opened fire on them, and that several of our party were killed and wounded, and several horses of ours were also shot, and that he believed that the commandant was going down in the morning to see if our column had burnt any houses, and that if it was the case, we would be shot.

I must here state that after clearing the Boers out of the ridges in the morning, we noticed a dense smoke rising at the drift – there were farmhouses on both sides – and I remarked at the time to one of my officers: 'Surely that is not a house burning' for our column did not burn houses or do unnecessary destruction. Maj. Paris was opposed to such acts of barbarism, and so was I; such are not in keeping with a white man's war, unless necessary in cases of treachery or otherwise. When the column arrived at our camping place, I ascertained that no houses were burnt, only a lot of chaff found in a hut, but later heard that some of our natives had burnt a house.

I had been suffering from colic during the afternoon and that night suffered severely. Our guards did what they could for me, but I past a bad night, towards morning I felt better. About daybreak Commandant Jacobs rode back, and I was told had gone to see if any houses had been burnt, and that we should meanwhile move further on to a farm a few miles ahead, which we shortly afterwards did and saddled off. Here, after a little palaver, a beaker of cocoa was given each of the prisoners, and some boiled green mealies. We enjoyed both considerably, we were all very hungry, having had nothing since the day before at noon.

About two hours after our arrival at the farm, a messenger arrived from Jacobs with the order that we were to proceed to Jagt Pan, south of Boshoff.

While halting at the farm, I constantly watched the hills in front and listened for the boom of cannon, for I felt sure a strong party would come in search of us; but we were doomed to disappointment, in spite of the fact our column was a strong one. I knew my men, now under the command of Capt. Browne (my son-in-law), would not leave me a prisoner if they could help it.

I was sent on horseback in charge of one guard; the man had been in the Free State artillery and had been wounded in the affair the day before through the calf of the leg; he showed me the wound, but did not appear to mind it. His name was Van der Merwe, he spoke English fairly, was kind, communicative and intelligent. As we were riding along he said:

'But I think you can talk Dutch, your eyes and your manner show me you are an Afrikaner.'

I replied in Dutch, saying:

'Yes, I am as you hear, I do speak and understand your language, read and write it as well, but I did not care to do so before.'

He laughed and said:

'You were 'slim' for our people are very bitter against the Cape Colonials who are fighting against us. Why did your people not remain neutral, and we should easily beat the English. You are like ourselves, you know the country and our mode of fighting. We fear your colonial forces. Your raw English we can manage, except your Tommy, your regular infantry soldiers; he can fight, he is a man and does not fear death.'

'Yes,' I replied, 'all are not equally trained, and I am glad you give Tommy his due; he is the best soldier we have of our regular forces, and what England wants more of is mounted infantry, men well-trained in both ways.'

He made disparaging remarks about the imperial officers, who he said, as a rule, do not understand their work. I passed this off, not wishing to show that I agreed with him on that point, which, alas, was only too true in so many cases. But this does not apply to all, for I have met some very fine officers, who were gentlemen besides.

Riding up to the man, who was on lookout point, he addressed him as follows: [attempting to imitate an English officer's accent]

'I say, you fellah, any 'Bahs' about?'

'What, Bahs! Yes, any quantity. Look over there, eyeglass. Get another pane [eyeglass] up, and you'll see a thousand or more woolies (sheep) over yonder.'

Then that young officer left.

After riding for about nine miles, we arrived at Van Zyl's farm, situated under some hills. The owner was an elderly man, who, after shaking hands most cordially with me, asked us into his house, where his wife, a quiet, good-natured sort, quickly set the table and brought us some food. Van Zyl sat talking to us at the table, and remarked to me that he hoped I would feel myself at home and not consider myself a prisoner in his house.

'You and I,' he said, 'cannot help these things. We are not the cause of the war; it is Rhodes' war, it is a war caused by the capitalists of the Rand. We only must do our duty, though we suffer for it, you for your side, I for mine.'

We remained at the hospitable farmer's house that night, as the other prisoners, who were on foot, did not arrive until some time after, and time was evidently no object. A most comfortable bed was given me, and the men were all cared for as well as lay in Van Zyl and his wife's power.

The next morning we went on to Jagt Pan, my guard Van der Merwe, and myself, going on ahead on horseback. As we came in sight of the pan, he said:

'Do you see that little koppie standing by itself over yonder, about nine or ten miles away?'

I said:

'Yes.'

'Well,' he said, 'if I were a prisoner and in your place, I would make my escape from Jagt Pan and go straight for that koppie; from there you can see Boshoff, which is only a few miles from it, that is just to the left of Villebois Kop.' (Meaning the Kop where the French officer Villebois de Muriel fell.)

'Thank you,' I replied, 'I do not think I shall try yet,' only too glad that I should have been to affect my escape, but I could not leave the men, and I knew that if all tried to escape we should not succeed.

We arrived at a house on the farm Jagt Pan, belonging to Ben Groenwald, who, with his wife and family, were very kind – in fact, no friends could have treated me with greater kindness. We remained at the Groenwald's place for three days. At night all were placed in a room leading off the stoep under the verandah in front of the house, but during the day I was free to wander about anywhere, having given my word that I would not try to escape. On the fourth day, it was a Sunday morning, we were all marched off north, and I was told we should meet Jacobs the next morning at an empty store about six miles distant. We camped at the store that night, and the next morning Commandant Jacobs arrived with his secretary, who spoke English well. I was called into the store, and, after greeting me, he said:

'I have orders to send you and the other officer' indicating Sgt. Pearse, (who had been called in with me) 'to see Gen. de Wet, and the other men will be let go free.'

I said:

'But why are you keeping the Sergeant? He is not an officer. Why not let him go as well?'

The sergeant touched me and said:

'No, sir, I go with you.'

I was allowed to write a letter home to Vryburg, which was first read by the secretary. Shortly after the other prisoners were sent off with a few mounted Boers, to be released near the colonial border on the road to Kimberley, and about an hour after a cart was driven up, we started on our way to somewhere. We were told that we were going to Gen. de Wet; but I cared not where it was. I had made up my mind now to escape; there were only two of us, and it could easier be affected than by having a lot together. Our first halt was at a farm about two hours (twelve miles) north of Boshoff, where we stayed that night and slept in an old wool shed on some bales of wool. The treatment here was by no means what we had experienced at Groenwald's or Van Zyl's. However, we got some food – meat only. We did not feel starved. The next morning at 6 o'clock we proceeded on our way with a fresh driver, and arrived at Bultfontein about 3 o'clock in the afternoon, and were at once sent over to the jail – the jailer went with us. I remonstrated with him as he opened a cell door and told us we were to go in.

'Who is in charge here?' I asked.

'The Landdrost Meneer Hugo,' he replied.

'Well, go and ask the Landdrost if I may see him.'

We were locked in the dark cell, no light, except what streaks came from a grating near the roof and through the chinks of the door. About half an hour later we heard voices outside, and then the key grated in the lock and the door was opened, letting in daylight once more, and with the jailer was Mr Hugo, the Landdrost. After introducing myself and my companion, I spoke about our being placed in jail; that we were not criminals but prisoners-of-war.

'Well,' he replied, speaking in English, 'my orders are to keep you both in jail, but I will take it upon myself to let you out during the day, and at night you will have to sleep in jail.'

We were allowed to accompany him over to the courthouse, where some food was brought us in a back room. We were not allowed to go any distance from the courthouse. A guard armed was always near us on the first day; the second day we were allowed greater freedom, and the third day we were not guarded at all. On the morning of the fourth day, about 10 o'clock, I noticed that there were several carts and horsemen in the village, and little knots of men were standing talking together, and remarked to Sgt. Pearse that they evidently scented danger, and that it was more than likely than one of our columns was in the vicinity. A young man standing nearby, whom I noticed before sitting reading in front of the courthouse, overheard what I said and remarked:

'You are, I believe, right, and they might turn up today.'

I made no remark, as I was wary and did not know who or what he was, but found out the same day from our jailer that he too was a prisoner, one of the National Scouts, who had been captured near Bloemfontein; that his case had been referred to De Wet; that the reply had come that day, and the next morning he was to be sent to Commandant-General Badenhorst for trial; that he probably would be shot, as he was a Cape Colonist who had assisted in the early part of the war, but had surrendered to Lord Roberts at Bloemfontein and then joined the National Scouts. Great bitterness, of course, existed among the Boers against his class.

I omitted to mention that we stopped a night, on our way to Bultfontein, at the house of Commandant-General Badenhorst. The wind blew very cold during the evening. We were placed alongside a cart in the open, with orders that we were not to move away from there or we would be shot. About 8 o'clock one of the guards came out from the open door of the house, which commanded a good view of us at the cart. I said:

'I wish you would ask your Commandant whether it is his custom to treat prisoners-of-war as he is treating us, and ask him to let us have a sail, or anything, as we have no blankets.'

He went inside and came out again directly, saying:

'The Commandant says that people who go to fight should take blankets with them.'

'You can tell your Commandant,' I replied, 'that he should teach his burgers better than to take all private belonging of prisoners-of-war.'

However, shortly after, an old Cape boy came near the cart and said in Dutch:

'Sir, shall I bring you a buck sail? There is one close by on that wagon.'

I said:

'Yes, bring it, for we are cold.'

The old boy brought the sail, and we were all right under its folds. A little after a white boy, about 12 years of age, brought us some meat and pumpkin in a tin dish without knives or forks, saying:

'Here, Khakis, is your food,' and threw it down near us.

On finding there were no knives or forks, I said:

'Bring us something to eat the food with.'

'Eat with your fingers,' he said, and went away.

I did not forget that place.

I digressed from details of my story of our experiences at Bultfontein. While speaking to the jailer about the unfortunate young man, who, I was informed, was a friend of Hugo, the Landdrost, and that he was pleading for him, I noticed the magistrate go hurriedly past into his private office, and followed him. As I entered, he said:

'Captain Smith, I'm going to send you away today to Theron's laager, who will send you on to near Smaldeel, where you will both be let go.'

I thanked him. Interrupting me, he said:

'Circumstances over which I have no command may place me in a similar position you are in today, and I may need your help.'

'If ever I am in a position to be of service to you, Mr Hugo, you may command it, and I can assure you it will give me great pleasure to be of use to you, as some return for your kindness to my companion and myself,' I replied.

I then went out and told Sgt. Pearse the good news. About an hour later, after we had finished our midday meal, the cart drove up which had to convey us to our freedom, and, after bidding farewell to the Landdrost, we started with the driver and one guard. On our way I conversed in Dutch with the guard, who rode beside the cart. Among other questions he put me was, 'Whether do you know Dennison of Dennison Scouts?'

'Yes,' I replied, 'I know him very well. He belongs to the Kimberley Column.'

'And where was he when you saw him last?' he queried.

I hesitate to remember when I last saw a mirror and replied:

'With the Kimberley Column on the 29th April.'

'Well,' he said, 'if we can only catch him, we shall be very glad, for we never get a chance when his scouts are with the English, and we know he is an Afrikaner like ourselves.'

'And what would your people do with him?' I asked.

'Some might shoot him at once, but not if any of the leaders were present. They would send him away to some safe place until the war was over.'

I nice prospect, I thought, if I should meet any Boer who knows me. But my lucky star was in the ascent, we met no one who knew me.

On arriving near Theron's camp about sundown, our guard rode off to the camp and told the other man to span out, that he would soon be back. He returned in about half an hour with two other men and a lead horse, and said:

'They will send two horses saddled for you directly.'

We waited, and at last, became impatient, I said:

'We can walk on so long, if you will direct us the road, and when you catch up to us with the other horses we can mount and ride on with you.'

'Very good,' said one of the two men, 'Do – we shall soon follow you; keep the road you are now on,' for we were standing in the road.

We bid goodbye to our guard and cart driver and walked on. It was a bright moonlight evening, and the air was refreshing. We had barely got on top of the rise above the valley we had left when the two men caught up to us with one horse only, and no saddle or bridle. They said the horses had evidently gone astray, as they had not yet arrived, but that if we could both mount the one horse bare back it would help us to make distance.

'Very well,' I said, 'no help for it; come along, Pearse,' and I leapt on to the horse, which was quiet quite.

And after some difficulty and much laughter, Pearse managed to get on board, and away we went at a slow canter, but after about two miles of it I said:

''Tis far enough, thank you, I prefer tramping,' and I knew poor Pearce felt very much in that direction as well.

'All right,' said one of the men.

We halted and all dismounted. Then, after I had been well-posted as to the road, which to take and which to leave – which, by the way, a Dutchman can describe in Dutch better and more explicitly than an Englishman can in Dutch or English, we bade goodbye to our guards and walked on in the cool moonlit air. After about two hours good walking, we saw a light in the distance which I remarked to my companion would be the farmhouse described to us by the two men, and there is the sluit where our road turns off. After walking on slowly a bit we found the road turning off to the right we had been told to take, which would lead us to the house. We walked on for about half an hour, and on getting within fifty yards of the dwelling, a little boy came out carrying a tin can, and on seeing us ran back to the front door at once which was the customary half-door of a primitive farmhouse, and leaning over he called:

'*Ma, hier is twee menschen.*' ('Ma, here are two men.')

A woman came to the door.

'Good evening,' I said, but she immediately withdrew and spoke to her husband, who came forward and greeted us in a most suspicious manner.

I explained our position and was not surprised at the action of the man or woman, for we were odd-looking mortals no doubt with the torn Boer hats on and no leggings. However, the man, on my telling him who we were, cordially asked us inside, and, while his wife got us some food, I briefly told him our story, and said:

'Now we shall want to start over to the railway siding' (which he had explained to me was Eensogevonden, south of Smaldeel) 'at daylight.'

'You shall not walk,' he said, 'for I have carts and horses, and will drive you over, and we can start after coffee, for there is a lot of time, as the train is due only at 9 o'clock.'

We might easily have walked on the night before to the camp at the siding, but I feared the pickets, who so often fire indiscriminately at any moving object at night. The two men who left us the night before had told us of this farmer, who they said, was a 'Loyal', meaning one who was friendly to the British, and directed us to him and the siding at Eensogevonden, as they said it was nearer than Smaldeel and the best route for us to take.

After finishing a hearty meal we sat talking to our kind host and his wife, and then turned in, a comfortable bed having been made up for us, and we slept soundly till the morning, when we started for the railway siding about 7 o'clock with the kind farmer in his cart, and arrived there about half an hour later, where we found a detachment of the North Lancashire Regiment, from whose officer, acting as Commandant, I received the necessary permits. The train from the north arrived about 9.30 and we started for Brandfort, and then on to Bloemfontein. On arriving at the latter place I immediately reported to Headquarters, and met Gen. Tucker, whom I had known in Pretoria previous to 1881 as 'good old Dan Tucker'. Every kindness was shown me at Bloemfontein, where I succeeded in equipping again, and then left by train for Kimberley. On arriving at De Aar I heard shouting as the train drew up to the platform, and heard my name distinctly so amid the noise, and, as I got out, was at once surrounded by the officers and men of the New Zealand Contingent, who were with the Kimberley Column when I was taken prisoner. A hearty shake of the hand from the officers, and such of the others who could reach me, while cheering welcomed me on all sides. They were going home, I heard with regret, for no corps had the scouts worked so well as with that of New Zealand – all good capable men and officers and friends besides. After partaking of some refreshment, their train left, conveying as fine a body of men – of the colonies abroad – back

223

home as served during the war in South Africa.

At the different stations all along the line I was met by hearty welcomes, and on my arrival in Kimberley not less so, as in camp a hearty cheer greeted me. I was once more among my men, and left a day or two after for Boshoff, at which place it was intended that I should attend the Court of Inquiry; but after agreeing the court should be held there, I ascertained that it was not for certain reasons wise. I thus requested that the court might be convened at Kimberley, to which Maj. Paris agreed. I heard of the evidence given at the inquiry on the other released prisoners, and that decided me, for one certain officer had tried to clear himself at my expense. On our return to Kimberley, the inquiry on myself was held, which did not, by any means, reflect credit on the officer in question, who shortly after left South Africa, and South Africa suffered no loss. Suffice it to say I was exonerated from any blame. A few days after I got leave to go to Vryburg on a visit to my family.

During my absence the Column marched for the Hoopstad district, and had an engagement with the combined commandos of Commandant-General Badenhorst and Commandants Jacobs and Erasmus, and drove them off, effecting considerable loss on the enemy. On this occasion four scouts were taken by the Boers, two of which – Hoffman and Hannay – both slightly off-coloured, were shot in cold blood; the other two were with the Boer wagons a few days later which were captured by De Lisle's column, and the two men released and sent back to Kimberley, where they rejoined the column. The engagement mentioned took place on Commandant-General Badenhorst's farm. On retiring after the engagement, the scouts were left to cover the rear, and, knowing the treatment meted me by Badenhorst they destroyed the house. Having found some gunpowder, they placed it under an organ in the house, after breaking up all that could be found to burn and packing it on top of the organ, they laid a train and ignited it. An amusing sketch was made by the late Lt. Nescham showing the blowing up of this house, and the Assistant Provost-Marshal going, both himself and his horse, coat, arms and all, back to discover the cause (for, as I have said before, house burning was not allowed on our column). The sketch in question was underlined with the words, 'Let's scatter and go, here comes the Provost'. Many were the amusing sketches made by poor Nescham during the war, a collection of which is in my possession.

I rejoined the column at Schmidt's Drift, and not very long after we started for Griquatown again with a convoy of wagons, and after safely delivering the stores at Griquatown we went on to Langburg, which Maj. Paris was determined to see. We had some skirmishing with Boers on the way and experienced a night attack besides, which was severe while it lasted. Two of our infantry picket were killed and a couple wounded. Our animals suffered severely; on my lines alone nine horses were killed and the yeomanry also lost heavily in horses. The night attack was near Postmasburg. We returned to about four or five miles south of Post-masburg, and left the majority of our wagons and marched for Langburg, arriving in full view of the apparently smooth rocky range. Our force consisted of detachments of the 74th IY, Diamond Fields Horse, Kimberley Light Horse, Ashburners Light Horse, my Scouts, two 15-pounders in charge of Lt. Nescham and about 400 mounted men besides the artillery. Also one pompom in charge of Lt. Kidd, DFA. Just before we got to the thorns at the foot of the mountain range, a troop of horses were seen being rapidly driven by some horsemen, followed by a cart, about two miles on our left in the direction of Langburg. The guns were brought to bear on them, on which the horsemen galloped off, leading them, while the cart with six horses harnessed to it succeeded, with the horsemen, in reaching the cover of the bush, and escaped. Despard of the 74th brought the horses in with a few of his men. When we got on to the level in the thorns, I noticed fresh tracks of horses, cattle, sheep, and goats everywhere; but no animals could I see anywhere and not a sound was heard, save the noise made by our men and horses – the gloom was ominous. Capt. Gorton rode up and joined me.

'You will, of course, close in directly and water your horses first,' he said (for we had been informed that we should get water at a dam near the foot of the pass in front of us called Winter Hoek).

'Not yet,' I replied. 'I do not like the look of things; too many spoors about here.'

'True, there does not appear to be much cover on the sides of the mountain; but we will know directly.'

He left me and rode forward; barely had he gone a few minutes, when a rattling fire was poured on us. The screen extended for about a mile in front of me, and the men dropped off their horses as usual and held their ground as soon as the firing started. Maj. Paris had also ridden up, thinking all was safe. I hastily dismounted and sent my horse back with my servant, then got all the horses back out of range of fire; we were about

800 yards from the Boers on the mountainside. The guns – two 15-pounders and a pompom – opened fire under the heavy pelting from the enemy, and under it all Lt. Nescham and his men coolly directed the fire of his guns, and Kidd with his pompom did the same. One of the guns was sent back some distance to get into a better position and cover our flanks, while the Kimberley Light Horse held some koppies covering our rear and flanks as well. The fire was returned hot and continuous from our side, but beyond a few Boers that crept over the pass or nek in a footpath, we saw no others in our front. The mountainside looked smooth, but had evidently many crevices from which the Boers were firing. Three of my men of the screen were wounded at the commencement of the firing and nine horses killed. Capt. Gorton, we presumed, had either been made a prisoner or been hit, as we could see nothing of him, and some time after ascertained, through one of the screen, that he was lying in the gorge, whether killed or wounded I could not ascertain. Some of my men tried to reach him, but could not on account of the heavy fire.

A dash forward was made by my left flank, under Lt. Brunton, and by the 74th, under Capt. Humby, on the right; but as nothing could be gained they were not allowed to advance again after the first run forward, but held the ground they had gained, lying flat in extended order. A man lying flat, even on bare veld is seldom hit, and they should never be too close together.

After about two hours' firing, Maj. Paris gave orders to retire, which was done without any confusion or unnecessary haste. Nothing was left behind that could be brought out. My wounded were fetched out by the ambulance, but Capt. Gorton was in the hands of the Boers. He had gone too far, and did not realise any danger until too late.

We got well out of range of the Boer rifles and then off-saddled. Capt. Gorton's servant was sent back by Maj. Paris with a white flag, and met some men of 'Conry's', a colonial rebel (the commando was that of De Villiers under whom Conry was serving; the whole lot were, in fact, rebels), bringing Gorton out. He was wounded through the flesh of the thigh. We were all pleased to see him so well out of it, for he was a most popular and good officer.

Maj. Paris had had his way; he had been to Langburg and come back again. Again and again he had expressed a wish to attack it, and had always been advised by myself and others who knew it, not to attempt Langburg, where a few Boers could defy an army. It required at least three good columns to sweep the long and almost inaccessible mountain range. Gen. Pretyman, then GOC, at Kimberley, had spoken to me before I followed the column, to which I caught up at Smitsdrift, about Langburg. I told him what I have above stated. He said:

'Tell Paris to keep away from it; he can do no good there.'

I told Maj. Paris, but what orders he got later I do no know. However, what might have been rather a serious affair for us turned out better than might have been. We arrived at our camp the next evening, and were met by the officer left in charge, who gave Maj. Paris some letters and then a wire to me, saying at the same time, 'I'm afraid this contains very bad news for you.' I would not look at it there, and not until I had left them and walked away did I open the envelope and read of my eldest son's death. I felt the blow almost too much to bear, and walked away beyond my lines to recover myself. The second boy gone in this war, both having fallen fighting for our cause, and both shot by rebels! My readers can better realise my feelings than I can describe them, and care not to dwell on the subject.

I got leave to go to Vryburg, and left the column between Campbell and Smitsdrift on our return in company with Maj. T. Rogers, DSO, of the Diamond Fields Horse, a fine man and good officer. We arrived at Kimberley the day following. It was on a Sunday morning. I got a warrant the next day and proceeded to Vryburg by train. After hearing particulars, and spending two days with my heartbroken daughter-in-law and her two little ones, I returned to Kimberley, and got further leave from Col. Garstin, who had succeeded Gen. Pretyman as GOC of the Kimberley District, to proceed to Grahamstown, where my wife and daughter were staying. While in Grahamstown I got a letter from Kimberley informing me that it was Lord Kitchener's wish that one regiment should be formed from the different units of the Regulars, and asking me whether, in the case the command was offered me, I would accept. I replied in the affirmative. Then after spending a few days with my family, including my eldest daughter and her little ones, at Port Alfred, we returned to Grahamstown, and I came on to Kimberley, and at once reported to Col. Garstin, who I found always most kind, and believe him to be a good soldier and a good Christian besides. Col. Garstin made no distinction between Regulars and Irregulars; if an officer or man did his duty, it was all the same to him what corps he belonged to. He proved a good superior and kind friend to me.

I was shortly after offered command of the combined units and accepted it, but a few days later got a similar offer from the CSO of Lord Methuen for the Vryburg District, and as it had always been my wish to work in my own district, I got permission from Col. Garstin to withdraw my acceptance of his offer and accept that of Lord Methuen, and left for Vryburg at once, and then on to Mafeking, where I met Col. Belfield, Lord Methuen's Chief Staff Officer, and after arranging some details returned to my quarters at the hotel. While in conversation with him the next day at his office a wire was brought in from the Commander-in-Chief (Lord Kitchener) that I was to go up to Pretoria at once, as he wished to see me. I started off by the next train for Pretoria, and arrived there on a Sunday, and reported the same day at Headquarters, where I was informed the Commander-in-Chief would see me the next day at 9 a.m. I spent the remainder of the day in visiting my friends, after having moved over to my sister's, who, with her husband and family, had lived in Pretoria for many years, and had also suffered in the earlier war of 1881, as so many of us had done.

The next morning at 9 o'clock I was at Headquarters, where, after waiting a short time in one of the offices, I was sent for by Lord Kitchener, who, on my saluting him as I entered, immediately rose from the table he was sitting at and, shaking hands with me, requested me to be seated. I read Lord Kitchener's face and formed the opinion of his character, and have no reason to think I was wrong. among other qualities, I felt sure he possessed a kind heart, which a casual observer might not suspect was hidden under the hard exterior. He told me his object in sending for me, and then gave me confidential orders regarding the rebels. I felt dissatisfied as I had looked forward to being put in a position to clear the Vryburg District; but I made up my mind to carry out the instructions given as fully as lay in my power, distasteful though the duty was. After Lord Kitchener's office, I had an interview with his Chief Staff Officer, Gen. Ian Hamilton, whom I found to be a most perfect gentleman in manners; and I felt also that I had met a soldier and a man on whom one could rely. We talked of the war of 1881, in which he took part and was wounded in the wrist at Amajuba.

On my return to Vryburg I was informed that 200 horses had been picked for me at the remount, Kimberley.

'And what am I to do with horses without men?' I asked. 'Lord Kitchener does not wish me to raise a force at present.'

'Not so,' said the officer who informed me about the horses, 'Lord

Methuen has arranged with the 'Chief' and you are to recruit at once.'

A few days later I got orders to proceed to Kimberley, there to meet Lord Methuen whom I met in the presence of Col. Garstin at the Kimberley Club, and was ordered by Lord Methuen to start recruiting at once. Matters were arranged with Col. Garstin about recruiting in Kimberley. All arrangements were made, and men engaged to recruit. I then returned to Vryburg to carry out Lord Kitchener's instructions, and started recruiting there as well, when suddenly I was sent for one morning to the staff office, and informed by Col. Vyvyan, CSO, to Lord Methuen, that Lord Kitchener objected to my raising a force at present. I met Lord Methuen a few days later, on his return from Kimberley. He said:

'Why did you call the force you are raising "The Western Border Rifles"? Why did you not stick to the old name, Dennison Scouts?'

'Dennison Scouts now form part of the Kimberley Regiment,' I replied, 'and the name "Western Border Rifles" was thought appropriate.'

'You must change the name to "Dennison Scouts",' the General replied, 'and all will be well; but put your shoulder to the wheel, and get men as quickly as you can.'

'Very good, sir,' I said, saluted, and retired to my camp, immediately paraded my men – about seventy-five all told – and told them the name of the corps was changed, that the old title would be used in future, and all willing to remain on under the altered circumstances were to step forward. The whole line immediately did so with three cheers, for the old title was the popular one. Thus from the 'Western Border Rifles' we became 'Dennison Scouts' again.

Men arrived from Kimberley, and recruiting was briskly carried on for a few days, when I was again sent for by the GSO, Col. Vyvyan, who said:

'I am very sorry, Maj. Dennison, to have to inform you that Lord Kitchener adheres to his former wire, and you will have to disband your men.'

I knew that Col. Vyvyan felt for me and also that in him I had a friend and one worth having – an officer respected by all who knew him, and one who had taken a most prominent part in the defence of Mafeking, though he, like so many others, did not get the credit deserved during the siege of that place.

When I got this, another rebuff, I felt hot, and said:

'Well, Colonel, where am I? I feel as if I were between the devil and deep blue ocean.'

229

However, there was no help for it; I had to disband, but meantime wrote a semi-private letter to Gen. Ian Hamilton informing him of my position, and also an official statement of my case, with a short allusion to past services, of which I give a verbatim copy as follows:

'CSO Headquarters Staff, Pretoria.
Perhaps the circumstances of my case are not fully known to the Commander-in-Chief, I therefore take the liberty of stating them in detail, as I am sure that when Lord Kitchener knows all he cannot fail to see that it is worthy of consideration.'

In December last, while on our way to Daniel's Kuil, I received the following wire from Kimberley:

'OC Kimberley District, to Major Dennison, Schmidt's Drift, December 9th, WE.398.
Intend to combine three local corps in district. In this case you will accept command on the understanding that your operations are confined to this district? Only please reply at once.'

Which I accepted. On my return to Kimberley I received from Col. Belfield a wire, offering me the same command under Lord Methuen, which, as I belonged to the Vryburg, and was most anxious to work there, I accepted, I accepted conditionally.
Correspondence as follows:

'CSOWD., Mafeking, to Major Dennison, Major Paris' Column, W. Road. 21st December, C.956.
A local regiment is being formed in this district to include Cullinan's Horse, Keely's Squadron, Brown's Squadron and others that may eventually be raised up to it is hoped a total of 600. Knowing you are anxious to return to Vryburg, which would be headquarters, this regiment and your local knowledge would be of greatest service, and all above corps have expressed willingness to serve under you, would you be willing to accept command FOC Kimberley has no objection? If you agree please communicate with me, and lay the matter before OC Kimberley District.'

To which I replied as follows:

'Major Dennison to CSOWD, Mafeking,
December 22nd.
I gladly accept if matters can be arranged. OC Kimberley District
is at present away; expected back today.'

I then wrote to CSO, Kimberley, on 23rd December, 1901, as
follows:

'Annexed wire from CSO, Mafeking, I am willing to accept
provided OC agrees to waive his claim on my services. I consider
Vryburg has a prior claim on me. Have wired as follows to
CSOWD, Mafeking: I gladly accept if it can be arranged. OC
Kimberley is at present away; expected back today.'

To which I got the following reply:

'The OC District will place no impediment in the way of your
accepting this offer.
(Signed) P. Holland Pryor. SCO, Major
Dated: Kimberley 23/12/01'

I went to Mafeking during the latter end of December last and met
Col. Belfield, CSOWD, who informed me that as two of the units
mentioned in his wire of the 21st December had been taken over by
the Cape Government, there would be a difficulty. Later on I met
Lord Methuen, on the 8th January, 1902, and Col. Belfield, in
Vryburg, when the whole matter was talked over and arranged,
pending confirmation by the Commander-in-Chief. I returned to
Kimberley, and there received the following wire on the
11th January, 1902:

'CSOWD,
Major Dennison, Kimberley.
Date: 11th January.
For some reason, of which Lord Methuen is unaware, Chief has
refused sanction to formation mounted corps this district.'

I then wired to CSOWD asking what I was to do, and also wrote to Lord Methuen and Col. Belfield, receiving no replies. Then went to Mafeking, on the 25th January, saw Col. Belfield, who told me he was awaiting communication from Lord Methuen about the proposed corps. I returned to Vryburg on 26th January. On the 28th I got an order to proceed to Pretoria, as the Chief wished to see me. I proceeded to Pretoria on the 29th January, arriving there on the 2nd February. I met Lord Kitchener on the 3rd, who gave me instructions re special work which I am now carrying out. On my return to Vryburg I was informed that 200 horses were awaiting me in Kimberley. On the 12th February I got from Col. Vyvyan CSOWD, the following wire:

'I have wired to GOC for definite instructions as to conditions of enrolment, pay, and establishment of corps, also about half-castes. Engage as many white men as you can get, but do not take half-castes at present.'

I then commenced recruiting; met Lord Methuen in Kimberley with Col. Garstin on the 17th February, when matters were settled. I was to recruit about a hundred men, white and coloured, when I was told on the 5th instant by Col. Vyvyan that it was finally decided, by order of the Commander-in-Chief, that the corps was not to be formed, and that the men enrolled could either join other corps or take their discharge. This is being done and I am stranded.

I served in 1879 in Zululand as second-in-command to the late Col. Weatherley, of the Border Horse, under Col. Sir. E. Wood. When Col. Weatherley fell I was appointed to command, and served in that capacity throughout the war with Secocoeni, under Gen. Sir Garnet Wolseley. During the Boer War of 1881 I kept open communication personally with the assistance of two native boys between Pretoria and Rustenburg garrisons until the cessation of hostilities. I lost my all during that war. Prior to the present war I was in charge of the Intelligence Department of this district. The day the Boers were expected at Vryburg I went to Kuruman and, acting on instructions from Col. Kekewich, assisted in the defence of that place with sixty-three men, under Capt. Bates, CP, and myself. We successfully defended the place against 800 and 1,350 Boers for seven weeks, were forced to surrender when a gun was brought to bear on us (we had nothing but small arms). One third of our force was hit, including myself. I was five months a prisoner-of-war in Pretoria. Then served as assistant MC of Rustenburg and Zeerust until the evacuation of both places. Then raised the corps of scouts which I have ever since commanded. What they have done is too well-known to require any comment from me, suffice to say that the Kimberley Column has never had a reverse while my scouts were with them, which can be borne out by Col. Milne, Gen. Pretyman, Col. Carstin, and Maj. Paris. I have tried to do my duty, have lost two sons in the war, and am still able and willing to work to the end. As I have curtly as possible sketched my case, and leave it to the Commander-in-Chief to judge whether my services and sacrifices justify the treatment received.

I shall esteem it a great favour if you will kindly let me know my position at present, and from which department I am to draw pay. I conclude I am to continue the duty given me by the Chief until further orders.

C. G. Dennison, Major.

Vryburg, 14 March, 1902'

In answer to the letter, Gen. Hamilton wrote me that it was the wish of the Commander-in-Chief that I should raise the nucleus of a corps by enrolling fifty Britishers and augmenting them from time to time with such of the surrendered rebels who preferred five shillings a day to scanty subsistence, and 'that my corps for the present would rather take the form of an intelligence corps than otherwise'. I now had positive instructions verified officially a few days later, and in a very short time had over a hundred men enrolled, consisting of fifty Britishers, principally South Africans, and the balance of the class I was instructed to enrol, viz. surrendered rebels, whom I would much rather have met in the field as enemies than have their service; but these were my orders and I carried them out.

It was about this time that two disasters followed quickly in succession, by which two columns of Lord Methuen's division suffered severely. The Kimberley Column, under Maj. Paris, had been transferred to Vryburg District, and had done some convoy work to Kuruman, besides making some captures of stock and prisoners and scattering the Boers about. Lord Methuen decided on taking the Kimberley Column with the local forces, consisting of some CP and specials under Maj. Berrage, and Cullinan's Horse, under Capt. Cullinan. The result was another unfortunate disaster to this apparently doomed commando – that known as the 'Klip Drift Disaster', in which the General was himself severely wounded. Many of our best men were killed, including Lt. Nesham, already mentioned, who nobly stood to his gun to the last and fell riddled with bullets. He died as brave men die, a glorious death, a soldier's death! The majority of the column were taken prisoners and later on released. I omitted stating that a detachment of the 1st Battalion Northumberland Fusiliers formed a part of the local contribution and fought, as I was informed, to the last.

No blame can be attached to any particular unit, excepting perhaps some supports who took the safest direction to avoid glory. The remnants of my old Scouts, under Capt. H. P. Browne, were placed to cover the rear, and in the dawn of the morning saw the Boers in strong force at a gallop, which was reported forward, and I believe extra supports were sent back. The Scouts were simply ridden down, shot, and taken prisoners, excepting eleven with a sergeant, who escaped. Some nine half-castes who were taken, where they stood with the whites to the last, were shot in cold blood. Some of the whites were robbed of their clothing, and in several instances their boots were taken from them, which was the case with Capt. Browne, who tied putties round his feet and arrived like others at the Kraaipan Siding, hardly able to crawl along with their feet blistered and bleeding, having walked between seventeen miles after their release.

I did not accompany the expedition, as my duties kept me at Vryburg, but had all the details from those of the officers who came out, by which I came to the conclusion that the fatal error had been committed in not keeping the wagons eight or ten abreast, as much as in a square as possible, with the guns at the four corners, supported by the infantry and the mounted men dispersed, as the occasion required.

I continued my work in accordance with the instructions received from Lord Kitchener regarding the rebels, and was enrolling them besides as fast as possible. The Klip Drift Disaster undid all I had done previously. While negotiating, I got the following note from Col. Vyvyan:

'Vryburg 6/4/02
Dear Major Dennison,
The General would be glad if, in dealing with the question of negotiations with the rebels, you would not work outside the

Western District without first obtaining his approval.
Yours Truly
C. B. Vyvyan'

Previous to the foregoing I received the following:

'Vryburg 21/2/02
Dear Major Dennison,
Lord K. wants to know (a) how many men you have got? (b) how many want to join you? Please let me know, also kindly tell me if Cullinan's Horse could be embodied in your corps and any of Hannay's Scouts? I conclude the present establishment of the corps could not be reckoned at more than one squadron whites and 150 bastards, exclusive of Cullinan's.
Yours Very Truly
C. B. Vyvyan'

And on 22nd February, 1902, the following note:

'Dear Major Dennison,
The GOC wishes you to go on recruiting and to equip and mount all your men enrolled without delay.
Yours Very Truly
C. B. Vyvyan'

On the 5th March 1902, I got orders that the corps was not to be formed, and that the men enrolled were to be disbanded. Then, later, came again came the order to enrol fifty Britishers, etc., etc., as I have in both cases before stated, and only reiterate to make the matter as clear as possible, and to show the false position in which I was placed through contradictory orders.

While busy carrying out the last order, and without any previous intimation, Maj. Paris came to my office one morning, having arrived from Mafeking the evening previous, and, after greeting me, said:

'I want to see you alone.'

'Very good,' I replied, 'let us walk down to the hotel.'

We did so, and finding that we could talk privately on a bench under the verandah outside, we sat down.

'Lord Kitchener,' said Maj. Paris, 'has been good enough to offer me the command of a regiment to be formed here of a thousand men, and I want to know if you will accept the command of a squadron under me?'

'What!' I indignantly replied, 'Accept the command of a squadron under you! No! Most emphatically No! Not for all the Generals in South Africa would I entertain such an offer. I consider it an insult!'

'No, my dear Dennison,' said Maj. Paris, 'You are one of the last men in the world I would think of insulting, and I must have you with me. Will you be my Second-in-Command?'

'Yes, Major Paris, I will be your Second. You will have the responsibility, and I should do the work.'

Matters were thus arranged, and this was the outcome of all my expectations regarding the command at Vryburg.

The corps raised by Maj. Paris absorbed Scott's Railway Guards, Cullinan's Horse, the Cape Police Specials, Hannay's Scouts, and Dennison's Scouts. About 900 men were raised, all told, but the life of the corps was a short one, for peace soon followed, and, excepting a bit of a skirmish outside the town, particularly the last of the war down West, the Western Light Horse saw no service in the field.

The Western Light Horse was disbanded the week following the notice of peace. Peace, after a war of two years and eight months' duration; the war that, it is to be hoped, has taught the little Englanders a big lesson, and all-powerful England that South Africans are not to be despised as a foe.

Chapter 22

It was my intention to have gone to England immediately after the war, but owing to having matters to settle that required my personal attention in South Africa I could not go. A Government billet had been promised me, and, in fact, I was led to believe that the Native Commissionership of Rustenburg in the Transvaal would become a permanency, but after repeated correspondence and a personal interview with Sir Geoffrey Lagden, I was doomed to disappointment: but was given in February last year a billet as Inspector of the Lands Department in the district of Rustenburg, under a young man of no South African experience. I felt this most bitterly at the time. He had seen no service during the war and knew nothing of the district or duties of a District Commissioner (he was Acting).

I had taken up four private horses; there were no horses belonging to the Department fit for the work. I used my own for the purpose, being told that an allowance would be made me for the use of them; this, after I had left, was got by threats of legal proceedings, and the forage used for the animals I paid for, though only getting at the rate of 3 shillings per diem each for them while in use. I was forced to leave the service of the Land Department by Dr Jameson, the Commissioner of Lands, for having assaulted the Acting District Commissioner, although, at the urgent request of friends, I apologised to him, he promising that he would not report the matter, which, after getting what he wanted, he did, but made such additions to his report as could only emanate from a man of his stamp. True, I had been guilty of an indiscretion, but did the fault which I had committed warrant the punishment meted out to me after the long services rendered, the sacrifices offered?

I had not tried to accumulate riches during the wars I had served in, I had ever tried to do my duty, and was I ever unsuccessful? All I undertook during this last, as well as the former wars, I was successful in. I know that my actions, assisted by my brave followers, saved the Crown many thousands of pounds during the last war, and yet, for one act was summarily dismissed the service without a hearing, without being allowed to raise any defence. That granted the most diabolical of criminals was denied me. This is not the justice of England, but that meted out by an arbitrary department administration. What I have suffered cannot make me disloyal, but what will be the affect on our children? The enthusiasm of the past to serve, to shed blood in the defence of the once-loved flag of the forefathers, will be a thing that once was; we may drift, as the united states of a South African nation, away from the ardent love we bore the Mother country. Once more, England, Beware! Your colonies are your future strength; do not lose their sympathy in any detail, the least of them is worthy of your most just consideration.

There are many besides myself in South Africa who have suffered; many who have fought and lost more than money or money's worth; and how have they been treated? A most searching inquiry by a combined commission – English and Colonial men – a few thousands wisely spent in time, means the gain of so much for the future. Such a commission of men, wisely chosen, temperate, unbiased men with practical knowledge and ability, and not anyone appointed on account of possession or influence gained otherwise than by worth, cannot but result in good to the Empire.

There has been a great tendency during the last war, as in former wars, but decidedly more so during the last great struggle, to place men at the Head of Departments who know absolutely nothing of the duties they have to undertake, and especially so was this noticeable in the Transport Service where the most ridiculous ignorance was displayed. Our Transport Officer in Vryburg had a number of wagons loaded and waiting to proceed to Kuruman. It had been raining heavily, and the ground was fairly saturated. This novice gave an order that the oxen were to be exercised by dragging the loaded wagons round the outskirts of the town. And it was done, the deep ruts cut by the loaded wagon wheels were visible for months after.

An order was passed that no private horses would in future be allowed for officers, and any who had such should hand them in to the remount for valuation and purchase, but the officer or officers should have the right of purchase at the same price given for them.

Some odd valuations and opinions as to the age were given at one certain remount I know of. Among others a mare of about four years of age was bought and on being examined by a young officer with an eyeglass, was passed as 'aged'.

'What do you mean?' said the owner, 'The animal is only four years old.'

'Do you know who you are speaking to, sir? I tell you the horse is as old as Adam; the bridle teeth are worn away.'

'The bridle teeth?' said the amused colonial officer. 'Put up another pane, and perhaps you'll see that this horse is a mare!'

'Ah yes, demme, four years old. All right, take it away; bring on the next horse.'

On another occasion a certain colonel happened to pass rather too close to a mule; the animal kicked him.

'You damn brute. Sergeant — , what is the number of that animal? Two hours pack drill every day for a week and spare diet. Do you understand?' was the order of the insulted colonel.

'Very good, sir,' replied the sergeant.

I never heard whether the example had the desired effect or not.

That England's Army needs reforming nothing has more vividly demonstrated than our last war in South Africa and the result of the War Commission. She has the finest material in the world, but in her officers, as a rule, that material has been spoilt. With our colonials the case is different, and I cannot agree with those who say that our colonial troops would be best offset by imperial men. No! Most emphatically No! If colonial forces are to continue being successful in war time they must be led by colonial officers and governed by their own commanding officers. The necessity of this has been too plainly proved during our last great struggle in South Africa. Every colonial, whether he be Australian, Canadian, New Zealander, or South African, who has taken part in it, will bear me out in this assertion, as well as the regular imperial officer who is honest to his convictions. How much more would have been done, and in far less time, if this course had been adopted, and besides the aggrandisement of mere puppets being made secondary (if it must exist at all) to the welfare of the cause. Jealousy, most deplorable, combined with incapacity, could not result in benefiting the cause.

Great has been the loss of life on both sides, and more especially on ours, during the war, and great the suffering throughout, physically and mentally; deep heartbroken sighs often escaped many of us as something occurs to bring to our minds those we have lost. Many, many are the stories told of suffering in the besieged towns – Ladysmith, Kimberley, and Mafeking. Vryburg Loyals, though not besieged, were in the hands of the enemy, and great was the rejoicing when relief came at last.

I give here an extract from my daughter Annie's diary:

'Sunday, 6th May – Today a Boer telegram stating that Lord Roberts had taken Bradfort, and that some of our troops have crossed the Vaal River, and are at Likathlong at last!

Monday, 7th May – Today will stand out green in our memories for many years to come. This morning early Charlie Rickett called out to us, while Mrs Browne and myself were still in our room, that the Acting Justice of the Peace had gone, and it was suspected our men were coming. This cheered us considerably after feeling so down all the previous week. Later in the day Mr Hendrik hoisted the Royal Ensign. Shortly after, six Boers came along and demanded his reason for hoisting the flag, and told him his presence was required at the courthouse. He went and explained that it was his birthday, and he always hoisted the flag on that occasion. He was told not to do so again. In the afternoon we were told that both the calligraphist and Public Prosecutor had gone and that the Vierkleur was down at last. A little later the courthouse bell rang loudly and cheerfully, so we guessed something had happened. Then came the glad, glad news that the Union Jack was about to be hoisted. Men threw their hats in the air. I think we cried with joy. All was excitement. Oh, it was nice after all the suspense! Our men looked overcome with joy to feel free Englishmen again. How the real Boer fled as the warning was given, 'The English are coming'! How others turned loyal British subjects in the twinkling of an eye! It was all very queer – very happy and very mixed. Hands were shaken; one pair seemed not enough. Yes, we have enjoyed today after all these months. We realise now what they meant. Flags were flying all over the town.

Tuesday, 8th May – Very little has happened today. Everybody looks happy. Tomorrow we hope to hear where our Englishmen are.

Wednesday, 9th May – Last night the town was in an uproar; men lost their heads and fired off guns and pistols until we – who did not know what was on – feared treachery on the part of the would-be loyal Boer, and imagined all sorts of horrors, and were up until after dawn fearing the worst had happened to our small town guard – hastily enrolled the day the Boers left. The dawn, however, only brought us gladness. Our anxiety was for nought. One of our men – Maurice – had returned and said a force of 15,000 would be here at noon, and the men were already mad to think that relief had come at last. At 10 a.m. we all – the whole town, English and those who 'would be' – decorated the houses with flags, and rode, drove, or walked as we best could to meet 'our men', all wearing the dear old colours, even the natives. It was a very glad day even to those of us who knew that among the crowd dear faces of some would be missing, but had left a record behind of bravery and manliness such as we shall always feel proud of, and the thought helped to take the sting away; for to all who had a drop of true English blood, honour is dearer than life always. After driving for some miles, we met a few of the scouts and learnt that the main body was still some miles behind, and could not be in before noon. So we returned home for lunch, and then went out again and met the troops just above the jail. Some of our own CP men were among them – brown and thin and tired they looked, but never were men more welcome. We could do but little cheering, we were so few, but it was all there, and some of them understood. H.P. Browne was among them, looking brown and well but thin, and was glad to be back home again. They all looked soldiers, every inch of them. Some were in Ladysmith during the siege, and some had gone to the relief, and now were going to relieve Mafeking. What a record for them all! ILH, CP, and DFH! Charlie Comley was among the ILH; Eldrid Peddle and Jimmy Robertson among the KLH. We went later to see their camp.

Thursday, 10th May – All day long men came begging for bread and milk to buy, and we could give them so little. In the afternoon we all, the Mansfields (four), Willmores (three), Mother and myself went to the camp and saw the artillery and those lovely English horses, great noble-looking animals. If only Father had been here! Both Rob and Angus Hannay are being left behind at the hospital and twelve others, sick with fever. Poor fellows, they are all so disappointed.

We saw Col. Rhodes, the Duke of Teck and all the other officers. The column left at 6 p.m. We stayed to wave them a goodbye and wished

241

them a safe return, but could hardly see them for the dust.

Friday, 11th May – It is all over for the present, only the new feeling of freedom and the flags remain to testify to the facts. They were here and it is not all a dream; they could not leave us any men for the protection of the town, so once more our Town Guard is on duty. Mr St. Quentin is Acting Administrator so long, Mr Gethin and Mr Morris are his clerks. Some rebels' houses were burnt by our troops as they came up to Vryburg. Meyers has been taken on to Mafeking, as prisoner, by our column.

Saturday, 12th May – Rumours that small parties of armed Boers are roaming about on 'mischief bent' have reached the town, and our men are arming some Cape boys to strengthen the town guard, and preparations are being made to supply the jail with food, water, firewood, ammunition, etc., in case of an attempt to attack the town on the part of the Boers, when our men, if obliged, can fall back on it. At the same time, on the ringing of the courthouse bell, all women and children are to rush to the hospital, but I don't feel that it will come to anything.

Sunday, 13th May – Sunday has dawned peacefully enough, no Boers ventured in.

Monday, 14th May – Nothing has happened today. All is so strangely quiet. It seems almost like a dream that 1,500 men were here last week.

Tuesday and Wednesday, 15th and 16th May, – No news.

Thursday, 17th May – Uncle Dan arrived from Barkly quite unexpectedly this morning (he was sent away some time ago by the Boers with a number of others through the Transvaal to Delagoa Bay). Letters from Harry dated from Warrenton, 13th instant; all well and hopes to be here soon. A dispatch today from Col. Rhodes to Mr St. Quentin states that they had a brush with the enemy twenty miles this side of Mafeking; five of our men killed and twenty-one wounded; enemy losses, fifteen killed and utterly defeated; and that they met Col. Plumer and his men a little further on. We are waiting anxiously for more news.

Friday and Saturday, 18th and 19th May, – No news.

Sunday, 20th May – News that Mafeking was relieved on Thursday last. Great rejoicing here, etc., etc.'

I give these extracts to show that there were some in Vryburg who had their sufferings also, not of a siege or much privation, but of mental strain. And, besides, all were not disloyal, as was the general impression. Many of the Boers were also loyal at heart, but were forced to take up arms.

I cannot here refrain from mentioning the late Acting Registrar of Deeds Mr M. C. Genis, an old friend of mine, who I know was a loyal man. He was imprisoned on suspicion, became ill in prison, and only when he became insensible was his family allowed to have him carried to his house, where he died. The imperial authorities were not responsible for this, and should these lines be read by a certain few, among whom counts one who should have been his friend, I am sure they cannot but feel that theirs was no noble victory over an innocent man. But there are such animals, and they seldom count among the brave.

My tale may appear to readers as erratic in some instances. Details do not follow in their regular course, but I have written mainly from memory, and here and there incidents of the earlier stage of the war crop up later, but whatever I have written is fact.

I have gone through more of warfare and danger than most men in South Africa; have been six times a prisoner since the early war of 1865 in the Free State, and twice wounded during the last war. Many, many of those who fought with me through the different wars of South Africa since I was a youth, have fallen; many friends and relatives besides, among whom I count my brother and my two eldest boys, Alec and Cliff; the latter fell in this last war, and the former, who served in my corps, died at Vryburg during the war, but I have been spared through the inscrutable will of Providence.

And now Mr Chamberlain, the great reformer of England's fiscal policy, is fighting the battle for the empire on a broad and open platform, which gives him scope better to wipe away the Little England feeling which so largely dominates Great Britain in England. May his efforts prove successful in building up the empire by rescuing its trade, now drifting away into foreign hands, simply for want of protective measures. People of England, cast aside the scales of prejudice from your eyes, and be convinced that protective measures, as far as foreign importations are concerned, are for your individual benefit and the prosperity of the empire. And in South Africa my native country, may the rule of a progressive government prove in truth the means of bringing about a united South African dominion, which shall in time become one of the strongest arms, if not the strongest, of England's colonies, when Progressive and Bond parties run on racial lines shall be of the past, and from one broad platform, dropping all former differences, work as one great South African nation in common cause for the building up to a greater, nobler standard, with all her faults, the greatest and grandest power of the world.

Editors' Postscript

The war ended and Dennison, having suffered all his disappointments and let-downs, still believed, through a euphoric fog of patriotism, that Britain could become 'the greatest and grandest power in the world'. This despite he having lost his billet with the Department of Lands, which would have seen him financially safe in his advancing years.

The editors have not attempted to trace Dennison's career subsequent to the publication of *A Fight to the Finish* – a time of British colonial consolidation in east and central Africa – and it is likely that Dennison, then 60 years of age, decided on one last venture to secure the future. As with many other 'displaced' volunteers of the Anglo-Boer War, he, at some time, headed north, finally ending his days at that Rhodesian town of pleasant sounding name, Plumtree, where he died in 1932, aged 88.

Index